Praise for *Mastering Blockchain*

Blockchain can be a daunting and elusive subject matter, especially for those who see the vast potential in this incredible technology. *Mastering Blockchain* brings within one's grasp a solid foundation of understanding, allowing for immediate actionable learning. This is in large part due to the incredible and nuanced understanding both Daniel and Lorne have earned through years in this space, as well as their active engagements with many in the community.

—*Dr. Jeff Flowers, Professor, CSM*
VP, Decentralization Foundation (d24n.org)

An excellent book which is easily digestible for beginners and crypto natives. Covers a wide scope of topics, including underlying blockchain fundamentals, crypto market infrastructure, regulations, and many others. Highly recommended.

—*Gavin Low, Investor*

Mastering Blockchain presents the history, technical fundamentals, and themes of blockchain in an easy-to-comprehend way. Technical and nontechnical entrants to the field will both find this an invaluable resource for getting up to speed on the broad range of topics in this fast-moving space.

—*Aaron Caswell, Expert Blockchain Engineer*

Get down in the trenches with Lorne and Daniel and find out what's really inside Bitcoin, Ethereum, altcoin, and other blockchains and forks.

—*Karen Kilroy, CEO, Kilroy Blockchain Corporation*

Mastering Blockchain goes from the basics to using blockchain in real-life implementations in enterprise-grade environments.

—*Jorge Lesmes, Global Head of Blockchain at everis (an NTT Data company)*

Daniel and Lorne cover an exceptionally broad range of topics in the blockchain universe with clarity. *Mastering Blockchain* is a terrific starting place for those trying to gain a comprehensive view of the incredible impact of this technology on the world.

—*Jeremy Allaire, CEO Circle Internet Financial Cofounder, Centre USD Stablecoin Consortium*

As someone who teaches blockchain, this book would be a great accompaniment to a course, providing a much more robust offering than almost anything I have come across.

—*Dr. Jimmie Lenz, Executive Director, Master of Engineering in FinTech and Master of Engineering in Cybersecurity, Pratt School of Engineering at Duke University*

After years of hype, pipe-dreams, and snake-oil, we now have a balanced, sensible, and comprehensive book on the essentials of blockchain technology. *Mastering Blockchain* is the O'Reilly book that IT professionals need in order to figure out where and how to use blockchain in serious production applications.

—*John Wolpert, Global Product Executive, Consensys Cofounder, IBM Blockchain*

Mastering Blockchain has managed to compile a vast amount of domain-specific knowledge into an easily understandable, concise reference. This book will be provided as reference material at Bitaccess for new hires to gain a quick, highly detailed, and accurate technical overview of the blockchain sector.

—*Moe Adham, CEO, Bitcoin ATM provider Bitaccess*

Mastering Blockchain

Unlocking the Power of Cryptocurrencies, Smart Contracts, and Decentralized Applications

Lorne Lantz and Daniel Cawrey

Beijing · Boston · Farnham · Sebastopol · Tokyo

Mastering Blockchain

by Lorne Lantz and Daniel Cawrey

Published by O'Reilly Media, Inc., 1005 Gravenstein Highway North, Sebastopol, CA 95472.

O'Reilly books may be purchased for educational, business, or sales promotional use. Online editions are also available for most titles (*http://oreilly.com*). For more information, contact our corporate/institutional sales department: 800-998-9938 or *corporate@oreilly.com*.

Acquisitions Editor: Michelle Smith	**Indexer:** Ellen Troutman-Zaig
Development Editor: Corbin Collins	**Interior Designer:** David Futato
Production Editor: Christopher Faucher	**Cover Designer:** Karen Montgomery
Copyeditor: Rachel Head	**Illustrator:** Kate Dullea
Proofreader: Piper Editorial Consulting, LLC	

November 2020:   First Edition

Revision History for the First Edition
2020-11-13:   First Release
2021-03-29:   Second Release

See *http://oreilly.com/catalog/errata.csp?isbn=9781492054702* for release details.

978-1-492-05470-2

[LSI]

Table of Contents

Preface. xiii

1. Origins of Blockchain Technology. 1
   Electronic Systems and Trust   1
   Distributed Versus Centralized Versus Decentralized   2
   Bitcoin Predecessors   7
       DigiCash   7
       E-Gold   8
       Hashcash   8
       B-Money   9
       Bit Gold   9
   The Bitcoin Experiment   10
       The 2008 Financial Crisis   10
       The Whitepaper   11
       Introducing the Timestamp Server   13
       Storing Data in a Chain of Blocks   13
   Bringing Bitcoin to Life   17
       Compelling Components   17
       Achieving Consensus   18
       An Early Vulnerability   20
       Adoption   21
   Summary   22

2. Cryptocurrency Fundamentals. 23
   Public and Private Keys in Cryptocurrency Systems   24
   The UTXO Model   25
   Transactions   26

The Merkle Root   28
Signing and Validating Transactions   30
The Coinbase Transaction   31
Bitcoin Transaction Security   31
Hashes   33
Block Hashes   34
Custody: Who Holds the Keys   36
Wallet Types: Custodial Versus Noncustodial   36
Wallet Type Variations   37
Security Fundamentals   39
Recovery Seed   40
Mining   41
Mining Is About Incentives   42
Block Generation   43
Consensus   44
Proof-of-Work   44
Proof-of-Stake   51
Other Concepts for Consensus   53
Stakeholders   54
Brokerages   55
Exchanges   55
Custody   56
Analytics   56
Information   57
Summary   57

3. Forks and Altchains. 59
Bitcoin Improvement Proposals   59
Understanding Forks   61
Contentious Hard Forks   62
The Bitcoin Cash Fork   65
Altcoins   67
Litecoin   68
More Altcoin Experiments   69
"2.0" Chains   70
NXT   70
Counterparty   70
Privacy-Focused Cryptocurrencies   71
Dash   71
Monero   71
Zcash   71

Ripple and Stellar   72
  Ripple   72
  Stellar   73
Scaling Blockchains   73
  SegWit   74
  Lightning   75
  Other Altchain Solutions   76
The Ethereum Classic Fork   77
Summary   78

4. The Evolution to Ethereum. **79**
Improving Bitcoin's Limited Functionality   79
  Colored Coins and Tokens   80
  Mastercoin and Smart Contracts   80
  Understanding Omni Layer   80
Ethereum: Taking Mastercoin to the Next Level   84
  Ether and Gas   85
  Use Cases: ICOs   86
  Decentralized Autonomous Organizations   87
  Key Organizations in the Ethereum Ecosystem   88
Decentralized Applications (Dapps)   90
  Use Cases   90
  Challenges in Developing Dapps   91
Deploying and Executing Smart Contracts in Ethereum   91
  The Ethereum Virtual Machine   92
  Gas and Pricing   99
  Interacting with Code   101
Summary   101

5. Tokenize Everything. **103**
Tokens on the Ethereum Platform   105
  Fungible and Nonfungible Tokens   105
  Is a Token Necessary?   106
  Airdrops   107
  Different Token Types   107
Understanding Ethereum Requests for Comment   108
  ERC-20   108
  ERC-721   112
  ERC-777   114
  ERC-1155   116
Multisignature Contracts   116

Decentralized Exchange Contracts   119
Summary   121

6. **Market Infrastructure**. **123**
Evolution of the Price of Bitcoin   123
The Role of Exchanges   125
   Order Books   126
   Slippage   128
   Depth Charts   129
   Jurisdiction   129
   Wash Trading   131
   Whales   131
   Derivatives   133
Cryptocurrency Market Structure   134
   Arbitrage   135
   Counterparty Risk   135
   Market Data   138
Analysis   139
   Fundamental Cryptocurrency Analysis   140
   Technical Cryptocurrency Analysis   142
Arbitrage Trading   144
   Timing and Managing Float   144
   Float Configuration 1   145
   Float Configuration 2   145
   Float Configuration 3   146
Regulatory Challenges   146
   Banking Risk   147
   Exchange Risk   148
   Basic Mistakes   148
Exchange APIs and Trading Bots   148
   Open Source Trading Tech   151
   Rate Limiting   152
   REST Versus WebSocket   152
   Testing in a Sandbox   152
   Market Aggregators   153
Summary   153

7. **Decentralizing Finance and the Web**. **155**
Redistribution of Trust   155
   Identity and the Dangers of Hacking   155
   Wallets   156

Private Keys	157
Naming Services	157
Decentralizing Finance	158
Important Definitions	158
Stablecoins	160
DeFi Services	163
Lending	163
Savings	163
Derivatives	163
Decentralized Exchanges	164
Decentralized Versus Centralized Exchanges	164
Flash Loans	173
Creating a Flash Loan Contract	174
Deploying the Contract	176
Executing a Flash Loan	177
Flash Loans for Arbitrage	180
The Fulcrum Exploit	180
Privacy	182
Zero-Knowledge Proof	183
Zcash	186
Ring Signatures	186
Web 3.0	186
Summary	187
8. Catch Me If You Can.	**189**
The Evolution of Crypto Laundering	190
FinCEN Guidance and the Beginning of Regulation	192
The FATF and the Travel Rule	194
Skirting the Laws	194
Avoiding Scrutiny: Regulatory Arbitrage	196
Malta	196
Singapore	197
Hong Kong	197
Bahamas	198
Crypto-Based Stablecoins	199
NuBits	199
Digix	199
Basis	200
Tether	200
Initial Coin Offerings	200
Founder Intentions	201

Token Economics   202
Whitepaper   202
Exchange Hacks   203
Mt. Gox   203
Bitfinex   205
Coincheck   206
NiceHash   206
Other Hacks   206
Bloomberg TV BTC Stolen   206
EtherDelta Redirection   206
CryptoLocker and Ransomware   207
SIM Swapping   207
Summary   209

9. Other Blockchains. 211
What Are Blockchains Good For?   211
Databases and Ledgers   213
Decentralization Versus Centralization   214
Participants   214
Key Properties of Distributed Verifiable Ledgers   214
Ethereum-Based Privacy Implementations   215
Nightfall   215
Quorum   215
Enterprise Implementations   215
Hyperledger   216
Corda   216
DAML   219
Blockchain as a Service   220
Banking   221
The Royal Mint   221
Banque de France   221
China   222
US Federal Reserve   222
JPMorgan   223
Permissioned Ledger Uses   223
IT   223
Banking   223
Central Bank Digital Currencies   224
Legal   224
Gaming   224
Health Care   225

Internet of Things	225
Payments	226
Libra	226
The Libra Association	226
Borrowing from Existing Blockchains	227
Novi	228
How the Libra Protocol Works	228
Summary	230

10. The Future of Blockchain. **231**

The More Things Change	232
Blockchains to Watch	233
How Monero Works	234
Mimblewimble, Beam, and Grin	237
The Scaling Problem	237
Sidechains	238
Sharding	238
STARKs	238
DAGs	238
Avalanche	239
Liquid	239
Lightning	239
Ethereum Scaling	245
Privacy	246
Interoperability	247
Tokenize Everything	247
Summary	247

Index. **249**

Preface

The goal of this book is to educate on all areas of the blockchain, using facts and data rather than bias or promotion. As authors we've researched using multiple data sources, and we've interviewed dozens of experts in the field to provide a more holistic and accurate view of what is really happening in the blockchain industry.

Conventions Used in This Book

The following typographical conventions are used in this book:

Italic
:   Indicates new terms, URLs, email addresses, filenames, and file extensions.

`Constant width`
:   Used for program listings, as well as within paragraphs to refer to program elements such as variable or function names, databases, data types, environment variables, statements, and keywords.

`Constant width bold`
:   Highlights important elements in program listings.

 This element signifies a tip or suggestion.

 This element signifies a general note.

Using Code Examples

Supplemental material (code examples, exercises, etc.) is available for download at *https://github.com/Mastering-Blockchain-Book*.

If you have a technical question or a problem using the code examples, please send email to *bookquestions@oreilly.com*.

This book is here to help you get your job done. In general, if example code is offered with this book, you may use it in your programs and documentation. You do not need to contact us for permission unless you're reproducing a significant portion of the code. For example, writing a program that uses several chunks of code from this book does not require permission. Selling or distributing examples from O'Reilly books does require permission. Answering a question by citing this book and quoting example code does not require permission. Incorporating a significant amount of example code from this book into your product's documentation does require permission.

We appreciate, but generally do not require, attribution. An attribution usually includes the title, author, publisher, and ISBN. For example: "*Mastering Blockchain* by Lorne Lantz and Daniel Cawrey (O'Reilly). Copyright 2021 Lorne Lantz and Daniel Cawrey, 978-1-492-05470-2."

If you feel your use of code examples falls outside fair use or the permission given above, feel free to contact us at *permissions@oreilly.com*.

O'Reilly Online Learning

 For more than 40 years, *O'Reilly Media* has provided technology and business training, knowledge, and insight to help companies succeed.

Our unique network of experts and innovators share their knowledge and expertise through books, articles, and our online learning platform. O'Reilly's online learning platform gives you on-demand access to live training courses, in-depth learning paths, interactive coding environments, and a vast collection of text and video from O'Reilly and 200+ other publishers. For more information, visit *http://oreilly.com*.

How to Contact Us

Please address comments and questions concerning this book to the publisher:

O'Reilly Media, Inc.
1005 Gravenstein Highway North
Sebastopol, CA 95472
800-998-9938 (in the United States or Canada)
707-829-0515 (international or local)
707-829-0104 (fax)

We have a web page for this book, where we list errata, examples, and any additional information. You can access this page at *https://oreil.ly/mastering-blockchain*.

Email *bookquestions@oreilly.com* to comment or ask technical questions about this book.

For news and information about our books and courses, visit *http://oreilly.com*.

Find us on Facebook: *http://facebook.com/oreilly*

Follow us on Twitter: *http://twitter.com/oreillymedia*

Watch us on YouTube: *http://youtube.com/oreillymedia*

Acknowledgments

Thanks to J.R. Willett, Preston Byrne, Joey Krug, Tom Menner, Daniel Feichtinger, Addison Cameron-Huff, Scott Robinson, Elliott Williams, Neal Reiter, Moe Adham, Alex Waters, Charlie Lee, Francisco Giordano, Casey Detrio, Ben Chan, Paul Brody, Tim Swanson, Jake Brukhman, Kevin Owocki, Witek Radomski, Michael Weiksner, Taariq Lewis, Gareth MacLeod, John Wolpert, Jeff Flowers, Karen Kilroy, Gavin Low Zhe Bang, Aaron Caswell, Jorge Lesmes, Colin Goltra, Reuben Bramanathan, Dee Goens, and Kara Miley.

CHAPTER 1

Origins of Blockchain Technology

The term *blockchain* may sound mysterious or even scary to the uninitiated. Its literal meaning—*a chain of blocks of information*—is perhaps the simplest way to explain blockchain. But what is it for? Why does anyone need something called a blockchain?

To find the answer we need to look back to an earlier time, closer to the start of the web. The internet is about storage and distribution of information to large numbers of people. Blockchain has a similar goal, and it builds on previous experiments looking for ways to improve that distribution.

Electronic Systems and Trust

Before blockchain, cryptocurrency, or the systems that use them, could ever be a reality, the internet needed to exist in a reliable and distributed manner, and it needed to be used by a lot of people. In its infancy in the 1960s, the internet was a simple, relatively small network, and it was primarily used as a tool for university researchers and the US government to share information digitally.

Over time, early internet pioneers made the system more usable. The biggest impacts came from the development of TCP/IP, which established a standard for communication, HTTP, which enabled web browsing, and SMTP, which delivered electronic mail. These *protocols* made the internet accessible not just to researchers, but to everyone, and on a growing number of devices, including computers and later tablets and smartphones.

The evolution of the internet has changed life forever—incredibly large amounts of information and services are now available in the palm of anyone's hand, much of it for free. However, using most online products or services requires a person or entity, known as a third party, to act as a trusted gatekeeper. These systems require two types of trust:

Intermediary trust
> A third party is relied on to make rational and fair decisions.

Issuance trust
> A third party is relied on to ensure the safety and security of any value.

Financial transactions are one major area where this trust is relied upon, since most money has become digital. For various reasons, the use of *fiat paper money*, or government-issued physical cash, is on the decline—people today utilize electronic financial tools like debit and credit cards more than ever before. In some countries, such as Sweden, payment systems are almost entirely electronic, with most customers using smartphones and cards at the point of sale (*https://oreil.ly/sGW0S*). But while for consumers the shift of payment interfaces from physical to digital is a relatively recent trend, the systems powering this accounting have long been electronic. Although cash is still readily available to most, money has largely gone from paper and coins to just numbers in a computer system, without many people even noticing.

When value is moved from physical items to a database, there must be an element of trust among the multiple parties involved. Huge payment companies around the world have been created based on the idea that people storing value digitally can trust these brands. However, trust hasn't always been a reliable factor in finance. In fact, the 2008 financial crisis gave people pause, and many began to think that perhaps blind trust and faith in financial institutions wasn't what it cracked up to be.

 Blockchain is an effort to reestablish lost trust. It uses technology—specifically cryptography—to automate and enforce trust in a third party.

Bitcoin was the first working system to use a blockchain. But before Bitcoin came into existence, several predecessors tried—and failed—to create similar concepts. One of the main reasons they failed was the inability to put together a truly *distributed* system on the internet.

Distributed Versus Centralized Versus Decentralized

The internet today is a mix of centralized and distributed applications, though it was designed as a distributed technology. Rather than building a centralized structure with one point of failure, early internet architects wanted to create a more resilient system. The idea for a distributed internet came from the goal (inspired by the military) of ensuring that if one part of the system were attacked, it would still be able to operate if properly distributed.

On a bike wheel (see Figure 1-1), many spokes connect to a single hub (the axle). This design facilitates a distributed approach—if some spokes are broken, the wheel can still work (*https://oreil.ly/awSTC*). *Distributed* means that no single point of failure can bring down an entire system, such as the network of computers that powered the early implementations of the internet.

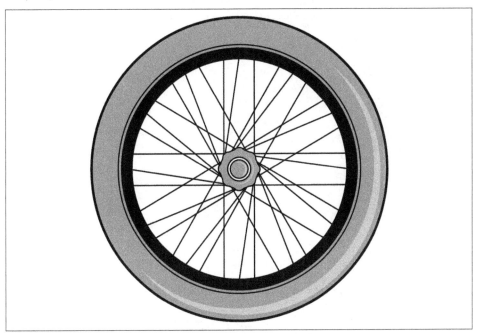

Figure 1-1. A bicycle wheel has a distributed design

The early internet as designed decades ago was distributed to protect the network from any type of disruption, and this system has proven itself to this day. In more recent times, centralized companies such as Google, Facebook, Apple, and Amazon have come to largely dominate the internet (*https://oreil.ly/qrTjl*). It is the hope of some that blockchain technology's distributed nature could help to mitigate the dominance of the web by these few powerful companies by giving individual users more control—a topic that will be explored later in this book.

In the field of computing, a distributed system is one where processing is not done solely on one computer. Rather, computation is shared across a number of computing resources. These systems communicate with one another using some form of messaging. Figure 1-2 illustrates a few different network designs (*https://oreil.ly/l_7Xr*). A distributed system has characteristics of decentralization, in that the failure of a single entity (or *node*) does not mean the failure of the whole network. The common goal is to use processing power to collectively accomplish a task by distributing responsibility across many computers. However, decentralization changes the concept of common goals and messaging. In a fully decentralized system, a given node does not necessarily collaborate with every other node to achieve its objective, and decision-making is done through some form of consensus rather than having this responsibility rest in the hands of a single entity.

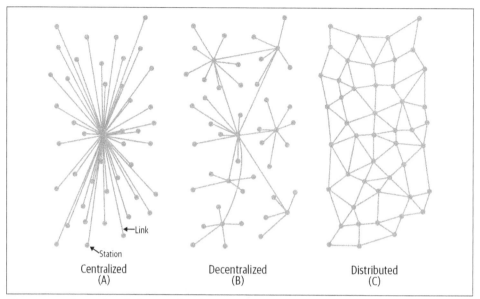

Figure 1-2. Centralized, decentralized, and distributed network designs

Figures 1-3 through 1-5 illustrate the differences between centralized, distributed, and decentralized systems in the form of databases that store information.

Centralized database

Paypal

From	To	Amount
Alice	Bob	$10
Jeff	Janice	$5
Debbie	David	$8
Henry	Heather	$12

Figure 1-3. In a centralized database, like PayPal, all nodes connect to a single, central node that is controlled by one entity

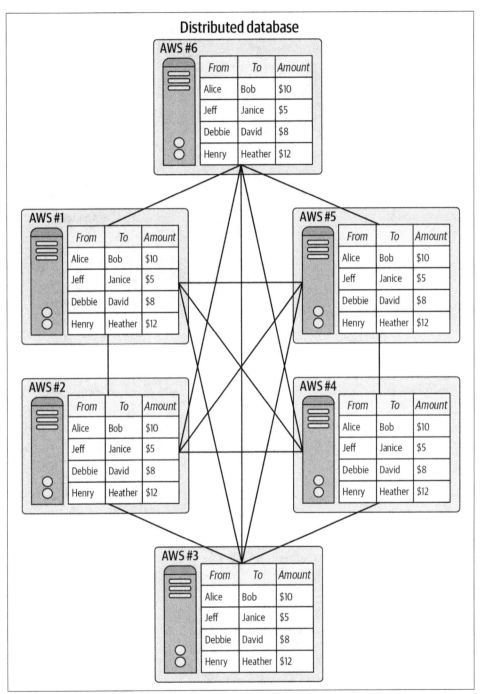

Figure 1-4. In a distributed database, like multiple databases hosted on Amazon Web Services (AWS), each node can maintain a replicated copy of the same data, each node knows the identity of other nodes, and all nodes are controlled by one entity

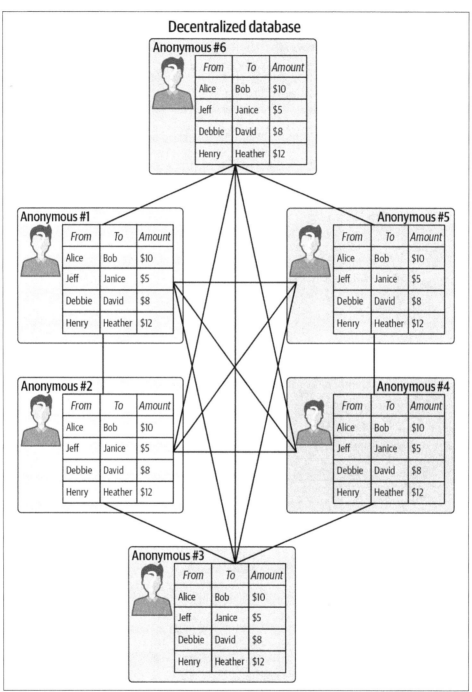

Figure 1-5. In a decentralized database, like Bitcoin's Blockchain, each node can maintain a replicated copy of the same data, each node may not know the identify of other nodes, and all nodes are controlled by many entities who may be anonymous

Bitcoin Predecessors

The internet's ubiquity has been disruptive and changed many industries. To name just a few examples, over the past few decades Wikipedia (*https://www.wikipedia.org*) has more or less replaced encyclopedias, Craigslist (*https://www.craigslist.org*) has taken the place of newspaper classified ads, and Google Maps (*https://www.google.com/maps*) has mostly rendered printed atlases obsolete.

Yet the financial industry was able to resist the internet's turbulent changes for quite a while. Prior to 2009, when Bitcoin launched, control of money had not changed much outside of the switch for users from analog (physical currency and checkbooks) to digital (electronic banking). Because of this shift the idea of digital money was a familiar concept, but control was still centralized.

Many pre-Bitcoin concepts were tried before ultimately failing for various reasons, but the ultimate goal was always the same: increased financial sovereignty, or better control for users over their money. Looking at a few of the early failures can bring the reasons for Bitcoin's growing popularity into greater focus.

DigiCash

Founded by David Chaum in 1989, DigiCash (*https://www.chaum.com/ecash*) was a company that facilitated anonymous digital payments online. Chaum is the inventor of blind signature technology (*https://oreil.ly/dNrAn*), which proposed using cryptography to protect the privacy of payments online. Cryptography uses encryption-based mathematics to obscure sensitive information and has long been used by governments worldwide as a communications tool. Chapter 2 covers cryptography and encryption in a bit more detail.

The DigiCash platform had its own currency, known as *cyberbucks* (*https://oreil.ly/Y-qfL*). Users who signed up for the service would receive $100 in cyberbucks, which were often referred to as *tokens* or *coins*. The company pioneered secure microchipped smart cards, similar to the system used in most credit cards today. It was also an early innovator in terms of the concept of a digital wallet for storing value (*https://oreil.ly/AWHhW*)—in this case, cyberbucks.

DigiCash systems were trialed by a few banks, including Deutsche Bank. A handful of merchants also signed up to accept cyberbucks, including the book publisher Encyclopaedia Britannica. In the 1990s commerce on the internet was very new, and because of concerns about fraud, most people were hesitant to even use credit cards on the web, much less adopt an entirely new type of payment system. However, many privacy-conscious users did begin using cyberbucks and even developed a mailing-list marketplace that was in operation for some time. It was never able to achieve traction due to lack of merchants, though, and DigiCash ultimately filed for bankruptcy (*https://oreil.ly/JKDS-*) in 1998.

E-Gold

A digital store of value established in 1996, E-gold was backed by real units of precious metal. Operated by a company called Gold & Silver Reserve, E-gold enabled instant transfers between its users on the internet. Everything on the platform was denominated in units of gold or other precious metals. By 2006 there were over 3.5 million E-gold accounts. At that time, the company was processing $5.9 million in daily volume (*https://oreil.ly/5eTLs*).

With denominations as small as one ten-thousandth of a gram of gold, the platform was the first to introduce the concept of making *micropayments*, or transferring tiny amounts of value, on the internet. Innovative for the time, E-gold also offered developers an API that allowed others to create additional services on top of the platform (*https://oreil.ly/Bum1H*). Merchants accepted E-gold as a form of payment alongside credit cards in online shopping carts. Support for mobile payments (*https://oreil.ly/X7DeN*) was introduced in 1999.

E-gold was technologically ingenious in the context of its features during the 1990s and early 2000s. However, the system was plagued with problems from the outset, which ultimately led to its demise. A centralized system, it had no mechanism to tie accounts to anyone's identity. As such, the platform was used for nefarious purposes, facilitating money laundering, online scams, and other illegal activity. The US government shut down E-gold (*https://oreil.ly/-MBZz*) in 2008, seizing its assets and establishing a system of redemption for account holders.

Hashcash

Invented by Adam Back in 1997, Hashcash introduced the idea of using proof-of-work to verify the validity of digital funds, including the concept of money that exists solely on the internet. *Proof-of-work* means that computers need to produce some kind of verifiable, computation-intensive output for electronic money to have any value (Chapter 2 explains this in more detail). Hashcash used cryptography to enable proof-of-work, and Back proposed using an algorithm called SHA1 (*https://oreil.ly/Tdpui*) in order to accomplish this.

In his initial proposal for Hashcash, Back referenced DigiCash and raised the idea that adding a fee or "postage" on emails with digitized currency could reduce spam. By utilizing a *hash,* or a function requiring computer processing, Hashcash would impose an economic cost, which would limit spam in email systems. For digital currency, the concept of using hashes would solve what's called the *double spend problem,* which enables a digital unit to be copied like a file and thus spent more than once. Computers, after all, make it easy to duplicate files; anyone can copy an image file and reproduce it over and over. The use of hashing is meant to limit that possibility with digital money by imposing a cost through proof-of-work, or computing power.

Although Hashcash was tested in email systems from Microsoft and the open source software provider Apache, it never took off (*https://oreil.ly/F-8P3*). Conceptually, Hashcash was a great example of how to introduce the digital scarcity required for internet-based money, but the technology itself wasn't really a good form of digital currency.

B-Money

Proposed by Wei Dai in 1998, B-Money introduced the concept of using computer science to facilitate monetary creation outside of governmental systems (*http://www.weidai.com/bmoney.txt*). Like Hashcash, B-Money suggested that digital money could be produced through computation, or proof-of-work. Similar to Adam Back, Wei proposed that the cost of creating digital money could be calculated from the computer power used to create it. This digital money would be priced based on a basket of real-world assets such as gold and other commodities and limited in its supply to protect it from inflation, or losing value over time.

B-Money advanced the idea of broadcasting transactions to a network. For example, if one party wanted to pay another, a message would be sent to the network saying, "Person 1 will send $X to Person 2." The system would be enforceable via a system of digital contracts. These contracts would in theory be used to resolve any disputes, similar to how credit card companies deal with problems like fraud. This system would use cryptography instead of a centralized system for both payments and the enforcement of contractual issues, enabling users of the network to be anonymous; no identity would be required.

The concept of B-Money brought together a number of components of digital cash. It applied the idea of contracts to provide order to an anonymous and distributed system. And it introduced the concept of using proof-of-work to create money. However, B-Money was mostly just a theoretical exercise by Wei. Its purpose was to explore the concept of nongovernmental money that could not be subject to inflation via a controlled money supply.

Bit Gold

Proposed in 2005 by computer scientist Nick Szabo, the idea behind bit gold (*https://nakamotoinstitute.org/bit-gold*) was to bring the scarcity of precious metals into the digital realm. Szabo pointed out that materials such as gold, while having value, are "unforgeable," or very difficult to counterfeit due to their rarity and fixed costs such as mining and transportation. He wanted to take the value of gold and make it digital.

Szabo's idea came after the advent of E-gold, which used gold to back digital value. However, his design utilized a "client puzzle function" type of proof-of-work. The system proposed using a "challenge string" generated on a user's computer that is then securely timestamped "in a distributed fashion." This would then be submitted to a "distributed property title registry" to digitally provide proof of ownership.

As with most of Szabo's ideas, bit gold was largely an intellectual exercise. Szabo was clearly conceptualizing a trustless version of E-gold with bit gold.

The Bitcoin Experiment

By 2008, the world was already relying on the internet as a distributed entity for a large number of services. With electronic maps and GPS apps, people looked to the internet to help them get from point A to point B. Email, texting, Skype, WhatsApp, and other communication apps allowed almost instantaneous connections with friends and family near and far.

In addition, people had begun buying more and more goods and services online rather than in-store. Credit and debit cards had become popular payment methods, along with PayPal and other services. However, as mentioned in the previous section, many still desired a tamper-proof, distributed way to transfer value via the internet— and amazingly, that had still not yet been devised.

The 2008 Financial Crisis

At the beginning of 2006, the world economy was humming along. It was a time of economic growth, but cracks were starting to show in the financial system that year. The US housing market for the first time saw a decline in values, as rules in lending had become so loose that many borrowers were unable to pay their obligations.

This led to banks scrambling because they had chopped up mortgages and other types of shaky loans into private securities that were traded and held like stocks or bonds among financial institutions. When many of those assets turned out to be worthless, it brought on a collapse of the financial system that resulted in governments around the world having to inject cash into the system to save the global economy.

In the US, modern housing bubbles had been controllable by the Federal Reserve raising interest rates (*https://oreil.ly/EV4AF*), as Figure 1-6 illustrates. However, the 2008 crisis could not be controlled, arguably because of lack of transparency in the financial system.

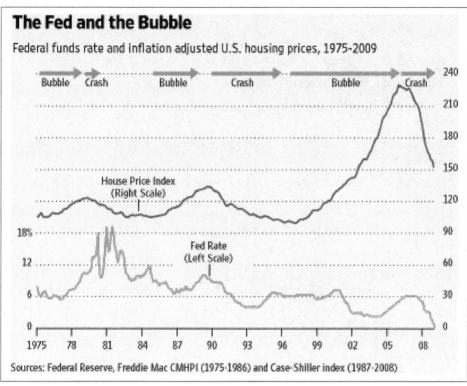

The Fed and the Bubble

Federal funds rate and inflation adjusted U.S. housing prices, 1975-2009

Bubble Crash   Bubble   Crash   Bubble   Crash

House Price Index
(Right Scale)

Fed Rate
(Left Scale)

Sources: Federal Reserve, Freddie Mac CMHPI (1975-1986) and Case-Shiller index (1987-2008)

Figure 1-6. Federal Reserve raising interest rates to control housing bubbles

Why is this bit of financial history relevant to a discussion of Bitcoin? Because although many of the concepts and technologies underlying Bitcoin already existed in 2008, no one had ever put together all the pieces of earlier e-money concepts to create a system that enabled digital trust and transparency.

The Whitepaper

On August 18, 2008, >the domain *bitcoin.org* was registered. Then, written by someone or a group using the pseudonym Satoshi Nakamoto, a whitepaper (*https://bitcoin.org/bitcoin.pdf*) was published on October 31, 2008, and shared on numerous software developer mailing lists. Titled "Bitcoin: A Peer-to-Peer Electronic Cash System," the paper provided a detailed proposal for creating a value system that existed only on the internet. The aim was to create a digital currency that could operate without any connection to a bank or central government, and to build a more transparent financial system that could prevent the catastrophic events of the financial crisis from ever happening again.

The Bitcoin proposal featured a number of ideas pulled from systems that preceded it. These included:

- Secure digital transactions, like the smart contracts outlined by Nick Szabo
- Using cryptography to secure transactions, like in DigiCash
- The theoretical ability to send small amounts of secured value, as E-gold was able to do
- The creation of money outside of governmental systems, as B-Money had proposed
- Using proof-of-work to verify validity of digital funds, as Hashcash was designed to do

The whitepaper also introduced several concepts that were new to many people, including:

Double spending
  The risk that a unit of currency is spent more than once via falsified duplication.

Proof-of-work
  A mathematical problem that must be solved using computational power.

Hashes
  A fixed-length output is produced so that data of different sizes and sequences can be organized.

Nonces
  A random number is used to ensure that a particular communication can only be used once.

Transcending the Mint-Based Currency Model

Government-backed currencies use the familiar *mint*-based model, in which a central authority, known as a mint, verifies that transactions cannot be double-spent. Currency is returned to the mint and is periodically destroyed in order to create new currency.

The Bitcoin whitepaper proposed eliminating that mint-based central authority by publishing each and every transaction on a digital-only network:

> To accomplish this without a trusted party, transactions must be publicly announced, and we need a system for participants to agree on a single history of the order in which they were received. The payee needs proof that at the time of each transaction, the majority of nodes agreed it was the first received.

Introducing the Timestamp Server

In addition to using proof-of-work to secure the Bitcoin network, Satoshi proposed using a timestamp system to verify transactions, similar to filesystems and databases. Taking the information generated during a transaction and running it through a hashing algorithm generates a fixed string of numbers and letters known as a hash. For Bitcoin, Satoshi proposed using the SHA-256 algorithm that is popular in cryptography.

Here's an example:

```
keccak256("hello") =
1c8aff950685c2ed4bc3174f3472287b56d9517b9c948127319a09a7a36deac8
```

Here that is again with one small change:

```
keccak256("hello1") =
57c65f1718e8297f4048beff2419e134656b7a856872b27ad77846e395f13ffe
```

Using a hash to store information is also key when preserving large amounts of information. As seen in this example, different inputs output a unique fixed-length string when hashed (*https://oreil.ly/ESWf0*). This makes it easier to reference some stored piece of data that can be retrieved by a hash.

Storing Data in a Chain of Blocks

In the mint-based model, a government or central authority uses standard accounting practices to keep track of transactions. The Bitcoin whitepaper introduces the concept of tracking transactions using a *chain* of signatures, or hashes. These are organized by blocks of time in chronological order.

This scheme, in essence, creates a unit of account that does not require any single entity to keep track of transactions. Instead, the chain of blocks, or *blockchain*, uses cryptographic mathematical trust to keep track of transactions in a digital system. The network does not require a complex structure, as it uses a peer-to-peer system to verify and publish these chains of blocks. Basically, it needs a distributed data structure for *storage* and a messaging system *protocol* that makes up a *public network* on the internet. As explained further in Chapter 2, a blockchain is made up of multiple blocks of transactions, and those blocks are connected to each other through hashes. Though many blockchains are available freely on the internet, some blockchains are not public—especially those used in some business settings, as detailed further in Chapter 9.

Here is the challenge Bitcoin sought to overcome: how can multiple parties who don't know each other and don't trust each other collaborate? Maintaining a global ledger where they all agree which transactions are valid and should be processed is Bitcoin's solution to this challenge. The Bitcoin blockchain is the global ledger that all parties in the Bitcoin network agree is valid and accurate. Disagreement can mean a fork in the chain and the creation of a new root, a subject that is covered in Chapter 3.

In a payments network, a *ledger* is a constantly changing document. Every time someone wants to send a transaction, a new row of data is added to the ledger. With Bitcoin, about every 10 minutes a new block of transactions is added to what can be defined as a ledger.

The following are important attributes of every Bitcoin block:

Block hash
   A unique identifier for the block. The block hash is generated from input data that provides a snapshot of the current state of the blockchain within 256 bits of data. This snapshot is like a technical version of a balance sheet for the entire Bitcoin blockchain. A Bitcoin block does not contain its own block hash, but it does contain the hash of the previous block it is building on, which is what makes the blocks *chained*. A block hash can be found by hashing the block header.

Coinbase transaction
   This is the first transaction of each new block mined on the network. It adds new bitcoin to the supply, which is given as a reward to the miner who adds the block to the chain. Miners are discussed further in Chapter 2.

Block height number
   This number identifies how many blocks there are between the current block and the first block in the chain (also known as the *Genesis block*).

Merkle root
   This is a hash that allows proof of the validity of the blockchain (Chapter 2 talks more about Merkle roots).

The name of a blockchain system is generally used as a proper noun, while its unit of account is a regular noun. Thus, a *cryptocurrency network* is capitalized ("Alice loves the decentralized aspects of Bitcoin"), but a *cryptocurrency unit of account* is lowercase ("Alice sent two bitcoin (or bitcoins) to Bob").

Figure 1-7 shows a Bitcoin block.

Block #170

Summary	
Number Of Transactions	2
Output Total	100 BTC
Estimated Transaction Volume	10 BTC
Transaction Fees	0.00 BTC
Height	170 (Main Chain)
Timestamp	2009-01-12 03:30:25
Received Time	2009-01-12 03:30:25
Relayed By	Unknown
Difficulty	1
Bits	486604799
Size	0.49 kB
Weight	1.716 kWU
Version	1
Nonce	1889418792
Block Reward	50 BTC

Hashes	
Hash	00000000d1145790a6694403d4063f323d499e655c53426834d4ca2f8dd4a2ee
Previous Block	000000002a22cfee1f2c846adbd12b3e183d4f97683f85dad08a79780a84bd55
Next Block(s)	00000000c9ec538cab7f38ef9c67a95742f56ab07b0a37c5be6b02808dbfb4e0
Merkle Root	7dac2c5666615c17a3b36427de37bb9d2e2c5ccec3f8633eb91a4205cb4c10ff

Transactions

b1fea52486ca0c62bb442b530a3f0132b826c74e473d1f2c220bfa78111c5082		(Size: 134 bytes) 2009-01-12 03:30:25
No Inputs (Newly Generated Coins)	➡ 1PSSGeFHDnKNxlEyFrD1wcEaHr9hrQDDWc - (Unspent)	50 BTC
		50 BTC

f4184fc596403b9d638783cf57adfe4c75c605f6356fbc91338530e9831e9e16		(Fee: 0.00 BTC - Size: 275 bytes) 2009-01-12 03:30:25
12cbQLTFMXRnSzktFkuoG3eHoMeFtpTu3S (50 BTC - Output)	➡ 1Q2TWHE3GMdB6BZKafqwxXtWAWgFt5Jvm3 - (Spent) 12cbQLTFMXRnSzktFkuoG3eHoMeFtpTu3S - (Spent)	10 BTC 40 BTC
		50 BTC

Figure 1-7. Bitcoin block #170, which records a transaction of 10 BTC sent from Satoshi Nakamoto to developer and early blockchain pioneer Hal Finney

Figure 1-8 illustrates why it would be hard to change a past transaction.

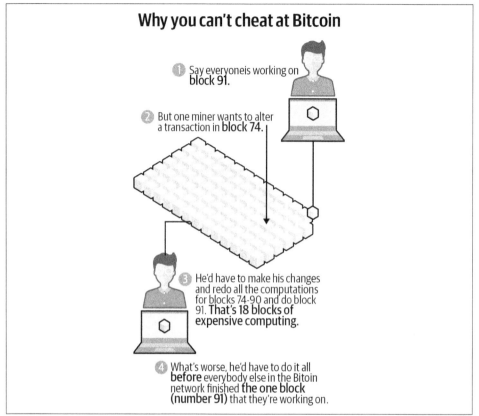

Figure 1-8. Why it's difficult to roll back bitcoin transactions

Satoshi Nakamoto's Disappearance

Many are naturally curious about the true identity of Satoshi Nakamoto. After the Bitcoin whitepaper's publication, Satoshi continued to be a figure in the community until 2012, helping bring Bitcoin into existence as a functional system.

Journalists have long tried to discover the identity of Satoshi Nakamoto (*https:// oreil.ly/BF0HI*). However, it is possible that it's not a single individual, but an amalgamation of a number of people working together who saw the financial crisis of 2008 as an opportunity to propose blockchain-based technology as a solution to the problems that caused the meltdown. Many in the cryptocurrency community are less concerned about Satoshi's true identity and more focused on the ideas that helped Bitcoin and blockchain come into existence.

As the earliest champion of Bitcoin, Satoshi Nakamoto was a major influence on the early open source Bitcoin developer community. This person or persons were active for roughly the first two years of Bitcoin's existence, communicating with people like Nick Szabo, Wei Dai, and computer scientist Hal Finney via message boards, developer lists, and the email address placed at the top of the whitepaper, *satoshin@gmx.com*. During their period of activity, Satoshi mined around 1 million bitcoin (*https://oreil.ly/Hbr1D*).

In December 2010, some members of the Bitcoin community began to advocate for the cryptocurrency to be used as a donation mechanism for the nonprofit (*https://oreil.ly/7Mjhp*) news-leaking organization WikiLeaks, which was struggling with traditional payment processing. The idea was that Bitcoin could help WikiLeaks fill a void. Satoshi disagreed via a post on a popular forum, arguing that WikiLeaks would prove to be too controversial and that they believed focusing on technical progression was more important. Within a week of the WikiLeaks idea surfacing, on December 13, 2010, Satoshi posted their last message (*https://oreil.ly/_ZYj9*) announcing a minor new release of the Bitcoin software client. One bitcoin was worth 20 cents at the time.

Bringing Bitcoin to Life

The initial Bitcoin concept as outlined in the 2008 whitepaper brought together technologies in cryptography, privacy, and distributed computing to rethink financial platforms. However, a lot of work remained to be done to bring these ideas to fruition. Fortunately, a number of computer programmers devoted to open source software and Bitcoin's ideals believed in its potential. Bringing the network to life was the next task, and it required the efforts of some early pioneers.

Compelling Components

Open source software means it's not proprietary—any developer can view the source code and modify it. In addition to being open source, cryptocurrency networks such as Bitcoin have three major components that make them uniquely attractive (*https://oreil.ly/h6Nsf*):

Value
> A unit of account, called bitcoin (often denoted as BTC), is used to record transactions on the ledger, also known as the Bitcoin blockchain.

Distribution
> As the Bitcoin whitepaper outlines, the Bitcoin network uses decentralized nodes in order to maintain a record of transactions.

Consensus
> Miners in the Bitcoin network use proof-of-work together to maintain the security and stability of this distributed record of transactions.

Those four components together made Bitcoin particularly appealing to a small group of determined developers, who were motivated to work together to create a resilient and secure model for value storage on the internet. Although not without its flaws, Bitcoin is considered to be leaps and bounds beyond previous attempts at achieving fully digital and distributed storage of value.

Achieving Consensus

On January 3, 2009, Satoshi Nakamoto "mined" the first 50 bitcoins, utilizing processing power to create the first Bitcoin block. Known as the *Genesis block*, this first block in the Bitcoin blockchain referred to the financial crisis as the purpose for bringing the network to life. In the coinbase, or transaction content input, the Genesis block has this information (*https://oreil.ly/msgF7*):

```
The Times 03/Jan/2009 Chancellor on brink of second bailout for banks
```

Bitcoin is a distributed network, which means people were needed to act as miners in the system. So, Satoshi produced the first Bitcoin client. Running the client allowed users to run nodes and mine Bitcoin blocks. "If you can keep a node running that accepts incoming connections, you'll really be helping the network a lot," Satoshi wrote in the message posting the software (*https://oreil.ly/2Kquz*), titled "Bitcoin v0.1 released - P2P e-cash."

A blockchain is a living, constantly updating document. As time goes on, more and more transactions are added to it. Users of a centralized payments network like PayPal trust that the central authority will update its ledger with new transactions as time goes on. But in a decentralized payments network like Bitcoin, there is no central authority—just thousands of anonymous miners powering the network.

So who should users trust to update Bitcoin's blockchain with a new block of transactions? Gaining that trust is called *achieving consensus*. It is a process that all the miners powering the network use for the following two purposes:

Block discovery
> To agree on which miner gets the right to add a block of transactions.

Validation of transactions
> To agree that the transactions included in that new block are legitimate.

Most blockchains used for cryptocurrency follow one of two approaches to achieve consensus (Chapter 2 covers these in more detail):

- Proof-of-work
- Proof-of-stake

Enterprise blockchains use other methods of consensus, which are discussed in Chapter 9.

Public/private key cryptography

Bitcoin uses public/private key cryptography to prove the validity of a transaction. *Private keys* in Bitcoin are used to digitally sign bitcoin transactions, which is the way the owner of a Bitcoin address proves to the network that they are the rightful owner of that address. Private keys authorize a transaction. They are kept secret, much like passwords.

Public keys in Bitcoin are only used to generate a Bitcoin address. The address is essentially a compressed version of the public key, making it somewhat easier to read. A Bitcoin address is a value that can be shared publicly with anyone, usually when asking someone to send bitcoin. In this way, it's a bit like an email address.

Generating keys

A private key is a 256-bit number that is chosen at random. Private keys are almost always shown in hexadecimal format. The private key is generated by a computer—most programming languages have a function to randomly generate a number.

A private key can be paired with a public key to make transactions on the Bitcoin network. Without a private key it is, by design, nearly impossible to do so (more on this in Chapter 2). In cryptography, a public key can be generated by running the private key through an Elliptic Curve Digital Signature Algorithm (ECDSA) secp256k1 function. A public key hash is then generated by running the public key through the cryptographic SHA256 and RIPEMD160 functions. The Bitcoin address is generated by first adding 00 to the public key hash and then running that value through a Base58Check function. Figure 1-9 illustrates.

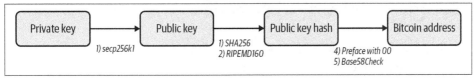

Figure 1-9. Process of generating a Bitcoin address from a private key

Some people use a Bitcoin client that has an option to generate an address, following certain rules (*https://en.bitcoin.it/wiki/Address*):

- Starts with 1, 3, or bc1
- Rest of string is between 25–34 characters long
- Valid characters include 0–9, A–Z, and a–z
- Most addresses do not include l (lowercase L), I (uppercase i), O (uppercase o), or 0 (zero), to prevent visual ambiguity

An alternative is to use *https://www.bitaddress.org*, a website that generates randomness in the address based on a user's mouse movement; however, users have to trust that the website's owners will not record their private keys. Most people generate a new Bitcoin address through an exchange like Coinbase, which does it for them using their internal software.

Generating transactions

Bitcoin transactions follow a unique type of accounting called UTXO, which stands for *unspent transaction output*. A transaction is basically a list of inputs and a list of outputs. Each input identifies a Bitcoin address that is acting as the source of funds, plus an unspent transaction that address has received in the past. It also contains a digital signature proving that the owner of that address has authorized the transaction. Each output identifies the Bitcoin address receiving the funds and the amount that address will receive.

We'll talk about the structure of a bitcoin transaction in the next chapter, and go over all of these concepts in more detail.

An Early Vulnerability

As a new protocol, Bitcoin was not without its share of issues early on. It was not easy to use, so not a lot of people downloaded the Bitcoin client. Some of the earliest proponents of Bitcoin were those who had already proposed some of the concepts it used. They included Wei Dai, who proposed B-Money, and Nick Szabo, whose bit gold concept led to a lot of development on securing transactions. Another early Bitcoin advocate was Hal Finney, who received the first bitcoin transaction from Satoshi Nakamoto.

A major security flaw was found less than two years into Bitcoin's existence. On August 6, 2010, a member of the community noticed an abnormally large output transaction and posted about it on a popular message board (*https://oreil.ly/qXQZ8*). "The 'value out' in this block #74638 is quite strange," developer Jeff Garzik wrote, as someone attempted to create 91,979,000,000 out of thin air. Example 1-1 shows the transaction.

Example 1-1. An abnormally large bitcoin transaction

```
CBlock(hash=0000000000790ab3, ver=1, hashPrevBlock=0000000000606865, hashMerkleR
oot=618eba, nTime=1281891957, nBits=1c00800e, nNonce=28192719, vtx=2)
  CTransaction(hash=012cd8, ver=1, vin.size=1, vout.size=1, nLockTime=0)
    CTxIn(COutPoint(000000, -1), coinbase 040e80001c028f00)
    CTxOut(nValue=50.51000000, scriptPubKey=0x4F4BA55D1580F8C3A8A2C7)
  CTransaction(hash=1d5e51, ver=1, vin.size=1, vout.size=2, nLockTime=0)
    CTxIn(COutPoint(237fe8, 0), scriptSig=0xA87C02384E1F184B79C6AC)
    CTxOut(nValue=92233720368.54275808, scriptPubKey=OP_DUP OP_HASH160 0xB7A7)
    CTxOut(nValue=92233720368.54275808, scriptPubKey=OP_DUP OP_HASH160 0x1512)
  vMerkleTree: 012cd8 1d5e51 618eba
```

The vulnerability was subsequently patched, and the blockchain was "forked" to diverge the chain (more on forks in Chapter 3). The fork was to make sure the blockchain did not reflect the erroneous transaction. To this day the vulnerability found in 2010 remains the largest security flaw in Bitcoin's history, a testament to the cryptocurrency community's growing strength.

Adoption

Satoshi's disappearance is often attributed to helping make Bitcoin a fully decentralized entity. This is because the creator is no longer a part of the system, unlike in the case of Ethereum and other blockchains, which tend to follow the direction of their creators and effective leaders.

It is perhaps no coincidence that around the time of the disappearance, Bitcoin was gaining some real traction. The community was growing steadily. Computer scientist Gavin Andresen, who eventually took a lead role after Satoshi's departure, created a "Bitcoin faucet" that gave out small amounts of BTC in the hopes of increasing adoption. Andresen gave a presentation to the CIA about Bitcoin and became chief scientist at the now-defunct Bitcoin Foundation, an early nonprofit devoted to the cryptocurrency.

On May 22, 2010, programmer Laszlo Hanyecz is credited with having made the first transaction for a good or service using Bitcoin. He paid 10,000 BTC (about $25 at the time) in exchange for the delivery of two pizzas. The date is celebrated in the community as Bitcoin Pizza Day.

In July 2010, Mt. Gox, a platform originally created for exchanging *Magic: The Gathering* trading cards by developer Jed McCaleb, began offering exchange of bitcoins (*https://oreil.ly/9kS54*). The concept of exchanging bitcoins for traditional currency started gaining momentum, fueling speculation and subsequent price appreciation.

Summary

Bitcoin has been fundamentally important to the birth of blockchain technology. However, the technological concepts it's based on and its growth did not come from nowhere, nor did they happen overnight. Most great ideas aren't created in a vacuum. Bitcoin certainly wasn't, and neither was blockchain.

Bitcoin's current level of maturity relies on a number of technologies that took devoted software developers decades to build, with this collective effort enabling blockchain technology to arrive at where it is today. The open source nature of Bitcoin and the community that grew around it also supported its early adoption. The fundamental aspects of cryptocurrencies come from Bitcoin—we'll explore these in the next chapter.

CHAPTER 2

Cryptocurrency Fundamentals

Like many emerging technologies, cryptocurrencies have ushered in a new way of thinking—about finance, in this case. As a result, new ways of storing value are being considered. Cryptocurrency has some similarities to fiat money, stocks, and bonds, as well as to precious assets such as gold. But the methods of acquiring, transferring, and storing cryptocurrency, or crypto for short, are very different from other assets.

> Major differences are involved regarding security and sending/receiving value in cryptocurrencies. It is possible to lose funds in these systems without recourse.

Using cryptocurrency can be confusing as it introduces a large number of new terms that even people in traditional finance are often unfamiliar with. Although today there are a number of services that make a lot of the basic underpinnings of crypto easier for consumers, becoming familiar with at least the basics of how cryptocurrency systems work can be helpful when trying to understand how these new systems are different. This chapter will cover some basic terminology and processes that will set you up for understanding the rest of the book.

> Although the examples here will primarily use bitcoin, most of these concepts translate to other cryptocurrencies as well. Ethereum introduces some new ideas, which are covered starting in Chapter 4.

Public and Private Keys in Cryptocurrency Systems

The use of cryptography, or encryption, goes back thousands of years. Its primary use has been to safeguard information. Up until the twentieth century, all that was needed for rudimentary cryptography was a writing implement and something to write on, which could be used to create rudimentary codes. In modern times, the use of machinery and subsequently computers fueled encryption's uses. For example, the success of the Allies in eventually breaking and deciphering German cryptography in World War II contributed to the end of that conflict.

Modern cryptography was used mostly by governments up until the 1970s. It was the invention of *public key*, or *asymmetric*, cryptography that allowed its use to become more widespread, along with the growing proliferation of computer networks. Public key cryptography allows anyone to easily encrypt a message using a receiver's *public* key, which is available to anybody; the message can then be decrypted using the receiver's *private* key, which (hopefully) only the recipient knows.

Cryptography has become crucial to major systems that underpin the internet. This includes the fundamentals underlying cryptocurrencies such as Bitcoin. For example, signing up for a hosted Bitcoin wallet generates a public key and a private key, and a Bitcoin address (we'll talk more about wallets in "Custody: Who Holds the Keys" on page 36). The Bitcoin address is a translation of the public key and is the identity of the wallet where funds can be received and from which they can be sent to other addresses. This address can be shared with anybody for receiving and sending, a bit like a username or email address. The private key is kept secret and is used to unlock stored cryptocurrency, somewhat like how you use a password to access your bank account. Here's an example of what they look like:

Private key	Kyc9JCPPKNPrMUopkCc7ng9PU5Bp9SGsjVkh8Hpfx4tCr5LGXgBf
Public key	033b368bfccf5921f8a5a42b81b0f5ecdc66583fac8dc13bcf860cf31290964c64
Bitcoin address	19PacjCFSSt9guX4zZ3GPpXpDrvDNQ7DC4

As mentioned in the previous chapter, Bitcoin private keys are used to digitally sign transactions. That's how the owner of a Bitcoin address proves to the Bitcoin network that they are the rightful owner of that address, and how they authorize a transaction. In the real world, a bank card user walks up to an ATM, inserts their card, and enters their personal identification number (PIN). That PIN is private—only the user is supposed to know it. For the ATM network, a valid PIN indicates that the ATM user has "signed" a transaction.

Bitcoin public keys are only used to generate a Bitcoin address. This address is essentially a compressed version of the public key, making it much easier to read. A Bitcoin address can be shared publicly with anyone, often when requesting that someone send bitcoin to that address.

A private key in Bitcoin is a random 256-bit number that is created by a random generator. Private keys are displayed in hexadecimal format. Once a user has a private key, it can be paired with a public key to unlock a Bitcoin address. Everything starts with the private key. From this, a user can generate a public key and Bitcoin address. As a reminder, Figure 2-1 illustrates the process for generating a Bitcoin address and which encryption algorithms are used at each step.

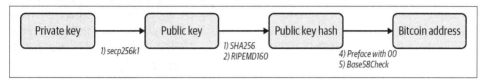

Figure 2-1. The process of finding a Bitcoin address from a private key

As you can see, the public key is generated by running the private key through an ECDSA secp256k1 function (*https://oreil.ly/UrWtL*). The public key hash is generated by running the public key through the SHA256 and RIPEMD160 functions. The Bitcoin address is generated by first adding 00 to the public key hash and then running that value through a Base58Check function (*https://oreil.ly/bJSdN*).

The UTXO Model

Bitcoin transactions follow a unique type of accounting called *unspent transaction output* (UTXO). A bitcoin transaction is essentially a list of inputs and a list of outputs. Each *input* identifies a Bitcoin address that is providing the funds, and an unspent transaction that address has received in the past. Similarly, each *output* represents the Bitcoin address receiving the funds and the amount that address receives. The difference between the input and the output is the *transaction fee*, which will be earned by the bitcoin miner. Each input also contains a digital signature, proving that the owner of that Bitcoin address authorizes that transaction. Figure 2-2 shows an example of a bitcoin transaction.

Figure 2-2. A sample transaction, and how it looks in a Bitcoin block explorer

In this example, there are four inputs. Two of the inputs come from the same address (*1HXpg8D9AMGFVZ9FEU2tkZYvAZ8xBhVudo*). However, these two inputs represent two different transactions that address has received in the past, one for 0.0027867 BTC and another for 0.0034977 BTC. The other inputs represent transactions that the addresses *14yPyVmGhNCSM9JgaabRZ8C3cT2RWEGd71* and *1MXDLBc2Tq2hnQ2x5qXTEPUen5xq9hDA39* have received in the past.

The inputs in this case total 0.0128 BTC, and the total amount output is 0.01145732 BTC. The difference between the two, 0.00134268 BTC, is paid to the miner who added the block the transaction is in to the blockchain (known as "mining" a block). The creator of the transaction pays this fee to incentivize the miner to include this transaction ahead of other transactions that are in the memory pool, where all valid transactions are waiting to be confirmed. We'll talk more about all of these concepts later in the chapter, but first let's take a look at how a bitcoin transaction is structured. Here's an example (*https://oreil.ly/lSJjm*) of a raw transaction:

```
01000000017967a5185e907a25225574544c31f7b059c1a191d65b53dcc1554d339c4f9efc0100000
06a47304402206a2eb16b7b92051d0fa38c133e67684ed064effada1d7f925c842da401d4f2270220
1f196b10e6e4b4a9fff948e5c5d71ec5da53e90529c8dbd122bff2b1d21dc8a90121039b7bcd0824b
9a9164f7ba098408e63e5b7e3cf90835cceb19868f54f8961a825ffffffff014baf21000000000019
76a914db4d1141d0048b1ed15839d0b7a4c488cd368b0e88ac00000000
```

The fields are described in Table 2-1.

Table 2-1. Anatomy of a bitcoin transaction

Field	Description
Version no.	4 bytes. Identifies which protocol version the node generating the transaction is using (currently 1).
Flag	If the flag is present, showing a value of 0001, then the node is using Segregated Witness (SegWit), which removes signature information from the transaction.
In-counter	The number of inputs.
List of inputs	List of input data.
Out-counter	The number of outputs.
List of outputs	List of output data.
Witnesses	If using SegWit, then this field shows a list of witnesses.
Lock time	4 bytes. If this field is not empty, it identifies the earliest time that the transaction can be added to the blockchain as determined by the network. This field can be represented as either a block height or a Unix-like timestamp.

Transactions

In cryptocurrency, *transactions* represent the movement of value from one address to another. Transactions that are published on the blockchain are said to be *confirmed*. Transfer of control of funds requires signing a transaction with a private key. The corresponding public key is then used by the recipient to verify the signature and validate the transaction. In most cryptocurrencies, users must also pay a small fee to the network in order for a transaction to go through. This fee, which usually goes to the miner who discovered the block in which the transaction is included, is to incentivize the miners publishing blocks to continue to secure the network. Online tools like the Bitcoin Fee Estimator & Calculator (*https://bitcoinfees.info*) can help you predict how big a fee you should include with a transaction to get it recorded on the blockchain within the desired time frame (see Figure 2-3).

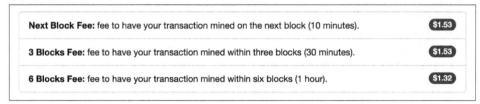

Figure 2-3. Estimating the fee to get a transaction included on the blockchain

Bitcoin transaction fees can vary depending on network capacity, how quickly confirmation is needed, and other factors. Because there is a limit on the number of transactions that can be recorded on a block—the current limit is 1 MB of data, or roughly 3,500 transactions per block—a higher fee may be required for greater urgency. There is essentially a competition in place for getting miners to confirm a transaction: higher fees mean faster confirmation. Figure 2-4 illustrates the series of events that occur in executing a bitcoin transaction (*http://learnmeabitcoin.com*).

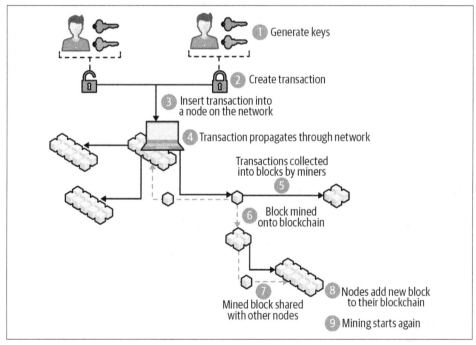

Figure 2-4. Series of events involved in executing a bitcoin transaction—"block mined onto blockchain" refers to miners adding a new block to be confirmed by the network

The Merkle Root

The *Merkle root* is used to show a snapshot of the state of all the transactions in the current block, stored in just 256 bits. The name comes from computer scientist Ralph Merkle, who came up with *Merkle trees,* which are digital signature data structures. The Merkle root has a special purpose aside from capturing the transaction snapshot. When a node in the network wants to ensure it has the exact same list of transactions as every other node, it does not need to compare each transaction individually. Instead, it only needs to compare its Merkle root with every other node's Merkle root. This allows for the building of light software clients that do not require storing the entire blockchain to validate their own transactions.

To calculate the Merkle root, you first create a Merkle tree, where the leaves are the transactions in the current block. Figure 2-5 shows the structure of a Merkle tree.

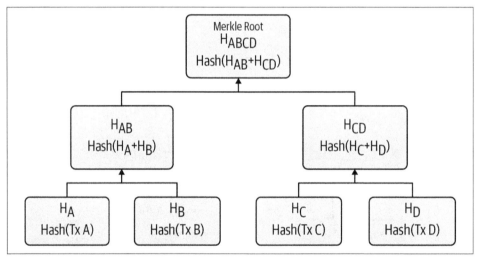

Figure 2-5. Flow chart of a sample Merkle tree

H_A is the transaction (tx) hash of the first transaction, H_B is the tx hash of the second transaction, and so on (we'll talk more about cryptographic hashes in "Hashes" on page 33). H_{AB} is the hash of H_A + H_B => $H_{A+B} = SHA256(SHA256 (H_A + H_B))$.

 The hash function for Bitcoin is double SHA-256.

By moving up the Merkle tree and generating hashes of all the leaves, you eventually reach the Merkle root (yes, the Merkle tree is an upside-down tree). If the number of transactions is odd, then the last transaction is replicated in order to continue this process. The Merkle root is an important value that helps to generate the block hash (see "Block Hashes" on page 34).

Figure 2-6 shows the Merkle root generated for a sample block, and Figure 2-7 shows the flow chart of this Merkle tree.

Block 125552 ⓘ

Hash	00000000000000001e8d6829a8a21adc5d38d0a473b144b6765798e61f98bd1d 📋
Confirmations	518,890
Timestamp	2011-05-22 01:26
Height	125552
Miner	Unknown
Number of Transactions	4
Difficulty	244,112.49
Merkle root	2b12fcf1b09288fcaff797d71e950e71ae42b91e8bdb2304758dfcffc2b620e3

Figure 2-6. Overview of Bitcoin block #125552

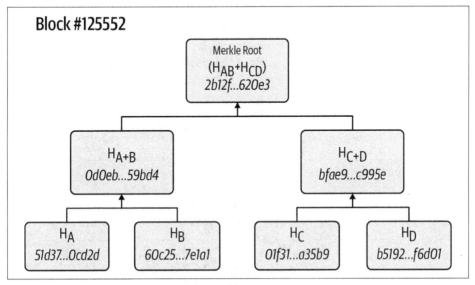

Figure 2-7. Flow chart of the example Merkle tree

Here's how we arrive at the Merkle root for this example:

This is the tx hash of the first transaction:

```
H_A = 51d37bdd871c9e1f4d5541be67a6ab625e32028744d7d4609d0c37747b40cd2d
```

This is the tx hash of the second transaction:

```
H_B = 60c25dda8d41f8d3d7d5c6249e2ea1b05a25bf7ae2ad6d904b512b31f997e1a1
```

This is the tx hash of the third transaction:

```
H_C = 01f314cdd8566d3e5dbdd97de2d9fbfbfd6873e916a00d48758282cbb81a45b9
```

This is the tx hash of the fourth transaction:

```
H_D = b519286a1040da6ad83c783eb2872659eaf57b1bec088e614776ffe7dc8f6d01
```

Thus:

```
H_{A+B} = 0d0eb1b4c4b49fd27d100e9cce555d4110594661b1b8ac05a4b8879c84959bd4
H_{C+D} = bfae954bdb9653ceba3721e85a122fba3a585c5762b5ca5abe117b30c36c995e
H_{A+B} + H_{C+D} = Merkle root =
   2b12fcf1b09288fcaff797d71e950e71ae42b91e8bdb2304758dfcffc2b620e3
```

The important takeaway here is that the Merkle root can be used to quickly detect tampering in blockchain nodes. If there has been any tampering or corruption of transactions in the blockchain on any given node, its Merkle root hash will no longer match that of the other nodes.

Signing and Validating Transactions

Each transaction input contains a signature that provides proof that the owner of the sending address has authorized the transaction. The signature is generated and encrypted using ECDSA, a cryptographic algorithm that takes the private key and transaction data as inputs, as illustrated in Figure 2-8.

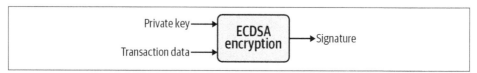

Figure 2-8. Encryption process to generate a transaction signature

When all the nodes are verifying the transaction, they can easily verify the validity of the signature by using an ECDSA verify function, as illustrated in Figure 2-9.

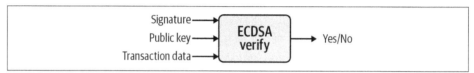

Figure 2-9. Verifying the signature on a transaction

The important thing is that the private key is not required to check whether the digital signature authorizing the transaction is valid or not. Therefore, all nodes can easily validate the transaction using public information, but they can't generate the signatures themselves because the private key is required for that.

The Coinbase Transaction

The first transaction recorded on every block is called a *coinbase* transaction. It is made up of two values:

Block reward
This is the reward a miner receives from the network for performing the work to discover a block and doing their part to provide processing power to the Bitcoin network. The reward comes in the form of new bitcoin being added to the world supply.

Transaction fees
This is the sum of all the transaction fees that are included in each transaction that gets added to the current block. There are often more transactions waiting to be processed than can fit into a block, generating a marketplace for transaction fees. The faster the miner wants a transaction to be processed, the higher the fee. The Bitcoin Fees (*https://bitcoinfees.net*) site shows what current average transaction fees are.

The coinbase transaction has only one input, called the coinbase, which is blank. It also has some other special properties—for example, the previous transaction is 32 bytes of 0, and the script signature is permitted to contain arbitrary data that the miner can choose, such as the nonce header overflow (see "The mining process" on page 47).

Figure 2-10 shows an example of what a coinbase transaction looks like in a Bitcoin block explorer.

Figure 2-10. Sample coinbase transaction

Bitcoin Transaction Security

Bitcoin transactions are *push* transactions, meaning that the sender—the one pushing the funds out of an account they control—is the one to initiate the transaction. In contrast, a *pull* transaction is initiated by the receiver. An example is a credit card transaction: in this case, the merchant who is receiving the funds initiates the transaction.

Pull transactions are significantly less secure because they require the sender to share their account details with the receiver. To compensate for this weakness, pull payment networks (like Visa) provide *chargebacks*, or the ability to dispute a transaction and ask for a refund.

As push transactions, bitcoin transactions are significantly more secure. When initiating a transaction, a sender never has to reveal any of their account information. The only way a fraudulent transaction can take place is if an unauthorized person gets a copy of someone's private key.

 The most common way for an unauthorized person to get hold of a private key is by breaking into an unsecured server or database.

With the technology available today, it is considered to be impossible to guess or reverse engineer what someone's private key is. The only way to guess a private key is through *brute force*—trying every possible combination.

A private key is a 256-bit number, which means there are 2^{256} potential combinations to try:

$$2^{256} = 1.15^{77} = 4 \text{ billion}^8$$

The combined total power of the Bitcoin network in 2020 is greater than that of any of the world's supercomputers. Currently the bitcoin hash rate—an estimate of how many hashes are being generated by all the miners trying to solve any given block—is 90 exahashes per second. That works out to something like pow(2,128)/(90000000000000000000*3600*24*365)=119,892,034,120 per year. (The use of pow(2,128) is because ECDSA, the cryptographic algorithm used to generate a bitcoin private key, can be cracked in proportion to the square root of the key size.)

So, if you harnessed the processing power of all the miners in the Bitcoin network, it would take them this long to go through every combination:

$4,589,678,828,851^{37}$ years

Brute force attacks are commonly used to hack into computer systems, with the attacker trying a huge number of possible user passwords. Bitcoin private keys are resistant to brute force attacks because there are so many possible combinations to try.

Hashes

A *cryptographic hash* is a function that encrypts any form of data into a fixed-size string. Hashes have the following attributes that make them attractive for blockchain:

- No matter the input, the resulting hash will always be a fixed length. For example, the hash generated by SHA-256 will always be 256 bits long.

- A hash is a one-way encryption, meaning it is easy to encrypt the data.

- Conversely, it is extremely difficult, if not impossible, to decrypt the hash back to the original input data. The only way to decrypt a hash without a private key is through brute force, which basically means trying every possible combination of input data and seeing if the resulting hash matches the valid hash.

- A hash is *deterministic*. This means every time the same input data is entered, the resulting hash will always be the same. It is also easy to re-create a hash later using the same inputs, and compare it to the original to see if any tampering or corruption of data has occurred.

- Any slight change to the input data makes the resulting hash look very different. This adds to the difficulty of decrypting a hash.

- Cryptographic hashes are *collision resistant*. It is extremely unlikely to find two different input values that yield the same hash value. This means every unique input will have a unique output.

There are many different cryptographic hash algorithms. Two of the most common are:

- *SHA-256*, commonly used by Bitcoin
- *Keccak-256*, commonly used by Ethereum

A common use case for a hash is a secure website storing a hash of your password in its database. Let's say your password for the website *www.store.com* is *FNj`{:;`k#F43rQ*.

For extra protection the website's database will store not the password, but a hash of the password. If the website uses the hash function SHA-256, the resulting string stored in the database will be:

```
SHA-256("FNj`{:;`k#F43rQ\") =
6586BC035202DFF98A67B814ACA615E613CBBFAE8FFA8F4A475DA0FAEF079C9D
```

Then, when you log in, the website only needs to verify the entered password by comparing the hash of the string you typed in to the hash stored in its database. This process makes the website more secure because if a hacker breaks into the database, they'll only get the hashes of customer passwords.

Block Hashes

A *block hash* is a snapshot of what the entire blockchain looked like at the moment that block was created. In accounting terms, it's like a balance sheet for the entire network. Every node in the network refers to the block hash to verify that its view of the network is the exact same as everyone else's (see Figure 2-11). If there's even one minor difference in a node's ledger, its hash will look significantly different. This is what makes blockchain *tamper-evident*; if the content experiences tampering or corruption, the resulting hash will no longer be the same.

In Figure 2-11, for example, Anonymous #4 has a different block hash than every other node—which means that node's view of the network is wrong. Verifying the block hash is a much faster process than each node checking what every other node's history of transactions would be.

A Bitcoin block hash is generated using a double SHA-256 hash function on the `Block_Header`:

```
SHA256( SHA256( Block_Header ) )
```

A `Block_Header` is made up of the data shown in Table 2-2.

Table 2-2. Anatomy of a Bitcoin block

Field	Description	Size (bytes)
Version	Block version number	4
hashPrev Block	256-bit hash of the previous block header	32
hashMerkle Root	256-bit hash based on all of the transactions in the current block	32
Time	Current block timestamp (*https://en.bitcoin.it/wiki/Block_timestamp*) as seconds since 1970-01-01T00:00 UTC	4
Bits	Current target (*https://en.bitcoin.it/wiki/Target*) in compact format	4
Nonce	32-bit number (starts at 0)	4

The two most important fields in the `Block_Header` are `hashPrevBlock`, which provides a snapshot of what the Bitcoin network looked like in the previous block, and `hashMerkleRoot`, a snapshot of all the transactions included in the current block.

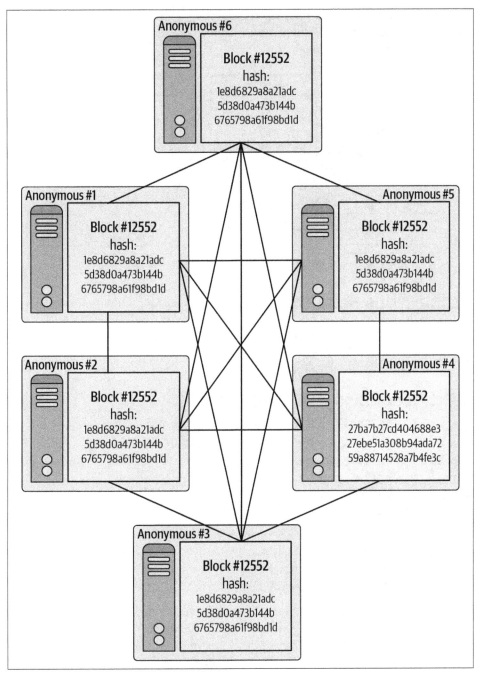

Figure 2-11. All nodes in the network maintain the same view of the state of the network by having the same blockhash

Including the previous block hash when generating the new block hash ensures that every block is connected, or "chained," to the previous block, as shown in Figure 2-12 —hence the name *blockchain*.

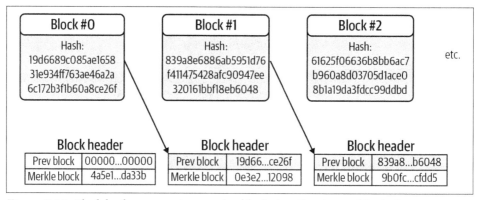

Figure 2-12. Block hashes connect successive blocks together in one big chain

Custody: Who Holds the Keys

In financial services, custody refers to the ability to hold, move, and protect assets. It's a good idea to know the concepts that support custody because of the number of different ways there are to store crypto assets.

Wallet Types: Custodial Versus Noncustodial

Similar to how people usually store value such as cash and credit cards in a folding piece of leather, cryptocurrency is stored in what is also known as a *wallet*. In this case, however, it's really just an interface for storing cryptographic keys and keeping them secure; the cryptocurrency itself does not physically exist on any device, and the wallet is used exclusively for storing the keys associated with it. Many people say crypto and blockchain are "secured by math," and this is what they are talking about.

In general, there are two types of cryptocurrency wallets: custodial and noncustodial. A *custodial* wallet is controlled by a trusted entity, with the user typically having to access its contents via a web interface. These sites store private keys for users; this way, users don't have to worry about them.

Exchanges are a common example of custodial wallets—they hold your cryptocurrency in an account, and they own and control the keys. One popular example is Coinbase (*https://www.coinbase.com*), which was founded in 2012 and is one of the oldest and largest custodial wallet providers in the market.

The obvious downside of this arrangement is that if the exchange goes bankrupt or runs away with the funds, there's nothing the user can do because they don't directly own or control the keys. Trust is therefore an important issue: users must trust the service to safeguard their keys and act responsibly.

Noncustodial wallets give users complete control of keys. However, there is a downside here too. The user is entirely responsible for the security of their private keys. If they lose them, that could result in complete and total inaccessibility of their funds. Blockchain.com (*https://www.blockchain.com*), founded in 2011, is one of the oldest and largest noncustodial wallet providers in the market.

 Using noncustodial wallets takes effort and is not recommended for people with no experience in computer security, but it can be done with fairly simple steps. We'll talk more about securing noncustodial wallets in "Security Fundamentals" on page 39.

Wallet Type Variations

The two primary wallet types can be implemented in a variety of ways:

- A *hot wallet* is connected to the internet, so keys are readily available for creating transactions. This means it's easy to move funds into and out of them. Many custodial wallets are hot wallets, including exchange wallets and web wallets.

- A *cold wallet* is one where private keys are stored completely offline. This could be on a piece of paper or some other physical object completely separate from the internet. Large cryptocurrency companies keep the majority of their funds in cold wallets for safekeeping.

- A *hardware wallet* lets individual users keep funds in cold storage. This device is a noncustodial wallet that is not constantly connected to the internet, which provides safer storage of cryptocurrency keys. Examples include Ledger (*https://www.ledger.com*) and KeepKey (*https://shapeshift.com/keepkey*), both of which support dozens of kinds of crypto assets.

    Pros

    — Support for multiple assets

    — Great cold storage method for large amounts of value

    Cons

    — Not as easy to use as other wallets

    — Funds are not as readily accessible

- A *paper wallet* is a type of noncustodial wallet where the private key is printed or written out and stored somewhere physically safe, offline. Examples include Walletgenerator.net (Bitcoin) and MyEtherWallet (Ethereum).

Pros

— Great long-term cold storage method

— Keys are offline, so risk of online theft is minimal

Cons

— Funds are not as readily accessible as with online wallets

— Physical damage could occur if keys are not stored properly

- A *web wallet* is a website-based wallet accessed via a browser. Examples include Coinbase (custodial) and Blockchain.com (noncustodial).

  Pros

  — Very easy to access from any computer

  — May have buy/sell capability

  Cons

  — User doesn't usually have control of keys

  — Must trust website operator for security

- A *desktop wallet* is software that runs on a Windows, Mac, or Linux computer. Examples include Electrum (Bitcoin) and MetaMask (Ethereum).

  Pros

  — User controls keys

  — Can be used mostly offline for better security

  Cons

  — No one desktop wallet is best for all cryptocurrencies

  — Desktop security must be maintained by the user

- A *mobile wallet* is an app-based wallet, found in the app stores for Android or iOS. Examples include Mycelium (Bitcoin) and Edge (dozens of assets).

  Pros

  — Great for sending transactions from anywhere

  — Many mobile wallets offer control of keys

  Cons

  — Security implications if someone were to get access to the user's device

  — Not a great method for storing large amounts of value

Security Fundamentals

It should go without saying that it's important to keep private keys private. If someone is able to access your private key, it won't be difficult for them to sign transactions on your behalf and empty out your wallet.

One of the most common ways people lose crypto funds is through authentication issues. That means exposure of either private keys or passwords associated with a cryptocurrency wallet. There are a few ways to help prevent this from happening:

Identity verification

> With so many different messaging services being used today, it can be hard to tell whether someone is who they say they are. Make sure to verify through personally known information who you are talking to, especially if someone starts making strange requests—like asking for cryptocurrency.

Two-factor authentication

> In addition to using a password, turning on two-factor authentication is a good idea. Two-factor authentication requires another source for verification, such as when a website sends a text message to your phone containing a code you must enter in order to access your account on the site. There are multiple ways of doing two-factor authentication, and some are more secure than others. SMS verification using an app like Authy or Google Authenticator is one way. It can also be done via a hardware device like the YubiKey that plugs into the user's computer. Note that the first option can be susceptible to porting (see below) if not done properly.

Types of attacks to watch out for include:

Cell phone porting

> Porting is a common type of attack where someone takes over your cell phone's number, allowing them to intercept incoming messages. This is often accomplished by calling the carrier and providing some personal information the attacker has learned. Because of the dangers of this attack vector, it's best not to use SMS verification for two-factor authentication. A good alternative is to set up a portable VoIP phone number that supports text, like Google Voice (*https:// voice.google.com*).

Phishing

> Phishing is a very effective way for hackers to take control of accounts (and cryptocurrency). The attacker typically claims to be from a familiar and trusted organization, like a government agency or a well-known company, and sends the user a message containing a link that encourages them to reveal personal information, such as a password. This might be a spoofed email that looks like it's from your boss and asks for your Social Security number, or the attacker could even ask an

innocent question first to establish trust. Although it may sound far-fetched, phishing is the most effective tool attackers have—all they need is to obtain some personal information. The best policy is to never give personal information out to anyone in response to an unverified email or text. Always try another means of communication, like a phone call, to verify the request as valid.

It's important to keep these fundamentals in mind. Even Steve Wozniak, the cofounder of Apple, was scammed out of bitcoins by letting a prospective buyer use a credit card to send funds to him via PayPal (*https://oreil.ly/WOGiT*). The card transaction was reversed, but the bitcoin had already been sent. Be very careful, as cryptocurrency is a major attraction for scammers!

Recovery Seed

A *recovery seed* is a series of words that can be used to retrieve a private key stored in a noncustodial wallet. Seeds are commonly used as a memory aid because it is very difficult to remember a private key, which is just a string of random numbers and letters. Seed phrases usually store enough information to allow the user to recover their wallet. An example seed phrase might look like this:

```
witch collapse practice feed shame open despair creek road again ice least
```

 It's very important to store the seed phrase for a noncustodial wallet somewhere safe. Indeed, for practical purposes, the recovery seed phrase *is* your "wallet," and with it an attacker can easily access your funds. Cryptocurrency gives you complete control over your balances, but it's up to you to secure them.

If you record your seed on paper, be sure to laminate it or otherwise make sure the writing does not fade. Using an etched metal seed storage device like the one shown in Figure 2-13 can also be useful, but it's important to consider factors like corrosion or humidity.

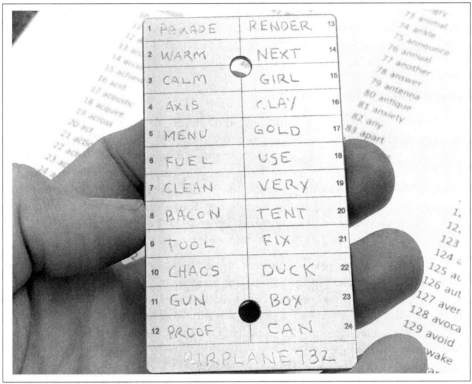

Figure 2-13. Sample cold storage, embedding recovery seed onto metal (image credit: http://www.coldti.com)

> The most common mechanism for generating a mnemonic to use as a wallet seed is BIP39 (*https://oreil.ly/Jr2JU*), the standard for creating phrases from addresses.

Cryptocurrency can and has been lost, whether a user controls their private keys or not. It's important to use secure communication tools, set up two-factor authentication, have a PIN with a cellular carrier, and be aware of phishing. Once cryptocurrency leaves a wallet, it's almost impossible to get it back.

Mining

In the beginning, cryptocurrency mining was solely a hobbyist's pursuit. Early adopters who wanted to support the Bitcoin network downloaded and ran the Bitcoin Core software (*https://bitcoincore.org/en/download*), and they were able to mine a few bitcoins here and there just by running the software on their computers.

In 2010, 1 bitcoin was worth $0.30, so miners weren't making much money—it was just a hobby. Block rewards at that time were 50 BTC, so if a miner discovered 1 block a day, they'd earn $15. However, that changed over time as the hobbyists gave way to serious professionals.

Mining Is About Incentives

Over time, as the price per bitcoin grew and interest in more professional mining hardware resulted in new equipment, the "difficulty" of mining also went up. It did not take long before just using a regular computer to mine was not enough. Miners needed special computer hardware known as *graphics processing units* (GPUs) to compete. Then they started using special microprocessors called *application-specific integrated circuits* (ASICs) to improve efficiency. Today, most cryptocurrency mining is done in huge data centers, with racks upon racks of machines requiring large amounts of power and cooling. So how did we get here?

It's all about incentives. In the beginning, miners were competing with one another using personal computers to solve what can basically be called puzzles. The reward for doing this was 50 brand-new bitcoins—and a new block would be published to the chain. Over time, however, the crypto rewards for solving these "puzzles" turned into serious revenue (Figure 2-14).

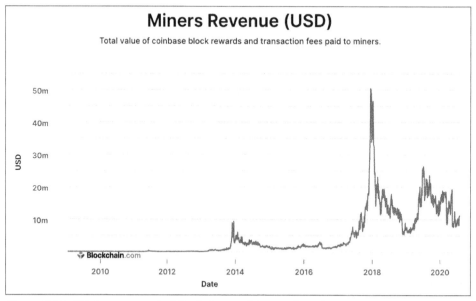

Figure 2-14. Mining revenue in bitcoin is as volatile as its price

There are massive benefits to mining bitcoins at scale. With access to cheap power and data centers, mining cryptocurrency can be profitable. As a result, mining has mostly moved beyond the purview of the hobbyist. New cryptocurrencies may arrive that welcome hobbyist miners, but Bitcoin has reached an enterprise level of large-scale data center–based mining.

Block Generation

Why does mining exist? Many cryptocurrencies require mining because they use a consensus algorithm called *proof-of-work* (we'll talk about consensus in the next section). The "work" is "proven" by running computations to solve a puzzle—in the case of Bitcoin, generating a hash that matches a specific pattern—which when completed reveals the address of the block being mined. A new block is added to the blockchain only once the current puzzle has been solved.

This process of proving work to generate blocks is called mining. The idea is that the sheer computing power necessary to mine blocks acts as a sufficient deterrent to make Bitcoin secure—and indeed the network has never been compromised. The amount of computing power needed to solve the cryptographic puzzles is increasing rapidly, as Figure 2-15 illustrates.

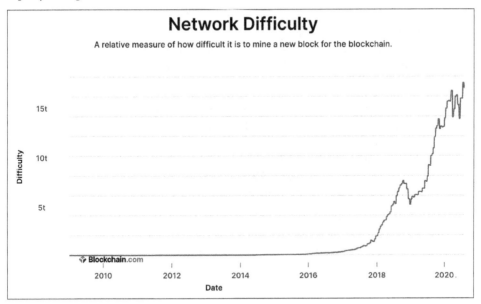

Figure 2-15. History of mining difficulty in the Bitcoin network

This is no accident. Bitcoin is designed to adjust its mining difficulty every 2,016 blocks, so as time goes along the puzzles actually get harder to solve. The math is designed so that as more miners join the network, the time gap between blocks being generated stays the same—around 10 minutes.

Consensus

Consensus is a way of reaching agreement between various participants who have shared values and goals, and it is an important component of how blockchain networks succeed. Though there are other ways of achieving consensus, in blockchain the two most popular are proof-of-work and proof-of-stake. Since we are focused on cryptocurrency and mining, this explanation will concentrate on proof-of-work and how it applies to Bitcoin. Note that enterprise applications that use blockchain generally do not use proof-of-work consensus and do not require miners.

Proof-of-Work

Proof-of-work enables cryptocurrency transactions to be confirmed and blocks to be published on the Bitcoin blockchain. First described in a research paper (*https://oreil.ly/rLEvs*) by Markus Jakobsson of Bell Labs and Ari Juels of RSA Laboratories, proof-of-work was initially created to bind economic value via computer processing to otherwise free services, like email, in order to stop spam. Because proof-of-work requires computing power, it reduces the incentive to attack or flood a system. The economic value provided in proof-of-work is directly correlated to the price of the electric power that is used in the mining process.

In proof-of-work cryptocurrency mining, a hash function is used to verify data. A hash is output on the blockchain as public proof using a *hash algorithm*. The computer speed at which this is done is known as the *hash rate*. With many cryptocurrencies, proof-of-work–based computer power is what secures the network—and that power has become quite substantial. Although hash rates fluctuate, Bitcoin has surpassed 70 million terahashes per second in the past (see Figure 2-16).

In cryptography, many different types of proof-of-work have been devised. For cryptocurrencies, a few are used. Bitcoin uses the SHA-256 hash algorithm, for example, while Litecoin uses a more memory-intensive cryptographic Scrypt algorithm.

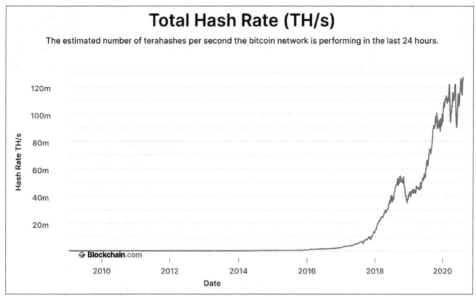

Figure 2-16. History of the hash rate for the Bitcoin network

Block discovery

About every 10 minutes, a new block of bitcoin transactions is confirmed by one miner. Since there are thousands of miners in the network, the network needs to achieve consensus on which miner gets the right to confirm the new block.

All a miner has to do to discover a new block is generate a Bitcoin block hash that is considered valid by the network, using the following criteria:

1. It is a hash of a valid block header.

2. The resulting block hash is a number that is lower than the current network target.

The *target* is a constantly changing number that must always be higher than a valid block hash. The *difficulty* is the average number of attempts required to discover a valid block hash. The *network hash rate* refers to how many times per second the miners in the network collectively attempt to generate a valid block hash.

The goal for the network, set in Bitcoin's initial parameters, is that a new valid block should be discovered approximately every 10 minutes. Over time, the number of miners using computer processing power to discover a block changes along with variables like electricity use and processing power, among other factors. The processing power they are consuming is called the *hash power*. The miners' computers are consuming this power to try to generate a valid Bitcoin block hash.

When the hash power of the Bitcoin network *increases*—that is, when more computer processing power is being applied to generate a valid block hash—it naturally takes *less* time for the network to discover a block. Therefore, in order to maintain an average of 1 block being discovered every 10 minutes, the Bitcoin network changes the network target to make it more or less difficult for the network of miners to discover a valid block hash.

The target value when the first Bitcoin block was generated was:

```
00000000ffff0000000000000000000000000000000000000000000000000000
```

This is the highest possible target value. When you compare the first block's hash to this, you can see that it is a (hex) number lower than the target at that moment:

Initial target	00000000ffff0000000000000000000000000000000000000000000000000000
Block #0 hash	000000000019d6689c085ae165831e934ff763ae46a2a6c172b3f1b60a8ce26f

A simple way to see which number is lower in hex is by counting how many zeros are at the beginning of the hash. The initial target has 8 zeros, whereas the first block hash has 10 zeros; therefore the block #0 hash is a lower number, and therefore it is valid.

When block #0 was discovered, there was little competition in the Bitcoin network to discover a block. So, the target value was high. The difficulty at that moment was 1, meaning that on average it would require 1 attempt to generate a valid hash. Ten years later, there are thousands of miners consuming significantly more hash power to discover a block. Therefore, the target 10 years later is a lower value, requiring more attempts.

Compare the target with a valid block hash from July 28, 2019:

Target	00000000000000000001f3a08000000015667e3e2c52a81e977a0b71f70e5af97
Block #587409 hash	00000000000000000000001f57b098911a90b164b9812304f4f7615cf9f91f66a
Difficulty	9,013,786,945,891.68 estimated attempts required to discover a valid block hash

Bitcoin is designed to have a new target recalculated by all the nodes in the network every 2,016 blocks (approximately 14 days). The new target value is calculated as the target value that would have generated the previous 2,016 blocks at intervals of exactly 10 minutes. This is the Bitcoin network's way of self-correcting the difficulty required to generate a valid block hash by the miners that participated in the network over the previous 2,016 blocks.

The main reason this difficulty process is in place is to ensure the supply of bitcoin is predictable and follows a specific schedule (see Figure 2-17). When each new block is created, new bitcoin is created as well, although over time this supply is diminished. With bitcoin, the size of the reward is also designed to get smaller as supply fills. Every 210,000 blocks, or approximately every 4 years, the block reward is cut in half. It went from 50 bitcoins to 25, then from 25 to 12.5, and so on, and will continue decreasing until 2140, when roughly 21 million total bitcoins (a hard cap) will have been mined.

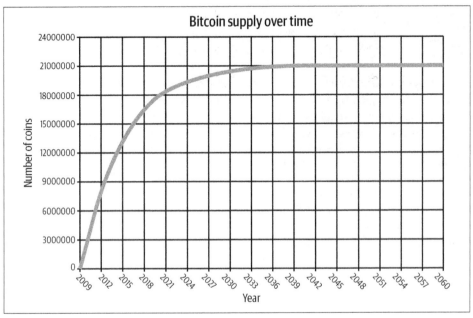

Figure 2-17. Bitcoin supply over time

The mining process

At every moment, hundreds of thousands of miners on the Bitcoin network are competing to discover the next valid block on the blockchain. Miners are incentivized to do this because of the block reward and transaction fees. As mentioned earlier, the miner needs to make sure the following are true to generate a valid block hash:

1. It is a hash of a valid block header.

2. The resulting block hash is a number that is lower than the current network target.

To generate a valid block hash, the miner needs to input the information shown in Table 2-3.

Table 2-3. Contents of a valid Bitcoin block

Field	Description
Version	The Bitcoin client version that the miner is currently using
hashPrevBlock	The hash of the last block that the miner sees at this moment
hashMerkleRoot	The hash of all the transactions the miner decides to include in the current block
Time	The block timestamp, calculated as seconds since 1970-01-01T00:00 UTC
Bits	The current Bitcoin network target
Nonce	Starts at 0; if the resulting hash is not valid, then add 1 and try the new hash

All the fields except for the nonce are taken from public sources of information. When a miner begins trying to discover a valid block, they initially set the nonce to 0 and then try to generate a hash that matches the block hash, which is randomly generated. Miners try over and over and to find this block hash, using hash power, meaning the more efficient a miner is at generating these hashes, the higher a hash rate they have.

If the resulting block hash is invalid, the miner adds 1 to the 32-bit nonce and generates a new block hash, which it hopes will be valid. If the miner runs out of nonce space, known as an *overflow*, they use script sig space in the coinbase transaction. If a miner finds a block hash that is valid, which includes satisfying the target criteria, then they have discovered a valid block. The process of continuously trying new block hashes is the proof-of-work every miner puts effort into, as shown in Figure 2-18.

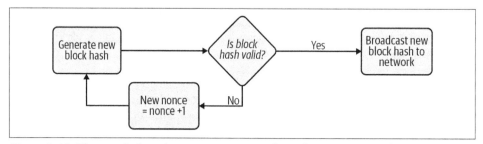

Figure 2-18. The proof-of-work process miners go through to attempt to discover a new block

After a miner discovers a valid block hash, the miner then broadcasts that new block hash to all the other miners in the network. There is a possibility that two different miners will discover a valid block and broadcast the new blocks to the network at the same time. It is then up to all the other miners in the network to achieve consensus on which new block will be added to the blockchain, as Figure 2-19 illustrates.

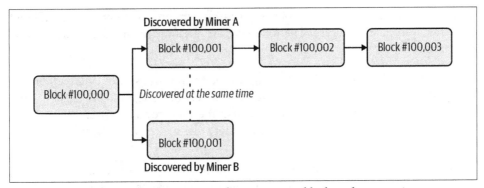

Figure 2-19. An event when two miners discover a new block at the same time

Before a miner adds a new block to the blockchain, the miner verifies that the following are true:

1. The block is valid.
2. All the transactions in the block are valid. This includes confirming the data signatures used to unlock transaction outputs.

Consensus is achieved when more than 50% of the other miners in the network include the same new block into their copies of the blockchain. The miners collectively "vote" on which block they recognize to be added at that moment to the blockchain, as well as verifying that all the transactions are valid.

 The *longest chain rule* dictates that miners follow the chain with the most work—in other words, the longest chain. If two versions of the chain are both the same length, as is the case when two different miners find a solution simultaneously, then miners stay on the first chain they see, and then switch over the moment they see a longer one. The longest chain rule is essential to most forms of consensus, especially proof-of-work.

Transaction life cycle

In a centralized payments system like PayPal, the life cycle of a transaction is pretty straightforward. You log in to the PayPal website or app, enter the transaction details, and press Enter. If PayPal responds with a "Completed" notification, then your transaction has been processed and you are done.

The transaction life cycle in Bitcoin is very different, and there are many different steps involved in the process. The following are the four main stages a transaction goes through:

1. *Broadcast.* The first step is generating a valid bitcoin transaction and then broadcasting the transaction details to the Bitcoin network. Most Bitcoin users will use an online wallet (such as Coinbase), and in the background there is software running a client connected to the Bitcoin network that enables them to see these transactions.

2. *Unconfirmed/Mempool.* As every miner in the network receives the transaction, it places that transaction into its *memory pool*, or *mempool*. The mempool is a collection of all the bitcoin transactions that are in an unconfirmed state and are still considered active. By default, if a transaction has been sitting in the mempool for more than two weeks, it is considered inactive and is dropped from the mempool.

3. *Confirmed by miner.* When a miner discovers a new block, the miner decides which transactions to include in that block, choosing from transactions that are sitting in the mempool. Miners choose transactions in order of transaction fees, starting with the highest ones. A transaction is considered confirmed by a miner when that miner adds a block containing that transaction to its blockchain. However, that miner cannot see the other miners' copies of the blockchain, and there is no assurance that the same block of transactions has been added to their chains.

4. *Confirmed by the network.* As a block is buried under newer blocks, the chances that the Bitcoin network has achieved consensus to include that block increase. A transaction is considered to be confirmed by the entire Bitcoin network when the network has achieved consensus to include the transaction's block in the blockchain.

Confirmations

Bitcoin wallets, and most people in the industry, consider a transaction to be safely confirmed by the network when that transaction has reached at least six confirmations. A *confirmation* involves a miner adding a block that contains transactions to the chain. Figure 2-20 illustrates the decision process of miners for including a block.

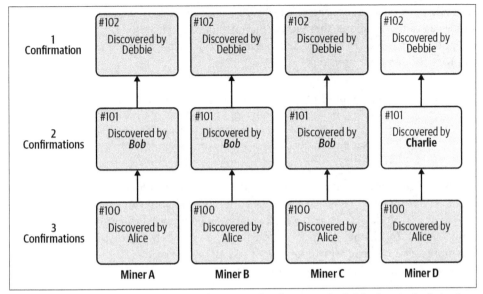

Figure 2-20. Example of proof-of-work miners deciding on which block to include in the blockchain

In Figure 2-20, block #100 has reached three confirmations. All four miners in the network have included the same block. At block #101, three of the miners (75%) have included the block discovered by Bob, but one (miner D) has included the block discovered by Charlie. At this moment, miner D does not realize yet that their view of the blockchain from block #101 on will have to change. If there is a transaction in miner D's block #101 that is not in the other miners' block #101, that transaction will not be included in the network's blockchain. This is why the more confirmations a transaction has, the more likely it is to be included in the Bitcoin network's blockchain.

> Many services have different cryptocurrency confirmation schedules. For example, some services require as few as three Bitcoin network confirmations before a transaction is considered complete, although the standard is usually six confirmations. Some services may require even more confirmations, depending on a variety of factors (including the type of cryptocurrency used).

Proof-of-Stake

Proof-of-stake is a consensus algorithm that aims to improve on proof-of-work by eliminating the need for mining. Instead, holders of a cryptocurrency "stake" their balances to gain voting rights and have a chance of being selected by the network to validate transactions. Staking therefore allows you to act as a node, or validator.

Though there are no expensive hardware requirements or difficult computational processes to worry about, there are economics in play with the cryptocurrency holders putting up funds. And there are incentives: those who stake are provided rewards in proportion to their holdings.

 In a proof-of-stake network, nodes are not considered miners because they are not doing work to discover a block. Instead, the role nodes have in the network is to *validate* transactions, so the nodes in the network creating blocks are called *validators*.

Instead of selecting the miner who can discover a valid block hash first by doing work, proof-of-stake consensus selects a node based on various staking criteria, which may include size of stake (the amount staked), age (which address has held onto the cryptocurrency for the longest time), wealth (which address has held onto the most cryptocurrency for more than X amount of time), etc. Alternatively, in some systems an address that has staked some of the cryptocurrency is selected at random.

Pros
- Because there is no mining, little energy is consumed in creating blocks, so less energy is wasted powering the network.
- Gives more control to those who are more invested in the network.

Cons
- Control of the network is tied to the distribution of wealth in the network. Most cryptocurrency wealth is concentrated among a small group, and therefore control of the network is more centralized than in a proof-of-work network.
- By giving more control to those who are more "invested" in the network, rather than the ones who are doing more "work," proof-of-stake could lead to more divergence between the rich and the poor than proof-of-work.

There has been a lot of criticism of the proof-of-work model. Although a novel idea for cryptocurrency when Satoshi Nakamoto proposed it, the hardware arms race to develop the most powerful ASIC has arguably made proof-of-work more resource-intensive than it should be. One side of this argument says Bitcoin has become an environmental problem because the amount of electricity required to confirm transactions and generate new bitcoin is no longer economically efficient (*https://oreil.ly/ttdDl*). Another side points out that most of the electricity consumed by Bitcoin is actually from renewable sources like hydroelectricity, which is where miners get cheap power.

Determining who gets to generate the next block in proof-of-stake systems is very different from in proof-of-work systems, and there are a few different ways to do it. Some cryptocurrencies use randomized block selection, which is based on a combination of stake size (the higher the better) and hash value (the lower the better). Another method is coin age–based selection, which is based on the number of coins staked and the number of days the coins have been held (possibly combined with the randomized selection method). The latest method of securely introducing randomness is by using the RANDAO random number generator (*https://oreil.ly/ WcsLC*) and verifiable delay functions (VDFs) (*https://oreil.ly/kE03f*) together.

A few cryptocurrencies currently use staking, including Dash, Neo, and Tezos, but it's still a relatively new concept and has not yet seen widespread use like proof-of-work. There are criticisms that proof-of-stake is not a secure consensus mechanism, as a *fork* would in theory create equal incentives on two different chains (*https://oreil.ly/ tjBAS*) (forks, which occur when a blockchain diverges, are covered further in Chapter 3). There is also the risk of a "fake stake" attack, where a staker with little to no balance could disrupt a network, as validation is much more complex to complete than with proof-of-work.

Another theoretical safety issue is the Nothing-at-Stake problem, where a miner freely creates several blocks, causing forks and denial-of-service attack possibilities. This has typically been addressed with *slashing algorithms* to reduce stake in order to penalize badly behaved validators.

Other Concepts for Consensus

There are other ideas outside of proof-of-work and proof-of-stake. Achieving consensus is still a new and evolving technology concept, and different ideas are being tested. This is why consensus algorithms are frequently decoupled from blockchains —in other words, the blockchain technology itself is not tied to one particular method of consensus. This way, third parties can build and market consensus algorithms to be added to commonly used blockchains.

Cryptocurrencies like Ripple and Stellar are active projects that use some very different types of consensus protocols, although it can be argued these systems are not entirely distributed. Both use what is known as *Byzantine agreement* (*https://oreil.ly/ 5R7yb*), a way for distributed nodes to cooperate to confirm transactions. Many of these nodes are controlled by the projects themselves, so they may seem centralized. However, both Ripple and Stellar bypass traditional banking and payments systems by having a blockchain-based unit of account. This allows users to save on the costs (*https://oreil.ly/SjTUT*) usually incurred in traditional financial systems.

Alternative methods

One approach being looked at is called *proof-of-storage*. Something that can be done computationally and is also resistant to ASICs, proof-of-storage uses the validation of storage through filesystems to verify transactions. Projects such as Permacoin, Torcoin, and Chia (*https://oreil.ly/66NFs*) are utilizing a version of proof-of-storage.

Another interesting approach to scaling is *proof-of-history*. For example, in proof-of-work, Bitcoin can be reimagined as a clock that ticks every 10 minutes (thanks to the difficulty adjustment), and the ordering of messages is not agreed upon until 10 minutes pass and the network reaches consensus. In proof-of-stake, everyone is receiving messages from the network, and they need to communicate with other's nodes to agree on the ordering and timing of these messages before they finally reach consensus, and the network progresses.

Proof-of-history is a way to create objective timestamps that nodes within the network can rely on, enabling them to optimistically trust the ordering and timing of the messages before consensus is reached. Consensus then comes in later: participants within the network vote on what they believe to be the main branch, and each time they do this, they commit to not voting on another branch for a set amount of time. The more they vote for a particular branch, their commitment to not vote on another branch grows exponentially. They're incentivized to consistently vote for what they believe to be the major branch because until they have stacked 32 votes for one particular branch, they won't earn any network rewards.

 In her paper "Practical Uses of Synchronized Clocks in Distributed Systems" (*https://oreil.ly/kQcL1*), Barbara Liskov of the MIT computer lab states, "Synchronized clocks are interesting because they can be used to improve the performance of distributed algorithms. They make it possible to replace communication with local computation."

Delegated proof-of-stake consensus is an energy-efficient form of consensus where users *delegate*, placing tokens with a "candidate," and use voting to help govern the network. There is also *voting-based* consensus, and *lottery-based* consensus is used in more private implementations of blockchain.

Stakeholders

In addition to a protocol network, wallets, and miners, there are other stakeholders in the cryptocurrency ecosystem. These may be centralized services or for-profit businesses, and they provide important functionality needed in the ecosystem. There are five categories of stakeholders that a typical user might interact with in cryptocurrency: brokerages, exchanges, custody services, analytics services, and information providers.

Brokerages

As services that help facilitate cryptocurrency transactions, *brokerages* act as intermediaries for buying, selling, and holding crypto in the ecosystem. This includes merchant payments. In name-brand services like the mobile apps Robinhood (*https://robinhood.com*) and Square's Cash App (*https://cash.app*), which allow people to purchase cryptocurrency, a brokerage transaction occurs. Robinhood acts as an intermediary, doing the work of acquiring cryptocurrency and storing it for the user.

For merchant transactions, companies like BitPay (*https://bitpay.com*) handle all of the processing. Any merchant that accepts bitcoin or other cryptocurrency usually has a brokerage take possession of the cryptocurrency. The merchant is then paid in cash by the broker since this is the primary way businesses pay for other expenses, like payroll, rent, inventory, and so on.

BTCPay Server (*https://oreil.ly/RT9E-*) is an open source, self-hosted solution for accepting bitcoin payments. It enables acceptance of cryptocurrencies via an invoicing function at checkout, and has a number of plug-ins for popular web platforms.

Exchanges

As on-ramps to the world of fiat-backed currency, exchanges allow people to directly trade with others. Exchanges like Coinbase Pro (*http://pro.coinbase.com/trade*) in the US and Bitstamp (*https://www.bitstamp.net*) in Europe have trading engines that match buyers with sellers. Trading pairs are typically in fiat, but can also be crypto to crypto. Example trading pairs include USD/BTC, EUR/BTC, and BTC/ETH. When compared to brokerages, exchanges offer increased risk, though the aforementioned exchanges have been around for many years and work with government regulators.

Exchanges have custody of users' keys and provide the trading engine. You must trust that a cryptocurrency exchange is reliable and will not manipulate the market or misuse funds, which is a problem in cryptocurrency.

In an effort to entice users to their platforms, some exchanges are also now offering staking and functioning on fractional reserves, topics that are covered in later chapters.

Custody

A number of businesses focus on long-term hosting and protection of cryptocurrency for users. These services, known simply as crypto custody solutions, usually charge a small fee for balances held or withdrawals. However, they are great services for those who don't ever want to worry about the custody of cryptocurrency. These businesses have worked for years to devise novel technologies to store crypto for users.

Two of the biggest names in the crypto custody business are BitGo (*https://www.bitgo.com*) and Coinbase (*https://www.coinbase.com*). Both are multicrypto asset custody providers, adding new cryptocurrencies all the time. Often these services offer various levels of hot, warm, or cold storage. With cold storage, it's important to note that it may take some time to withdraw cryptocurrency from the service.

Analytics

Cryptocurrency blockchains produce a voluminous amount of information. There are a number of products and services on the market to take this raw data and put it into a format that is easy for people to use. The most common tool is called a *blockchain explorer*. It allows users to better view transactions. Two popular services are Blockchain.com (*https://www.blockchain.com*) for Bitcoin and Etherscan (*https://etherscan.io*) for Ethereum, which let you see the full contents of a block. Figure 2-21 shows a transaction in a blockchain explorer.

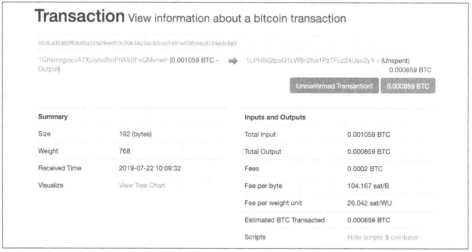

Figure 2-21. Screenshot of a Bitcoin transaction from a blockchain explorer

There are also companies that do deeper dives into following cryptocurrency transactions. One of the largest is Chainalysis (*https://www.chainalysis.com*), which helps exchanges and other stakeholders identify transactions. There are also free tools to help people follow trading patterns, such as TradingView (*https://www.trading view.com*), a charting tool that has cryptocurrency charts for almost all the major assets on most of the global exchanges.

Information

The blockchain industry is changing on a daily basis. New companies, new ideas, and brand-new cryptocurrencies seem to pop up all the time. CoinDesk (*https://www.coin desk.com*), which was founded in 2013, is one of the oldest and largest organizations dedicated to providing news and other research on the industry. Major publishers like the *New York Times*, the *Wall Street Journal*, and Bloomberg also do a good job of covering the cryptocurrency industry with dedicated beat journalists.

Conferences are great educational resources, but can be expensive. For the budget-conscious, Meetup.com (*https://www.meetup.com*) is a great source to find local cryptocurrency events. Using the search terms *bitcoin*, *ethereum*, or *blockchain* will usually turn up some local meetups, most of them featuring speakers talking about current events, best practices, or interesting technical topics.

Summary

The basics of cryptocurrency can be a lot to take in at first. We hope this chapter hasn't been too overwhelming. A good understanding of the material covered here will set you up for better understanding in the chapters ahead. The world of cryptocurrency is changing fast, but the basics seem pretty much here to stay. The next chapters cover a range of topics that build on this early material. It's perfectly fine if you find yourself coming back to this chapter as a reference!

CHAPTER 3

Forks and Altchains

Cryptocurrencies are still very much in a research and development stage, and developers have been trying for years to create another Bitcoin—a popular cryptocurrency network with a strong community behind it.

Whether because of scalability, functionality, or speculation, there have been a number of proposals for *forking* (more on this soon) the Bitcoin code into a new cryptocurrency with similar properties. Some of these ideas are quite novel, while others are simply a play to engineer value.

Bitcoin Improvement Proposals

Why not just change Bitcoin itself? It's not that easy. There is a *governance process* that must be followed to update the Bitcoin protocol.

This is typical of software products: there is usually an internal process to identify continuous improvement opportunities. The process takes into account criteria such as who owns the product and who has a final say in its development, and determines when new features should be added.

Bitcoin Core is open source—the client software is open to everyone and is intended to be owned and managed by the Bitcoin community. *Bitcoin Improvement Proposals* (BIPs) are the community's process to continuously manage and update the Bitcoin Core code. Instead of decisions being made by a designated committee or team, they are made by the entire community.

Anyone from the community who has an idea for improving Bitcoin can propose a new BIP. They must then champion the BIP to get consensus from the community that their proposal should be approved.

The life cycle of a BIP is as follows:

1. Someone from the community comes up with an improvement idea and proposes it to the BIP editors.

2. If the editors approve, they create a new BIP and put it into draft status.

3. If the miners signal support for a BIP, it moves into final status. It is the miners who need to be convinced to adopt a new BIP or not, because they are the ones who have to upgrade their software.

4. Once a BIP is in final status, the rest of the community must upgrade to the new software.

In order for a BIP to be accepted by the community, it must satisfy the following criteria:

1. It follows the correct format specified in the initial proposal outlining the process, BIP-0001.

2. It includes code that implements the change.

3. At least 95% of the past 2,016 blocks to be discovered were created by miners using the new BIP.

With that in mind, Bitcoin's democratic process looks like this:

- Anyone can propose a new bill.

- The miners are voters, and the more hash power a miner has, the more votes they get.

- The bill gets pushed into law if more than 95% of the hash power adopts the change.

Figure 3-1 sketches out the BIP process.

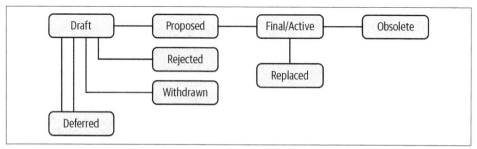

Figure 3-1. The Bitcoin Improvement Process

All BIPs are viewable on GitHub (*https://github.com/bitcoin/bips*).

Understanding Forks

Once the Bitcoin community started to come together for the common good of the network, many programmers decided to *software fork* the technology, allowing them to create their own *altcoins*. *Forking* involves taking the Bitcoin Core software, changing some parameters, and launching it on mailing lists and message boards. The result is *alternative coins*, also known as *altcoins*. Some of these altcoins are so different from Bitcoin that it is better to refer to them as *altchains*.

Forking can actually mean a few different things in the cryptocurrency world. Here are some terms you may come across:

Software fork
> This is a general term in technology systems and open source software. A software fork is when a developer takes a piece of open source software and changes some parameters to meet their needs. For example, the hundreds of different versions of the open source operating system Linux were created through software forks.

Soft fork
> As it pertains to blockchain technology, a *soft fork* is an upgrade to mining software that makes a change to the network but does not require that all miners participate. This makes the upgrade compatible with older software, and is usually done to upgrade transaction functions.

Hard fork
> As it pertains to blockchain technology, a *hard fork* is an upgrade to mining software that makes a change to the network that requires the participation of all miners. Hard forks typically implement key security or functionality changes, and the upgrades are incompatible with older software.

Contentious hard fork
> In blockchain technology, a *contentious hard fork* is a backward-incompatible upgrade to mining software that makes a change to the network that is not accepted by all miners. Because some miners disagree with the fork and therefore don't upgrade to the new software version incorporating the proposed changes, the blockchain effectively splits in two. All past records are the same on each branch, but beginning from the time of the contentious hard fork, the two chains have different transactions recorded on them and their software is incompatible.

Contentious hard forks can be problematic, so let's dig into them a little more deeply.

Contentious Hard Forks

When a contentious hard fork occurs, the main blockchain of a cryptocurrency splits into two separate blockchains. This is what happened with *Bitcoin Cash*, a chain that diverged from Bitcoin in 2017, as illustrated in Figure 3-2.

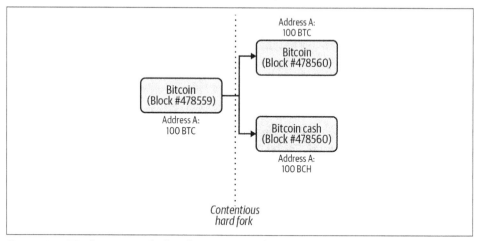

Figure 3-2. Blocks generated after the Bitcoin and Bitcoin Cash fork

Each blockchain inherits the history of the main blockchain before the fork. This includes every previous transaction, every address balance, every block hash, and so on. At the moment of the fork, the two blockchains have identical histories. *After* the fork, each blockchain creates its own new blocks and its own new record of transactions, and blocks can be mined by different miners.

In Figure 3-2, Address A has a balance of 100 BTC before the fork on the main Bitcoin blockchain. After the fork, two new chains split off of the main chain: Bitcoin (BTC) and Bitcoin Cash (BCH). Address A maintains a balance of 100 on both of the new blockchains, so it has 100 BTC on the Bitcoin blockchain (worth about $270,000 at the time of the fork) and 100 BCH on Bitcoin Cash (worth about $24,000). The previous Bitcoin chain (BTC) still exists as it did prior to the forking code being presented. Once the Bitcoin Cash nodes start accepting > 1 MB (megabyte) blocks, the Bitcoin Cash chain forks itself away from Bitcoin, creating the new chain.

Miners

Miners are the ones who contribute hash power to keep the network running. When a contentious hard fork occurs, the miners then decide which blockchain they want to support by either keeping the same software used by the preforked blockchain or changing to the software used by the forked blockchain. Figure 3-3 illustrates.

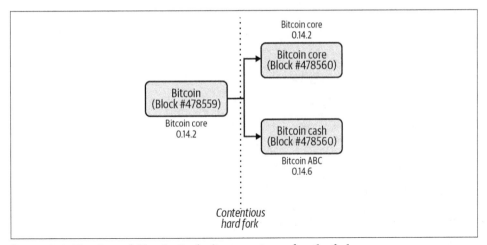

Figure 3-3. Bitcoin and Bitcoin Cash client versions after the fork

In the case of the Bitcoin Cash fork, the miners who wanted to support Bitcoin Cash changed their software to Bitcoin ABC v0.14.6 at block #478560, and began contributing their hash power to the new network. The miners who wanted to support Bitcoin continued using the same Bitcoin Core client, 0.14.2.

> Hash power is important to the survival of a proof-of-work–based blockchain. The more hash power is being contributed to a network by multiple parties, the more expensive it is for a single entity to take control of the network, and therefore the more decentralized the network is. And the more decentralized a blockchain network is, the more trust people have in it and in the security of that network. For example, say one blockchain has nine thousand nodes and another has just nine hundred nodes. The network with more nodes is more decentralized and will inspire greater trust.

So what happens then? When a contentious fork occurs, the community considers the blockchain with the highest hash rate after 2,016 blocks to be the "winning" blockchain, and the prize is that that blockchain gets to retain the prefork name. These names are extremely important because they are the names given to the blockchains on exchanges and have a big impact on the price of the cryptocurrency.

Today, Bitcoin has forked into three substantially different blockchains that the community continues to follow. They are Bitcoin, Bitcoin Cash, and Bitcoin SV (more on SV in a bit). As Figure 3-4 shows, Bitcoin's hash rate (*https://oreil.ly/map8E*) is by far the highest.

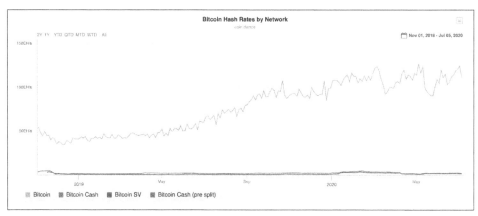

Figure 3-4. Hash rate of each network as of July 2020—Bitcoin's hash rate is superior to its forks

Replay attacks

When a hard fork happens, both new blockchains become potentially vulnerable to what is called a *replay attack*. This occurs when an attacker takes data from a legitimate transaction on one blockchain and "replays" or mirrors that transaction on the second blockchain.

Two blockchains are vulnerable to replay attacks if they both have the exact same process for generating a transaction signature. Figure 3-5 shows what could happen if the Bitcoin and Bitcoin Cash blockchains were vulnerable to replay attacks.

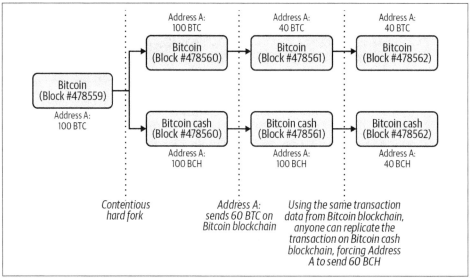

Figure 3-5. How a replay attack can happen after a fork

The sequence of events is as follows:

1. Address A broadcasts transaction instructions to the Bitcoin network that say to send 60 BTC to Address B.

2. The broadcast includes transaction data (that is, inputs and outputs) as well as a transaction signature. The transaction signature—a digital signature that ensures a transaction on the network is authentic—can only be generated by Address A using its private key and proves to the network that it has authorized the transaction on the Bitcoin network.

3. Since Address A has publicly broadcasted its transaction data and transaction signature, anyone can broadcast that same information out to the Bitcoin Cash network, and the network will process it because the two chains are similar.

Fortunately, when the Bitcoin Cash fork happened, the new software Bitcoin Cash miners were using included changes that prevented replay attacks from happening on either blockchain. Specifically, the Bitcoin Cash software added a new field called `SIGHASH_FORKID` to the structure of transaction data sent on its network. This field must be present in a Bitcoin Cash transaction in order for it to be valid. When the transaction signature is generated, one of the inputs to the encryption algorithm is the transaction data. Since the transaction data is structured differently on the two blockchains, signatures generated on the Bitcoin Core blockchain are different from those on the Bitcoin Cash blockchain and are not valid on the other chain.

Now that you've got a little background on forks, let's look at the Bitcoin Cash fork in a bit more detail.

The Bitcoin Cash Fork

For a long time the cryptocurrency community considered the possibility of a split in the Bitcoin blockchain to be a bad thing, and there was uncertainty about whether the Bitcoin blockchain could survive with the community divided. But a debate over the future of Bitcoin and its ability to be used as money caused a rift between developers around 2015. One side wanted Bitcoin to be used as peer-to-peer electronic cash, as laid out in Satoshi Nakamoto's original Bitcoin whitepaper. The other side wanted to limit the ability for there to be large volumes of transactions in Bitcoin's blocks. This ultimately led to a split in the Bitcoin blockchain and the creation of the new Bitcoin Cash blockchain. And this is where the BIP came in.

Despite the implementation of solutions like SegWit and Lightning (discussed later in this chapter), there continued to be a group in the Bitcoin community that were unhappy with how the network was scaling, and particularly the issue of block sizes. Bitcoin's block size was 1 MB, which limited the number of transactions in a block, and despite the proposed solutions, one group still maintained the easiest path forward was to increase the size of individual blocks. This group believed in Bitcoin's original "peer-to-peer electronic cash" concept and wanted to see fast, cheap transactions, which larger blocks would facilitate. The other group, which had implemented SegWit and Lightning, believed that increasing the block size would make it too hard for individuals to run the Bitcoin Core software, as the overall blockchain would get too large and slow down the network. This disagreement threatened to stymie the decentralization of the network.

When the two sides failed to come to an agreement on scaling Bitcoin, ultimately a contentious hard fork was arranged. Mining hardware manufacturer Bitmain developed a plan for forking the community into two different blockchains. The mining pool ViaBTC coined the term *Bitcoin Cash* to reflect the idea that larger block sizes would make the new cryptocurrency more spendable, like cash, with lower fees and faster confirmation of transactions.

On August 1, 2017, the contentious hard fork occurred, creating Bitcoin Cash. The new blockchain featured 8 MB block sizes, giving each block roughly eight times the amount of transaction storage as Bitcoin offered. Most of the other features of the original Bitcoin chain remained, including the hard cap at 21 million units of cryptocurrency and the SHA-256 proof-of-work. In addition, anyone holding bitcoin at the time of the contentious hard fork received the same amount of Bitcoin Cash (*https:// oreil.ly/hYqrW*). Bitcoin Cash's 8 MB block size, which was increased to 32 MB in May 2018, was designed to accommodate more transactions and features. While it has not garnered the traction many proponents expected, despite the controversy, Bitcoin Cash remains the most successful Bitcoin software fork.

A Fork of a Fork: Bitcoin SV

Bitcoin Cash itself faced another scaling debate before long. In November 2018, the Bitcoin Cash network split in two (*https://oreil.ly/Nm6Jt*), forking into separate chains called Bitcoin Cash and Bitcoin *Satoshi's Vision* (SV). The argument this time was a bit different. On one side was a group called Bitcoin ABC, which stood for *adjustable blocksize cap*—they wanted the ability to change the block size to whatever number they wanted and implement *smart contracts*, a programming functionality that exists in Ethereum and other "2.0" altchains (see the next section). The SV group wanted to keep their network away from smart contracts and create a more stable cryptocurrency, which they claimed is what Satoshi Nakamoto had originally proposed. The SV group also wanted the block size to be set at 128 MB and stay at that number. The differences proved irreconcilable, leading to another hard fork.

Altcoins

The term *altcoin* is usually used to refer to forks of the Bitcoin Core software. The early altcoin frenzy began in 2011, after Bitcoin had gained some degree of traction, had gone through its vulnerability attack, and developers had begun to trust the technology. Here are some of the earlier altcoins:

Ixcoin

This fork was an early *premined* altcoin (see the next section for more on premining). After generating 580,000 coins ahead of time, the founder(s) launched Ixcoin on message boards and mailing lists with the idea that the original developer(s) would generate a lot of value for the existing premined coins. Suspicious of the premine, which enables some to enrich themselves before a blockchain goes live, the community forked Ixcoin into I0coin, which did not gain any traction even without premining.

Solidcoin

This fork sped up transaction confirmations with 3-minute block times, as opposed to Bitcoin's roughly 10-minute confirmation time. With Solidcoin, fees were also constant, whereas Bitcoin's are variable based on the sum of transaction fees in one block. However, fixed fees in Solidcoin created spam in the network, as attackers could simply attach fees to transactions and fill up blocks. The original developer decided they wanted more control, so they relaunched the project as Solidcoin v2 and required every other block to be mined by a centralized party. The project eventually lost traction.

GeistGeld

This fork drastically reduced the block time (the rate at which blocks are generated) to just 15 seconds. However, this became problematic as it was actually too fast for miners. It led to the creation of large numbers of orphan blocks that were not ultimately accepted into the chain, causing their transactions to be left behind, never to be confirmed. This made transactions difficult to complete on the network. The developers of GeistGeld also launched Tenebrix, the first cryptocurrency to use *Scrypt mining*. Scrypt is a more memory-intensive proof-of-work algorithm designed to deter the use of ASICs for mining.

Namecoin

Namecoin's purpose was to act as a decentralized version of the Domain Name System (DNS), the system used to direct web traffic. When a user goes to *google.com*, for instance, DNS translates that address into a numerical location on the internet. The developers of Namecoin struggled to make the project both a cryptocurrency and a decentralized DNS, and it failed to gain traction. However, their idea of creating such a system and making the naming system more redundant raised the possibility of cryptocurrency being used for more than just transfer of value.

Primecoin

The proof-of-work for cryptocurrencies like Bitcoin typically involves solving random math problems, but Primecoin promoted the idea that finding prime numbers could prove to be useful. A prime number is a number that is only divisible by 1 and itself, and finding prime numbers becomes more difficult as numbers grow larger. Prime numbers are used in encryption systems, and as computers become faster at calculations, larger prime numbers need to be discovered (*https://oreil.ly/YTZsF*). Primecoin became known as the first cryptocurrency to have a proof-of-work with a use beyond just confirming transactions, with the work focusing on searching for chains of prime numbers.

Litecoin

The best-known altcoin from the early era is Litecoin. In 2011, Charlie Lee, a developer at Google, began spending time playing around with the Bitcoin code. He had observed that other projects had launched with interesting ideas but had continually failed to succeed, for various reasons. One factor Lee identified was that the developers of early projects often remained anonymous, like Satoshi Nakamoto, but unlike Satoshi, they didn't introduce groundbreaking new concepts; they only tweaked the Bitcoin code.

Another issue was *premining,* when a project mines or obtains cryptocurrency before its actual release as a public chain. If the developers of premined projects remained anonymous, it was hard to believe the projects would remain viable long-term because an anonymous founder who had premined could simply walk away at any time, taking their funds with them. Also, many of the early altcoins did not brand themselves well.

Lee thought deeply about creating something better. He thought of Bitcoin as a store of value similar to gold, and he wanted to create its silver complement. He also wanted to make his project "lite" so block times would be faster. Lee ultimately decided to give Litecoin four times the supply of coins of Bitcoin. In addition, the block time was set to be four times faster than Bitcoin's.

Lee also decided to not premine, and to use the (in 2011) ASIC-resistant Scrypt algorithm to attract hobbyists. (ASICs are used in numerous technical applications—they use a specialized chip design to perform one task very well. Scrypt is another proof-of-work algorithm, similar to Bitcoin's SHA-256 with some different properties.) With Litecoin using Scrypt, people could mine both bitcoin and litecoin at the same time on their computers. But eventually Scrypt would restrict bitcoin miners who wanted to use ASICs to profit from Litecoin because the algorithm was different.

Developing Litecoin took Lee one week of planning and four hours of coding. It is still one of the top 10 cryptocurrencies by market capitalization.

More Altcoin Experiments

Lots more altcoins have been launched since the early era. A few interesting examples include:

Dogecoin

Invented by programmer Billy Markus and marketer Jackson Palmer in 2013, Dogecoin is the realization of an internet meme crossed with cryptocurrency. Tweeting as a joke (Figure 3-6), Palmer suggested creating a cryptocurrency based on the internet meme of a Shiba Inu dog (*doge*). The idea gained traction, and an ecosystem formed around Dogecoin. Dogecoin is relatively inexpensive to acquire because there is no cap on the total number of coins, which keeps its price low.

Figure 3-6. Dogecoin started with a simple tweet

Unobtainium

Derived from an engineering term for an extremely rare element, Unobtainium was established in 2013. As its name suggests, the cryptocurrency has a very small number of coins in circulation—a cap of 250,000 units was set, to be mined over 30 years. Though an interesting experiment to try to create low inflation, Unobtanium experiences volatility like most other cryptocurrencies, and its daily trading volume is low (in the hundreds of dollars).

Coinye

Introduced in 2014, not long after Dogecoin, Coinye or Coinye West was the plan for a Scrypt-based cryptocurrency using rapper Kayne West as its meme/mascot. Almost immediately after the plans were announced, the developers received a trademark infringement notice from Kanye West. Although the team rushed to launch the coin, the legal pressure forced them to shut the project down.

PotCoin

Many banks still consider cannabis to be risky, so businesses with a license to sell pot often have to jump through many hoops. PotCoin, released in 2014, was the first attempt to create a cryptocurrency for the cannabis industry. Initially it was just a copy of Litecoin, but the project eventually moved to *proof-of-stake velocity*, which encourages staking, where a cryptocurrency holder profits from just holding it, and regular *signing*, which meant making transactions. Although PotCoin tried a number of marketing initiatives, market volatility and regulation made adoption difficult.

"2.0" Chains

In addition to forks from Bitcoin, there are also projects that have been built from the ground up. Indeed, many altchain ideas need to be built foundationally in order to accomplish the goals they intend to achieve. This section describes a few notable examples.

NXT

Launched in 2013, NXT was a very early "Bitcoin 2.0" or "blockchain 2.0" project. The idea was to create a more programmable, flexible blockchain. Instead of just having a cryptocurrency and a public ledger, NXT aimed to provide a platform for people to build applications on top of the system. It was one of the first to introduce the idea of a *colored coin*, which would tag or "color" a cryptocurrency to represent real-world assets such as property, stocks/bonds, or commodities. The NXT project was largely created and developed by an anonymous person or group. While it didn't really take off, the concepts it introduced were important for other blockchains that came afterward.

Counterparty

Labeled as another of the first "Bitcoin 2.0" projects, Counterparty was launched in 2014. Like Mastercoin (discussed in Chapter 4), it was built on top of the Bitcoin blockchain but aimed to offer a lot more programming capabilities than its antecedent. Most notably, programmers were able to create their own crypto-based blockchain assets on the platform. It featured smart contracts, which contain code that provides a blockchain application with business logic, giving developers more control over when and under what conditions a block would be written to the blockchain (this concept is also explored more in the next chapter). Counterparty also has its own cryptocurrency, called XCP. Interestingly, to raise funds for the project, the developers took in around $1.6 million in bitcoin and "burned" it (*https://oreil.ly/9bc71*).

Privacy-Focused Cryptocurrencies

As we've mentioned, having a lot of data on a blockchain is not always ideal. After cryptocurrencies began to proliferate, many people grew concerned about how much financial data was being kept on the blockchain. Because of this, *privacy-focused* cryptocurrencies began to emerge. Two of the earliest projects in the privacy-focused area were Dash and Monero.

Dash

Launched in 2014, Dash is a software fork of Bitcoin. It went through less-than-reputable days when it was originally branded as a cryptocurrency called Darkcoin and was accepted as payment in online marketplaces where illicit goods were sold. The Dash protocol has an option for transactions called PrivateSend, which makes them untraceable by "mixing" them with the transactions of other users. In 2018, Dash implemented its own new type of ASIC-resistant proof-of-work, called X11 (*https://oreil.ly/xegwl*).

Monero

Also launched in 2014, Monero uses something called the CryptoNote protocol for proof-of-work. CryptoNote uses a technology called *ring signatures*, a type of digital signature that can be used, for the purpose of hiding certain information, by a group of users owning keys. This system makes it impossible to tell whose key was used for signing, providing anonymity. Concepts like *stealth addresses* to hide destinations as well as *ring confidential transactions* to hide balances also lend to the privacy focus of Monero (*https://oreil.ly/gRBAr*).

Zcash

Launched in 2016, Zcash is one of the most well-known privacy chains available today. Research has proven that in some instances, using hashes can compromise privacy in cryptographic systems. These systems could include blockchain-based cryptocurrencies, since they use hashes on a publicly viewable ledger. Zcash uses a technology called *Zero-Knowledge Succinct Non-Interactive Arguments of Knowledge* (zk-SNARKs) in order to enable privacy for its users.

zk-SNARKs allows users to transmit information between one another without having to share their actual data. Though that may sound confusing, there are instances where one party may not want to share private information with the other. For example, blockchain transactions allow both senders and receivers to easily see which exchanges, wallets, and other stakeholders the parties they're transacting with use. zk-SNARKs prevents this.

Zcash has a fixed supply of 21 million units, just like Bitcoin. And like with Bitcoin, transactions can be transparent; users must implement a *z-addr* in order to "shield" a transaction. During Zcash's launch, the price of one coin reached over $1,000 because of the hype surrounding the technology (*https://oreil.ly/nCNqh*). However, most transactions on the Zcash network don't use the privacy capability; research has shown only 3.5% of Zcash coins are held in shielded addresses (*https://oreil.ly/OMWaN*).

We'll talk a little more about these and other issues of privacy in Chapter 7.

Ripple and Stellar

There has been a good deal of criticism directed toward Bitcoin-based proof-of-work consensus, which has trickled into other cryptocurrencies due to software forks. One of the problems with the existing mechanisms is that there is an increasing degree of centralization (*https://oreil.ly/2p2ZG*) happening in cryptocurrency networks such as Bitcoin. For example, over 65% of all Bitcoin mining is done in China (*https://oreil.ly/F-iER*), according to the Cambridge Centre for Alternative Finance. Ripple and Stellar, which share some founders and technical traits, are cryptocurrencies that don't use proof-of-work mining and have had some success.

As Bitcoin mining continues to require ever-larger amounts of computer processing power, the number of entities controlling that power dwindles, and a larger share of the mining is thus done by only a few entities.

Ripple

Initially released in 2012, Ripple is one of the earliest and longest-lasting alternatives to Bitcoin. Unlike a number of alternative cryptocurrencies from that time, the identities of Ripple's founders are known: Jed McCaleb (*https://oreil.ly/XXAQn*), who founded the Mt. Gox bitcoin exchange, is one, along with Arthur Britto and David Schwartz. There was even a company, Ripple Labs, formed to support the Ripple blockchain and its native currency, XRP. Ripple Labs is the largest contributor to the code for XRP and its blockchain, more commonly referred to as a *ledger*.

While early on Ripple was an open source competitor to Bitcoin, with third-party "gateways" that functioned as a method of anonymous exchange, in 2014 the company pivoted to supporting banks as a faster and cheaper settlement network with a cross-border focus. Instead of using traditional proof-of-work, Ripple introduced a new type of consensus known as the XRP Consensus Protocol (*https://oreil.ly/qf4ZR*). It uses *Byzantine fault-tolerant agreement,* which requires nodes to come to agreement on transactions.

Ripple has hundreds of partnerships with various companies in the banking and payments sectors. The best-known strategic partnership is with the money remittances company MoneyGram, in which Ripple has made a $50 million equity investment (*https://oreil.ly/4svT4*). MoneyGram uses Ripple's On-Demand Liquidity product to facilitate cheaper and faster cross-border payments.

Stellar

Launched in 2014, Stellar was founded by Jed McCaleb and Joyce Kim, who had both previously worked at Ripple. The Stellar protocol is supported by the 501(c)(3) non-profit Stellar Development Foundation, created with the aim of providing a low-cost payment network for underbanked or unbanked individuals across the world.

In the early days, Stellar used a similar consensus mechanism to Ripple's. However, the Foundation changed the protocol in 2015, switching to SCP, a system devised by Stanford professor David Mazières. One of the reasons for switching from the Ripple-designed consensus mechanism was that the Stellar blockchain unexpectedly forked in 2014 (*https://oreil.ly/d4d2O*), creating two separate networks and causing problems with transactions.

After the departure of Joyce Kim, the Foundation began a long pivot, founding a company called Lightyear.io (*https://oreil.ly/XvlKy*) in 2017 (which became Interstellar (*https://oreil.ly/T9MVK*) in 2018 after acquiring the blockchain company Chain) to promote and encourage adoption of the protocol. Like Ripple, Stellar is focusing on cross-border payments, albeit with a more unbanked and underbanked bent, attempting to provide services to those who lack financial access.

Scaling Blockchains

In technology terms, *scaling* is the ability of a network to dynamically change resource allocation while improving or maintaining efficiency. Scaling has been a challenge as Bitcoin has grown: as more transactions end up on the blockchain, the network needs to continue providing a cheap and easy way to transact.

As configured today, Bitcoin's blockchain can only handle three to seven transactions per second (*https://oreil.ly/Erx-4*). Compare that to Visa's payment network, which can complete 65,000 transactions per second (*https://oreil.ly/ld6Vc*). What's more, when the Visa network needs to scale, its administrators can just adjust the allocation of resources. Visa owns the data and applications that run on its servers and controls access through central administrators.

But unlike Visa, which is centralized, Bitcoin is distributed. It runs across many computers and has no central point of control. In order for the Bitcoin network to grow, many industry stakeholders have argued that something needs to change—namely, the number of transactions that can go in each public printing of the ledger needs to be enlarged. Whether this can be done through larger blocks, less information in each block, or a larger number of blocks has long been debated (*https://oreil.ly/STmZM*).

Some stakeholders promote moving things *off-chain*, an option we'll explore in Chapter 10. Despite this, there is still a great need for technical solutions for scaling blockchains. We'll look at a few of the solutions that have been implemented here, and come back to this topic in the final chapter of the book.

SegWit

By 2015, a bottleneck in the Bitcoin infrastructure had become apparent—there were many more transactions waiting to be processed than could fit into each Bitcoin block. For example, 10 transactions might be requested per second, but no more than 7 of these could be processed. When there's a bottleneck, 7 transactions get processed and the other 3 remain in the mempool, which contains pending transactions. This became problematic in that it slowed transaction times on the network. It also meant Bitcoin fees could become very expensive as users would have to compete to have their transactions recorded in a block, causing a "fee market." One proposition to counter this problem was to implement a technology called *Segregated Witness*, or SegWit (*https://oreil.ly/IA5qs*).

SegWit was originally proposed in 2015 by Bitcoin Core developers Eric Lombrozo, Johnson Lau, and Pieter Wuille. It moved some data, known as the *witness portion*, to a different part of each transaction. That data was then excluded from the block size calculations, effectively reducing the overall space needed for each transaction in a block (see Figure 3-7). This allowed more transactions to be stored in each block, effectively increasing the transaction throughput. It also solved the *transaction malleability problem*, an exploit that could allow an attacker to change the unique identifier of a bitcoin transaction (*https://oreil.ly/o3tC6*) before it is confirmed into a block. By July 2017, miners on the Bitcoin network had "locked in" an upgrade to the core software to implement SegWit. In August 2017 SegWit was *activated*, meaning it was put into use on the network.

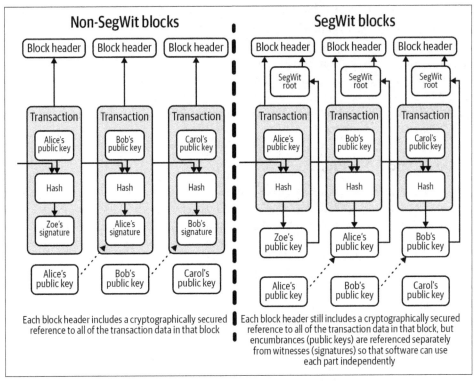

Figure 3-7. Technical comparison between SegWit and non-SegWit blocks

Lightning

The implementation of SegWit also created the technical preconditions for another scaling solution called the Lightning Network, proposed by Joseph Poon and Thaddeus Dryja in 2016. Lightning puts some bitcoin transactions on a separate "channel," taking them trustlessly off the main Bitcoin blockchain. This allows Bitcoin to continue to grow without the need to fill up the blockchain with so many transactions. That means more uses for Bitcoin—such as consumer payments and microtransactions, which have become problematic as blocks become full and fees increase—might now be possible (*https://oreil.ly/kh5_y*).

So how does it actually work? Instead of requiring miners and blocks to confirm transactions, the Lightning Network uses signatures between parties to digitally verify the sending and receiving of cryptocurrency (not just Bitcoin—Stellar has implemented a version of Lightning as well). This is done via the use of *bidirectional payment channels* (*https://oreil.ly/bChIR*). Users must create a channel on the network and post what is known as a *funding amount*, which does appear on the blockchain. The network uses a multisignature system called Hash Time Locked Contracts to enable multiple parties to transact with one another.

It is possible that the Lightning Network has some security risks. For example, Lightning experienced a distributed-denial-of-service (DDoS) attack in 2018, taking down 20% of the network (*https://oreil.ly/BHO7S*). The exploit used as many nodes as possible in order to block connections from occurring. Another problem with Lightning is that nodes must stay open for transactions to happen between two parties. In addition, there are concerns about the prevalence of fraud on the network, which may necessitate the inclusion of "watchtower" nodes to monitor transactions for possible fraudulent activity.

Other Altchain Solutions

The most common solutions to increase the speed at which blockchain transactions can be processed are called *state channels* and *sidechains*. The Lightning Network is an example of the former in Bitcoin. An example of an implementation in Ethereum is a project called Raiden. State channels don't use a separate blockchain, whereas sidechains do; an example is the Plasma implementation (*https://oreil.ly/cnei8*). Recently, there has also been a lot of talk about Rollups—specifically Zero Knowledge (ZK) Rollups, which present and publicly record validity without a verifier knowing the actual information for privacy purposes, and Optimistic Rollups, which use smart contracts to aggregate transactions off-chain and therefore store more information in each block.

Rollups is a scaling solution similar to Plasma, except Plasma has a data availability problem. With Rollups, thousands of transactions can be "rolled up" off-chain, which helps with scalability. It is estimated that the realistic throughput for Optimistic Rollups is around five hundred transactions per second (TPS, a metric used to define the speed of a blockchain), whereas ZK Rollups can manage around two thousand TPS. Of course, there is more to it than TPS, such as different security models and trusted setups, but discussing those is beyond the scope of this book.

Another scaling solution that Ethereum and other projects like Zilliqa and NEAR have been exploring for some time is *sharding*. This involves splitting the entire network into multiple network segments, termed *shards*. Each shard contains its own independent state, meaning a unique set of account balances and smart contracts.

Sharding allows the system to process many transactions in parallel, thus significantly increasing throughput. Although this helps with scaling, there are also some problems associated with it, such as the risk of a *single-shard takeover attack,* where attackers are able to take over a single shard due to the reduced hash power, and *cross-shard communication complexity,* where messages sent across shards may not be synchronized. When the network is sharded, essentially the security is also sharded, or reduced to individual parts. Ethereum intends to solve this via random sampling of validators on each shard (*https://oreil.ly/z-8yM*).

The Ethereum Classic Fork

The Bitcoin Cash fork was planned, and the developers of the new blockchain had the foresight and time to implement replay protection into their software. The first Ethereum fork (more on Ethereum in the next chapter) that created Ethereum Classic was another contentious fork, yet the software updates did not include replay protection.

The Ethereum Classic fork happened in June 2016, in reaction to a $50 million hack that exploited critical vulnerabilities in the implementation of a smart contract called The DAO (the DAO hack is also discussed in Chapter 4).

The Ethereum community was divided into two groups:

- One group wanted to update the Ethereum code to reverse the DAO hack.
- One group wanted to keep the software as it was because reversing the transaction would mean that a single entity could control the network, which would diminish the value of the network being decentralized.

On Ethereum block #1,920,000, most Ethereum miners updated their software to the new code that reversed the hack, and that blockchain is still considered to be Ethereum in 2020. The Ethereum miners who continued using the same prefork software began mining the forked blockchain, called Ethereum Classic.

The updated software issued to Ethereum miners to reverse the hack was developed and published quickly and did not include replay protection. Both blockchains were vulnerable to replay attacks for five months. During this time it was up to wallet holders to implement a workaround to protect against replay attacks.

One way in which wallet holders protected themselves was to send the funds on each blockchain to different addresses that they controlled. As seen in Figure 3-8, if a user has 10 ETH in Address A, they will generate Address B on the new Ethereum blockchain, and generate Address C on the Ethereum Classic blockchain. On the Ethereum blockchain they will then move 10 ETH to Address B, and on the Ethereum Classic blockchain they'll move the 10 ETH to Address C. After the funds are distributed to separate addresses, if someone attempts to do a replay attack on their funds, it won't work because the balance of funds on each blockchain will be different.

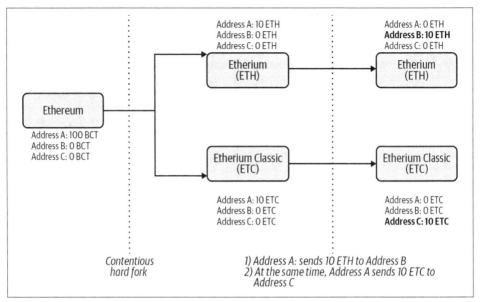

Figure 3-8. Protecting against replay attacks on Ethereum (ETH) and Ethereum Classic (ETC)

Exchanges that had the resources and expertise to protect against replay attacks were not affected. However, some individuals did lose funds due to the vulnerability. The Ethereum blockchain implemented replay protection in November 2016 through Ethereum Improvement Proposal 155 (EIP155), which was included in something called the Spurious Dragon hard fork.

Summary

Altcoins and altchains are fascinating explorations of what can be done with block-chains and cryptocurrencies. While numerous variations have been proposed, the majority of the projects described in this chapter build off the foundation of Bitcoin or Ethereum. Understanding what has already been tried is important. Many developers who come into the ecosystem may think a concept hasn't been attempted before, but a little history lesson might tell them otherwise.

CHAPTER 4

The Evolution to Ethereum

In its early days, Bitcoin was considered an all-encompassing technological marvel. Over time, however, developers began to realize that blockchain technology could support additional features. This led to the introduction of new concepts built on top of Bitcoin, and then an entirely new blockchain known as Ethereum.

Improving Bitcoin's Limited Functionality

Bitcoin was the first decentralized consensus protocol to apply the concept of *scripted money*—that is, the idea that cryptocurrency transactions could transmit funds depending on the true/false status of running a limited program. Initially, many saw bitcoin as "programmable money," but scripted money is a better analogy due to its limited functionality. Similarly, in the early days bitcoin was typically viewed as a currency, but along the way it began to be looked at as more of a *store of value* and sparked many debates on the difference between the two.

The evolution of Bitcoin led an influential and ardent group of followers in the developer community to advocate for a cautious and limited approach to protocol changes, for security and safety reasons. Protocol changes like block size increases were viewed with skepticism. These advocates wanted to maintain the core goals of remaining decentralized and being inclusive, to the extent that anyone could run a full node on cheap hardware with a low-throughput internet connection.

As we touched on in the previous chapter, however, some Bitcoin developers prompted a movement toward scaling solutions. Bitcoin became the foundation for what would become programmable money as developers began to devise ways to build on top of it, then later build entirely new blockchains.

Colored Coins and Tokens

Colored coins enable real-world assets such as equities (e.g., stocks) or commodities (e.g., gold) to be represented and managed on the Bitcoin blockchain. Bitcoin's scripting language is intentionally designed as *Turing incomplete*, meaning the available built-in commands are limited to reduce complexity in the network. Because of this, colored coins are built on top of, rather than directly on, the Bitcoin blockchain.

Bitcoin is limited in scope. However, its blockchain enables the storage of small amounts of data or metadata. The representation of some other asset can be attributed to the value of some amount of bitcoin via an address (for example, *17VZNX1SN5NtKa8UQFxwQbFeFc3iqRYhem*). The concept of colored coins introduced the idea of *tokens,* which are units of value built by programming a unique ledger on top of an existing blockchain. Tokens often look and act like other cryptocurrencies, with the exception that they are powered by another blockchain network. Tokens were foundational to the development of Ethereum's ecosystem, and the advent of colored coins on Bitcoin led to tokens on other blockchains.

Mastercoin and Smart Contracts

The evolution of Bitcoin's scaling solutions advanced in 2013 with the development of Mastercoin (*http://www.mastercoinfoundation.org*). Mastercoin was built on top of Bitcoin to add features not originally included in Bitcoin's core protocol. This allowed for more sophisticated programmable money concepts beyond Bitcoin's simple functionality. One of these was the concept of *smart contracts*, which are complex programs that run on blockchains.

Mastercoin introduced the notion of additional cryptocurrencies (*https://oreil.ly/oEFfK*), or tokens. Before Mastercoin, it was not easy to create new cryptocurrencies outside of software forks. The ability to allow money sent to a wallet to be rerouted to another wallet via smart contracts was not a feature of Bitcoin. In essence, Mastercoin, though now considered primitive, became a study of the capabilities of Bitcoin and exploring new functionality.

Mastercoin (and its inventor, J.R. Willett) is also credited with providing the first *initial coin offering* (ICO), a blockchain-based fundraising mechanism created to fund the initial protocol development.

Understanding Omni Layer

Omni Layer (*https://www.omnilayer.org*) is an open source, decentralized asset infrastructure built on Bitcoin. It is the successor of the work produced by the Mastercoin Foundation with the funding from its ICO in 2013. Omni Layer is an ongoing project, with its reference implementation known as Omni Core.

Omni Core essentially enhances elements of Bitcoin with additional features. It also provides smart contract capabilities, enabling developers to automate currency functions in a decentralized and transparent way. Smart contracts let transactions and agreements execute on the blockchain, performing functions beyond currency operations. These functions include the ability to use tokens to create new cryptocurrencies built on top of other blockchain protocols (among other properties explained in Chapter 5). Figure 4-1 illustrates the basic structure of how Omni works.

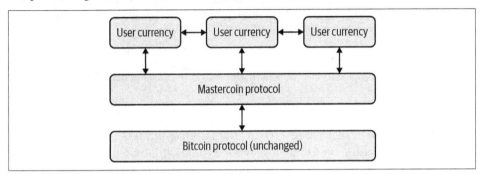

Figure 4-1. Overview of Omni Layer's technical stack

Tokens created on Omni include MaidSafe (*https://maidsafe.net*), a decentralized autonomous data network first proposed by engineer David Irvine in 2006. MaidSafe later implemented Omni Layer by using smart contract technology to enable an ICO, creating the MAID token, which is used within the network.

Tether

The most well-known project built on Omni is Tether (*https://oreil.ly/sM9CP*). It encompasses a use case that is incredibly important in the cryptocurrency world: how to represent a stable asset class in an ecosystem of volatile tokens. Tether is a digital blockchain cryptocurrency, and its aim is to provide a stable reserve currency pegged to the US dollar. According to the Tether whitepaper, one Tether token is pegged to one US dollar.

Real-world assets do present a problem when represented on a blockchain. That is, how do you actually peg the value of that asset in tokenized form? Tether claims to be backed by the US dollar, but unfortunately other than its website listing balances (*https://oreil.ly/4Qjjs*), there is little evidence that there really is one US dollar in a bank account for every tether in circulation. The company behind Tether promised to do a full audit of its one-to-one peg to the US dollar, but in 2018 it dissolved its relationship with its accounting firm (*https://oreil.ly/i3Nz1*) without explanation. The total outstanding tether on the market arbitrarily fluctuates, and tether has even lost its one USD to one tether peg in the markets (*https://oreil.ly/5mYlZ*) only to recover without much explanation.

While Tether is an interesting early use case for tokenization and implementation of Mastercoin's successor Omni Layer, it is still very experimental. It shows that backing a digital blockchain cryptocurrency such as tether with real-world assets such as the US dollar is still highly speculative and a work in progress.

How Omni Layer works

The Omni Layer team set out to build all the features that J.R. Willett promised in his "Second Bitcoin Whitepaper" (*https://oreil.ly/fbRRU*). These features included the following:

Custom currencies
    Anyone can create currencies where the ledger is managed by the Omni Layer network.

Decentralized exchange
    Instead of using a centralized exchange to facilitate the exchange of two currencies between parties, the Omni Layer code executes this trade.

When launching a proof-of-work–based blockchain, it is important to build a strong network of miners to dedicate *hash power* (computer infrastructure) to processing transactions. The larger the network, the more decentralized, trustworthy, and secure it becomes.

Omni wanted to focus its efforts on making tokenization and other smart contract features work on a decentralized blockchain without the burden of building that network effect. By building a second-layer protocol on top of Bitcoin, Omni benefited from the large network effect Bitcoin already had.

Adding custom logic

Bitcoin performs *logical operations*—rules that maintain the blockchain, proving that the fundamental concept of achieving consensus works. Omni adds custom logical operations to the Bitcoin blockchain.

After March 2014, Bitcoin added the OP_RETURN field, which enables the attachment of additional data to a bitcoin transaction. Once the OP_RETURN field was added to Bitcoin, every Omni transaction began storing a record within the OP_RETURN field of a bitcoin transaction.

Figure 4-2 shows an example Tether transaction recorded on the Bitcoin blockchain. This is a small transaction of five tether, also known as USDT. The transaction ID on the Bitcoin blockchain is:

c082fad4ee07a86c3ff9f31fb840d878c66082ad76ca81f0cafc866dee8aa9fc

Figure 4-2. Example of an Omni transaction on the Bitcoin blockchain

This is a Bitcoin transaction (*https://oreil.ly/svm8A*) that contains Omni Layer metadata. The only difference in an Omni transaction is the OP_RETURN field. Omni uses OP_RETURN because it provides enough space and is simple to use. The metadata in the OP_RETURN field translates to five USDT being sent. Figure 4-3 shows the same transaction in Omniexplorer (*https://oreil.ly/8WEPB*). Notice that the transaction ID is the same.

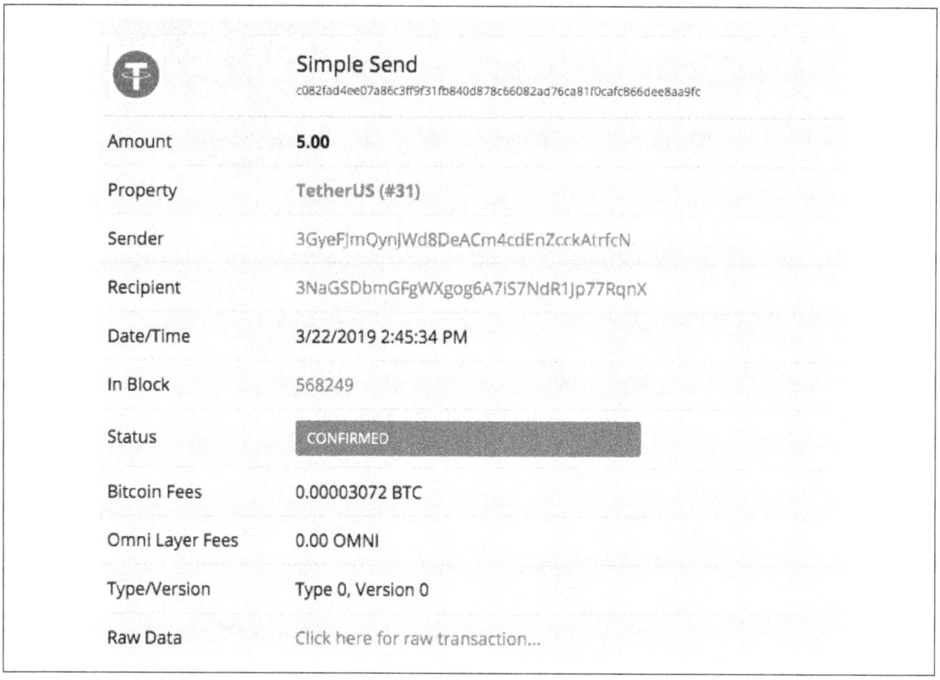

Figure 4-3. How the Tether transaction in Figure 4-2 looks in Omniexplorer

The value of the OP_RETURN field, 6f6d6e69000000000000001f000000001dcd6500, is the Omni Layer metadata that records the UDST transaction. The metadata is encoded in hex format, and Table 4-1 converts it into ASCII or decimal format.

Table 4-1. Translating OP_RETURN

Value stored in OP_RETURN (hex)	As ASCII or decimal	Description
6f6d6e69	omni	Omni flag to identify that it's an Omni transaction.
00000000	Simple send	Transaction type.
0000001f	31	Property type is 31, which is USDT. You can view all of the Omni Layer properties on the Omniexplorer site (https://www.omniexplorer.info/properties/production).
000000001dcd6500	5.00000000	Amount to send is 5.00000000. Omni Layer transactions all contain eight decimal places.

Ethereum: Taking Mastercoin to the Next Level

Ethereum represents an evolution in the design of and thinking about cryptocurrency networks. It's a more functional and general computation protocol that draws upon concepts from Bitcoin and Mastercoin, among other projects.

The Ethereum concept was first proposed by Vitalik Buterin in 2013. After lobbying the Mastercoin Foundation to make changes to its protocol (*https://oreil.ly/_Fq6p*) and add more functionality, and noting their reluctance to do so, Buterin began working with Gavin Wood and subsequently other founders to create the Ethereum protocol.

The aim of Ethereum was to take Mastercoin to the next level—that is, to create a decentralized, open computer system secured with consensus. Although Buterin envisioned Ethereum having an alternative to Bitcoin's proof-of-work mechanism, which he deemed wasteful, it currently uses a similar proof-of-work algorithm to Bitcoin called *Ethash*. Ethereum is expected to move to a proof-of-stake security model in the future—an ambitious project that changes the mining paradigm within the protocol, which is discussed more in Chapter 10.

Ether and Gas

The unit of account in Ethereum is *ether*. This cryptocurrency behaves in a similar fashion to bitcoin, with similar transaction address nomenclature. Ethereum addresses start with the sequence 0x. The blockchain has much faster confirmation times, save for periodic network congestion, and Ethereum is known to be a much faster transfer mechanism than Bitcoin.

As described in Chapter 2, Bitcoin uses an unspent transaction output (UTXO) structure to track the balances in accounts. Ethereum tracks the balances in the account state. UTXO is like having physical cash—bills and coins. Ethereum's approach is like having all your funds in a bank account. With UTXO, it's a lot more complex to make payments and calculate an account's balance.

For example, let's say you're at a coffee shop. You have three $1 bills in your pocket, and you want to buy a coffee for $1.50. You can't give the cashier $1.50; you have to give them two of the $1 bills and receive $0.50 back in change. Afterward, if you want to know how much money you have to spend, you have to calculate the value of all the bills and coins in your pocket.

It's the same thing with Bitcoin. Suppose your Bitcoin address has received three separate 1 BTC transactions, and you want to send 1.5 BTC to a friend. Like with physical cash, you can't send 1.5 BTC; you have to send 2 BTC. This is because each of those 1 BTC transactions you received in the past must be spent as a whole amount. So, you send two of the previous 1 BTC transactions, and in return you get 0.5 BTC change. This process occurs in a single bitcoin transaction.

Ethereum transactions are a lot simpler, similar to sending and receiving funds stored in a bank account. If your Ethereum address receives three separate 1 ETH transactions, your balance showing on the network will be 3 ETH. There is no need to calculate your account balance by adding up the different transactions yourself. And if you want to send 1.5 ETH, you can just send 1.5 ETH; there's no need to send more and receive change.

Ethereum also offers additional functionality. It takes elements from Bitcoin and Mastercoin to create *application-based* blockchain transactions, meaning it provides more functions than just account-based sending and receiving. Ethereum has another unit of account called *gas*. Gas enables developers to run applications on the Ethereum platform—these applications are known as *decentralized applications*, or *dapps* (discussed in detail later in this chapter).

Gas also solves one of the dangers of operating a programming language in a blockchain. Developers can run dapps on Ethereum without encountering what is known as the *halting problem*, or the inability to prevent code that runs indefinitely or in *infinite loops*. Ethereum requires gas to be used for computations of executed code within a smart contract, so that a dapp is as efficient as is possible. With every Ethereum transaction, developers specify a gas limit so if there's an infinite loop, the transaction will eventually run out of gas, and the miner will still earn the fees for running the transaction.

Use Cases: ICOs

There are a number of applications for a computerized transaction protocol using smart contracts. The concept of Ricardian contracts (*https://oreil.ly/OwjiK*) as proposed by Ian Grigg in 1996 provides insight into the realm of use cases for this technology. Innovations include using a cryptographic hash function for identification and defining legal elements as machine-readable by a computer. By being able to execute a set of instructions (via a smart contract) and associate it with an accounting system (via a blockchain), the Ethereum platform can be used to run a number of different dapps.

During the early years after Ethereum's release, it took time for a developer ecosystem to grow. But developers realized that one of its most powerful capabilities was the possibility of raising cryptocurrency funds in an automated and secure fashion, utilizing smart contracts—the already-mentioned ICO. For example, a project needing to raise money to launch a concept could set up a smart contract to take in ether. In return, it could give the donors a redeemable cryptocurrency built on top of Ethereum.

The legality of ICOs is questionable, and many projects have been ended prematurely because of legal problems they have caused. This issue is discussed in more detail in Chapter 9.

The idea of raising cryptocurrency funds to launch a project didn't begin with Ethereum. Entrepreneur Erik Voorhees raised money (*https://oreil.ly/HdGAx*) using the rudimentary mechanism of accepting bitcoin in return for digital "shares" in order to fund the blockchain-based gambling site Satoshi Dice in 2012. Mastercoin also used this concept, albeit in a much more organized fashion.

The ICO for MaidSafe was so oversold that donors eventually had to redeem incoming bitcoin with mastercoin instead of safecoin (*https://oreil.ly/dXxuZ*). Technical glitches such as this highlighted the need for a more reliable platform for crypto fundraising. Over time, as Ethereum matured, its smart contract platform coupled with the ability to create tokens on top of the Ethereum blockchain made it an ideal automated fundraising apparatus for jump-starting various cryptocurrency projects.

Decentralized Autonomous Organizations

In an effort to further the ethos of decentralization in the Ethereum ecosystem, the concept of a *decentralized autonomous organization* (DAO) was proposed as a way to utilize smart contracts to replace the governance of centralized authorities. Much like how the ICO concept replaces the centralized functions of an *initial public offering* (IPO), DAOs use cryptocurrency fundraising projects to create a distributed governance system whereby ICO investors have voting rights commensurate with ownership of tokens purchased in an ICO.

This concept was put to the ultimate test in a project known as *The DAO*. Launched in April 2016, The DAO was a smart contract–based ICO project built on Ethereum that was designed to run autonomously. Decisions made on the investment of raised funds into technology projects were to be based on the voting rights of token holders. The DAO was able to raise over $154 million (*https://oreil.ly/wtKJ_*) via Ethereum-based tokens from eleven thousand investors.

Forking Ethereum and the creation of Ethereum Classic

After its launch, a number of vulnerabilities were discovered in The DAO's smart contract code. One of these issues included a recursive call vulnerability (*https://oreil.ly/vPK-u*). The programmers had identified a flaw in the code: when funds were withdrawn from a wallet, the balance was only updated at the end of the function call. If the same function could be called again before the initial call completed, it would be possible to keep withdrawing the same funds over and over—a problem known as *infinite recursion*.

They immediately announced that the bug had been identified and would be fixed, but before they were able to roll out their update, on June 17, 2016, this vulnerability was exploited by an attacker who was able to steal over $50 million in ether from The DAO. There was no recourse for The DAO's developers to update the deployed contract code itself, because it was stored immutably on the blockchain. The only way to rectify the situation was to deploy a new contract and move the remaining funds over —a cumbersome and painful process.

This event led to the Ethereum Foundation forking the Ethereum blockchain, in order to undo the damage. It created two distinct versions of Ethereum: the original blockchain with the stolen funds still credited to the attacker, known as Ethereum Classic, and a forked version that retracted said funds, which continued to be known as Ethereum. This hard fork moved the stolen funds to a recovery address so their rightful owners could reclaim them.

The fork meant changing the Ethereum blockchain so that The DAO hack had effectively never happened, violating the principle of immutability. This was a controversial decision that was resisted by some members of the community, who chose to continue with the unaltered version of the blockchain. Ethereum Classic is a smart contract blockchain that still exists today, but its developer community is small and not as robust as Ethereum's.

Other Ethereum forks

The DAO hack warmed up the cryptocurrency community to the idea of forks. In addition to creating Ethereum Classic, the Ethereum blockchain has been forked several other times (*https://oreil.ly/kV0Xr*) to compensate for vulnerabilities and other changes in code. The Ethereum project understands the need to experiment, and when upgrades that are deemed important for the entire community become apparent, forking is seen as a better alternative than maintaining the concept of immutability. The Ethereum ecosystem has no qualms about forking its blockchain and gathering enough momentum for such changes to be successful. This attitude stands in stark contrast to other chains, like Bitcoin, where immutability is sacrosanct.

Key Organizations in the Ethereum Ecosystem

In the Ethereum ecosystem, multiple stakeholders and organizations support the vision that Ethereum is building, and each organization supports it from its own angle.

The Ethereum Foundation

As a leader in developing the roadmap and implementing further changes to the Ethereum platform, the Ethereum Foundation (*https://ethereum.org*) wields significant influence in the community. It also funds scalability projects related to the platform, including Plasma (*https://oreil.ly/SrG8m*), a solution that aims to increase the number of transactions on the platform without sacrificing the security of the network.

The Ethereum Foundation's predecessor was formed as a Swiss nonprofit entity, and initiated Ethereum's ICO. After raising over $18 million (*https://oreil.ly/3TzPj*) from the community in bitcoin, the Swiss entity transferred those funds to the Ethereum Foundation, which has been the key provider of funding for the aforementioned development efforts.

The Enterprise Ethereum Alliance

Announced in early 2017, the Enterprise Ethereum Alliance (EEA) (*https://entethalli ance.org*) aims to band together corporate entities interested in deployment of Ethereum blockchain solutions. Members of the EEA include IBM and Microsoft, which supports running Ethereum blockchain services on top of Azure.

One of the main goals of the EEA is finding blockchain-specific use cases in corporate business environments. Many large organizations are wary of the cryptocurrency aspect of blockchains because of compliance and other regulatory concerns. A good deal of the Ethereum-related work being done on the corporate side involves forking it to create a *private blockchain* that separates the token from public cryptocurrency markets. Chapter 9 discusses private and permissioned blockchains further.

Parity

Parity (*https://www.parity.io*), a London-based software solutions company, was formed by Gavin Wood, one of the original founders of Ethereum who contributed code very early on in the formation of Ethereum's protocol concepts. Parity has deployed several developer tools to make Ethereum easier to deploy, including reference frameworks.

The company is known for falling victim to the "Parity hack" in 2017, where $30 million worth of ether was stolen by an unknown attacker. This was the second-largest Ethereum hack (after The DAO); it exploited a vulnerability in Parity's multi-signature wallets that enabled the attacker to send two transactions, one of which included abstracting logic to change a wallet address in the code (*https://oreil.ly/jeGwj*).

ConsenSys

Founded by Ethereum cofounder Joseph Lubin, ConsenSys (*https://consensys.net*) is an organization that develops enterprise applications, invests in startups, builds developer tools, and offers blockchain education for the Ethereum network. The organization focuses on the development of dapps. Its offerings include the Truffle Suite, a framework that makes Ethereum development easier, and Gitcoin, a GitHub-inspired bug bounty tool for the Ethereum blockchain.

ConsenSys also has a mission to create consumer-friendly tools within the Ethereum ecosystem. One of the most well-known of these is MetaMask, a browser-based Ethereum wallet that makes using decentralized applications easier. ConsenSys also funds projects that create dapps and other useful applications.

Decentralized Applications (Dapps)

We've mentioned already that applications that run via a smart contract on a blockchain are known as decentralized apps, or *dapps*. Dapps are typically architected with a backend using a smart contract running on a blockchain and a thin frontend UI that interacts with it. It's similar to a client/server architecture, where the server is the smart contract. These types of applications make the blockchain more programmable and more functional.

A dapp is basically any computer program that runs on a smart contract platform, and the largest platform for this today is Ethereum. As we discussed in Chapter 1, in computer science, a *distributed system* is one in which the components are located on disparate computing resources, and a system is in place for communications to occur between these resources. Examples of distributed systems include many telecommunication networks and the web.

There are other platforms that provide the capability for dapps, but Ethereum is by far the largest platform for developers to execute distributed code.

Use Cases

A key feature of a dapp is immutability, meaning no centralized authority can change the code after it has been published to the blockchain. For this reason, use cases for dapps are generally found where there is a bottleneck in centralized systems. Many centralized applications, for example, are not censorship-resistant. In many centralized apps, a third party decides what users can and cannot see. Often these decisions are subjective, seemingly arbitrary, and made without input from users. With the use of a backend platform such as Ethereum and the web, developers can deploy applications that are permissionless, which greatly differ from their centralized counterparts.

Another feature of dapps is that they enable efficient and secure transfer of digital assets through the use of blockchains. For example, today many applications offer censorship resistance (think BitTorrent (*https://www.bittorrent.com*)) and privacy (through encryption). However, what dapps enable beyond these two properties is that transfer of value can be executed quickly and programmatically.

 Dapp platforms are relatively new. There's still lots to learn about how best to create them, and the infrastructure for doing so is still in its growth stages. Dapps are not yet widely used. In fact, there's some question about their traction and staying power, and the purposes of some dapps today seem nefarious. Many of them are designed to avoid regulatory scrutiny, and there are numerous gambling, gaming, and decentralized exchange dapps in use.

Challenges in Developing Dapps

There are several design challenges (*https://oreil.ly/7kI4n*) inherent to creating dapps today, including concerns about deployment, user experience, speed, and scalability. These issues currently exist across all dapp platforms, including Ethereum.

When a developer deploys a smart contract for a dapp, they need to be sure that its code does not contain critical flaws. It is not easy to update contracts. Most smart contract platforms, including Ethereum, do not permit redeploying to the same address. In addition, upgrading usually entails difficult data migration of the state that the smart contract manages.

Developers can test their dapps on one of four Ethereum testnets. Responsible dapp developers will spend months getting their contracts audited by professional security auditors (Quantstamp, OpenZeppelin), who then publish their reports to the public. During this time, they will also invite people in the community to audit their smart contracts through GitHub.

Unlike with centralized apps, where a user's experience is continuous, deploying new smart contract code could cause a break in the user experience. Also, the speed of dapps relies on the speed of the blockchain and its confirmation times. This issue was brought to the fore on Ethereum in late 2017 with the dapp CryptoKitties, whose popularity led to an enormous number of transactions congesting the Ethereum network (*https://oreil.ly/h3N1u*). This made the dapp virtually unusable until enthusiasm died down.

Now that you have some background, let's dive a bit more deeply into authoring, deploying, and working with Ethereum smart contracts.

Deploying and Executing Smart Contracts in Ethereum

Smart contracts have come a long way since the concept was first proposed in the 1990s. Omni Layer proved that running a dapp on top of a blockchain was possible, but it had many limitations, the biggest of which was who was given permission to author and deploy the dapp. If someone wanted to deploy a dapp, they had to convince the platform's developers to add it to the Omni Core code. In effect, Omni Core was the dapp where all code was deployed. The development of code was centralized, and only Omni Core developers could update it. Developers who wanted to deploy dapps on their own had to explore other options, such as forking Omni Core and making their own client that ran on top of Bitcoin—not an easy endeavor.

Other limitations of Omni Core included the following:

Blockchain scaling and speed depended on Bitcoin and its core developers
Omni Core still has limited influence over the future of the blockchain it runs on.

The Bitcoin blockchain is not designed for program execution

It's optimized for store of value, and its limited scripting language means that it will never be suitable for sophisticated smart contracts built directly on top of the blockchain. For example, the OP_RETURN field has a storage limit of 80 bytes, which limits the types of programs you can run in Omni Layer.

The Ethereum Virtual Machine

The Ethereum Virtual Machine (EVM) makes it easy for developers to create dapps and for the network to execute them. The purpose of the EVM is twofold:

1. Allow developers to deploy smart contracts to the blockchain
2. Instruct miners on how to execute EVM smart contract code embedded in the software that they run

Authoring a smart contract

Developers can use a few different languages to author a smart contract. The most common language is Solidity (*https://oreil.ly/oUDzV*).

ConsenSys has released a suite of tools to make it easy for developers to author, debug, and deploy smart contracts with Solidity, called the Truffle Suite (*https://truffleframework.com*).

To interact with a smart contract, you need an Ethereum wallet. The most popular wallet is MetaMask (*https://metamask.io*), which is a browser extension. This wallet stores a copy of your seed and private keys locally on your machine.

The seed and private key are not stored centrally. It's important to make a physical copy of the mnemonic seed (e.g., on paper) and store it in a safe place for redundancy. In addition, using a hardware wallet rather than relying on private keys being held locally by the wallet software can help increase security. For more on wallet choices, see Chapter 2.

Before deploying your smart contract to the main Ethereum network, it is wise to test it on one of the most common testnets:

- Ropsten (*https://ropsten.etherscan.io*)
- Rinkeby (*https://www.rinkeby.io*)
- Kovan (*https://kovan-testnet.github.io/website*)

- Görli (*https://goerli.net*)

Smart contract developers need to spend ether in the form of gas to deploy and change the state of a contract. All Ethereum testnets have *faucets* where you can get testnet ETH (tETH) for free. These testnets make for an ideal staging environment for smart contracts.

Deploying a smart contract

After a developer has written a smart contract, they can publish it to the *mainnet* or production environment, or any of the testnets. Publishing is done by sending a smart contract transaction to the Ethereum network. The easiest way to generate this transaction is by using the Ethereum Remix tool (*https://remix.ethereum.org*).

Remix is a cloud-based integrated development environment (IDE) for smart contract development. It supports the Solidity and Vyper languages, and since it's a website there is no need to install software. It lets developers write, debug, compile, and distribute smart contract code to the Ethereum network, including the mainnet and testnet environments.

Figure 4-4 shows what deploying the *Mastering_Blockchain_Guestbook.sol* (*https://github.com/Mastering-Blockchain-Book*) smart contract on Remix looks like. In this case, it's being deployed to the Ropsten network.

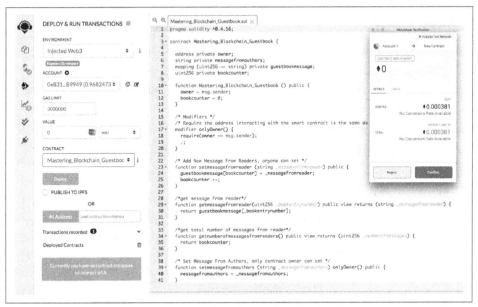

Figure 4-4. Deploying the Mastering_Blockchain_Guestbook.sol smart contract to the Ethereum network via Remix

To deploy the smart contract, you must click the Deploy button. Remix then sends the transaction data to MetaMask, which asks for your authorization to complete the transaction.

After the transaction is authorized, MetaMask pushes a smart contract creation transaction to the network. Figure 4-5 shows what this looks like.

Figure 4-5. Details of the transaction (https://oreil.ly/Y2eSZ) that created the smart contract

Note the following in this transaction:

- The value of the transaction is 0 ether, indicating that no ether were transferred.
- The transaction is being recorded in block #5357662.
- The miner who discovered this block receives a transaction fee of 0.00137715 Testnet ETH (tETH).

After the Ethereum network processes a transaction, it stores the smart contract on the Ethereum network in bytecode format, which takes up less space, as illustrated in Figure 4-6.

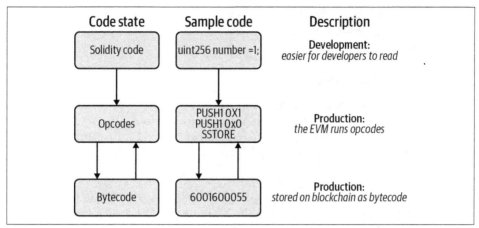

Figure 4-6. Different layers that smart contract code goes through when going from development to production

Since the smart contract code is on the Ethereum testnet, it is viewable by the public (*https://oreil.ly/tHshF*) (see Figure 4-7).

Figure 4-7. Viewing the smart contract code after deployment on etherscan.io

When a smart contract is created, it is given an Ethereum address. This Ethereum address can hold an ETH balance and send/receive ETH just like a normal Ethereum address can.

Interacting with a smart contract

Now that the Guestbook smart contract has been deployed to the Ethereum testnet, it's possible to begin reading data from it and writing data to it. To read data from the contract you just ping the network directly, like making a call to a public API. However, to write data to the contract, you must send a transaction to the contract address.

All read/write interactions with a smart contract require a reference to the contract's *application binary interface* (ABI). The ABI is like an API for a smart contract. ABIs are machine-readable, meaning they are easy to parse by client software to understand how to interact with the contract code. An ABI documents all the functions and their attributes.

Here is the ABI for the Guestbook smart contract:

```
[{"constant":true,"inputs":[{"name":"_bookentrynumber","type":"uint256"}],
"name":"getmessagefromreader","outputs":[{"name":"_messagefromreader",
"type":"string"}],"payable":false,"stateMutability":"view","type":"function"},
{"constant":true,"inputs":[],"name":"getnumberofmessagesfromreaders",
"outputs":[{"name":"_numberofmessages","type":"uint256"}],"payable":false,
"stateMutability":"view","type":"function"},
{"constant":true,"inputs":[],"name":"getmessagefromauthors",
"outputs":[{"name":"_name","type":"string"}],"payable":false,
"stateMutability":"view","type":"function"},
{"constant":false,"inputs":[{"name":"_messagefromreader","type":"string"}],
"name":"setmessagefromreader","outputs":[],"payable":false,
"stateMutability":"nonpayable","type":"function"},
{"constant":false,"inputs":[{"name":"_messagefromauthors","type":"string"}],
"name":"setmessagefromauthors","outputs":[],"payable":false,
"stateMutability":"nonpayable","type":"function"},
{"inputs":[],"payable":false,"stateMutability":"nonpayable","type":"constructor"}]
```

Reading a smart contract

Let's read the data in the Guestbook smart contract (*https://oreil.ly/thsoP*). You should see something like Figure 4-8.

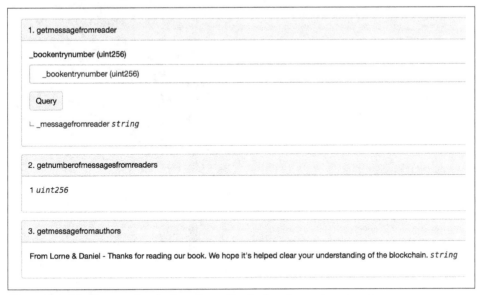

Figure 4-8. Viewing read-only functions of a deployed smart contract

This figure shows the three read functions that the Guestbook smart contract has. The first function requires an input to return data, and the other two don't.

Writing a smart contract

Let's now write some data to the Guestbook smart contract (*https://oreil.ly/VxE2M*). This will look something like Figure 4-9.

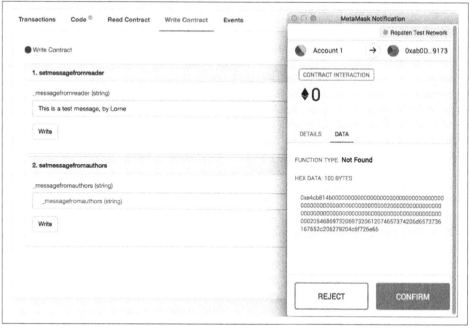

Figure 4-9. Calling a write-only function of a deployed smart contract

The MetaMask browser extension will provide you with the choice to connect to the website or not. After connecting to the website, you can start writing data to the contract. Notice that two things happen when you click Confirm:

- Etherscan generates a new transaction, populating it with the correct data, and pushes it to your MetaMask wallet.
- MetaMask then asks for authorization to send that transaction.

After you click Confirm, your transaction gets pushed to the Ethereum network.

Executing a smart contract

As part of block discovery, Ethereum miners add transactions to blocks in much the same fashion as Bitcoin miners. There are two main actions a transaction can trigger:

Payment
Send ETH value from address A to address B.

Execution

Execute the smart contract.

If the following are true, then the miner will execute the smart contract code through the EVM:

- The receiving address is a smart contract.
- The data payload contains data.

The earlier test message example created a transaction (*https://oreil.ly/SEAH8*) where the receiving address is the *Mastering_Blockchain_Guestbook* smart contract, and the data payload contains the following data:

```
Function: setmessagefromreader(string_messagefromreader)

MethodID: 0xe4cb814b
[0]: 0000000000000000000000000000000000000000000000000000000000000020
[1]: 0000000000000000000000000000000000000000000000000000000000000020
[2]: 546869732069732061207465737374206d6573736167652c206279204c6f726e65
```

Gas and Pricing

As we've discussed, gas is a unit of account used in the Ethereum ecosystem to calculate how much ether miners are paid to process transactions. When a miner executes a smart contract transaction through the EVM, the miner executes *opcodes*—instructions at the machine level—that are written in the smart contract. Each opcode that it runs has a gas price associated with it.

Figure 4-10 shows examples of opcodes and gas prices.

Value	Mnemonic	Gas used	Subset	Removed from stack	Added to stack	Notes
0x00	STOP	0	zero	0	0	Halts execution
0x01	ADD	3	verylow	2	1	Addition operation
0x02	MUL	5	low	2	1	Multiplication operation
0x03	SUB	3	verylow	2	1	Subtraction operation
0x04	DIV	5	low	2	1	Integer division operation
0x05	SDIV	5	low	2	1	Signed integer division operation (truncated)
0x06	MOD	5	low	2	1	Modulo remainder operation
0x07	SMOD	5	low	2	1	Signed modulo remainder operation
0x08	ADDMOD	8	mid	3	1	Modulo addition operation
0x09	MULMOD	8	mid	3	1	Modulo multiplication operation

Figure 4-10. List of gas prices by opcode

Gas is necessary because it rewards miners for processing a transaction through a smart contract. It also defends the network against spam and denial-of-service attacks. Gas is paid in ETH. The miner receives the usual fixed block reward for discovering the block, plus the ETH received from gas for processing all the smart contract code.

When structuring a transaction, there are two gas-related fields you need to input:

Gas price
> The amount of ETH paid for each unit of gas. If a user wants their transaction to be processed immediately, they can pay a higher gas price to incentivize the miner to choose their transaction over other transactions waiting to be processed.

Gas limit
> The maximum amount of gas you are willing to pay the miner to process your transaction. The amount of gas specified here should be sufficient to run all the opcodes the contract function is expected to perform.

 Wei is the smallest unit of ether (ETH), which is 10e-18 ETH. The US dollar is divisible by two decimal places. ETH is divisible by 18 decimal places. Just as the US dollar has the penny as its smallest unit of value, a wei is the smallest unit of value in Ethereum. A satoshi is the smallest unit of value for Bitcoin.

Here are a few more of the denominations:

- 1 wei = 1 wei
- 1 kwei = 1,000 wei
- 1 mwei = 1,000,000 wei
- 1 gwei = 1,000,000,000 wei

 ETH Gas Station (*https://ethgasstation.info*) is a very useful site for calculating what gas price you should pay based on the current network usage.

In the earlier Guestbook smart contract example, where we wrote a test message, the amounts were as follows:

- *Gas limit:* 128,050
- *Gas used by transaction:* 85,367 (66.67%)
- *Gas price:* 0.000000001 ether (1 gwei)

Interacting with Code

Here are a couple of popular methods for programmatically interacting with the Ethereum network:

Web3.js

The most common way developers make their websites interact with MetaMask and smart contracts is through Web3.js (*https://oreil.ly/6PAvl*), a Node.js library.

Infura

Another popular option is Infura (*https://infura.io*), which provides a REST API to the Ethereum network. This API is structured in a way that is familiar to developers. The advantage of using Infura is that the learning curve to deploying is much lower because it handles access to Ethereum. The disadvantage is that developers must trust Infura to secure and pass along data properly.

Summary

The Ethereum ecosystem developed quickly from an idea publicly proposed in 2014 to the full-fledged network it is today. Thanks to its smart contract properties and the vast number of resources and tools being created in the ecosystem, many developers now choose to build on Ethereum rather than Bitcoin. Ethereum and Bitcoin do share some technology, but their advancement is certainly going in separate ways.

CHAPTER 5

Tokenize Everything

The advent of Bitcoin gave developers an opportunity to explore different types of cryptocurrencies. Yet it was Ethereum, a totally new technology, that gave coders the ability to easily create new cryptocurrencies on top of its blockchain, known as *tokens*. Today, there are tens of thousands of cryptocurrencies, mostly thanks to Ethereum. The Ethereum network sparked the proliferation of the concept of "tokenize everything" via initial coin offerings (ICOs), which allow a project to raise cryptocurrency funds and give investors tokens in exchange. This chapter looks at how that happened. We'll begin by introducing a few notable examples:

Mastercoin

Developer J.R. Willett began working on the Mastercoin whitepaper in 2011. His aim (*https://oreil.ly/tVC-J*) was not "to bootstrap an entirely new blockchain, as every other cryptocurrency does," but rather "to create an entirely new network of currencies, commodities, and securities on top of Bitcoin itself." Willett eventually realized that community backing in the form of investment via bitcoin might help foster adoption. So, he held the first "token sale," or ICO, in 2013. This enabled Mastercoin to raise 3,700 BTC, or about $2.3 million (*https://oreil.ly/UXrMe*) at the time.

Ethereum

As described in the previous chapter, the beginnings of Ethereum trace back to November 2013, when Vitalik Buterin began emailing around a whitepaper proposing a new protocol based on elements of Bitcoin, Mastercoin, and other projects. This document was disseminated throughout the cryptocurrency community, and developers and backers began to accumulate. Buterin made a public announcement of the Ethereum project in February 2014.

A Swiss-based nonprofit foundation was created to initiate the ICO, and starting in July 2014, for 42 days Ethereum conducted a crowdsale. Approximately 60 million ether tokens were sold, raising some 31,000 BTC (around $18 million at the time). This became the template for many other ICOs in the future.

Gnosis

A decentralized prediction market platform, Gnosis shares some concepts and some personnel with the Augur project, an early Ethereum-based offering that had its ICO in 2015. The Gnosis multisignature wallet is still one of the most widely used in the Ethereum ecosystem, especially for applications such as cold storage of tokens.

The most interesting aspect of the Gnosis project's ICO was the Dutch-style auctioning system it employed. This novel concept enabled tokens to decline in value over the time of the ICO, encouraging investors to wait until the end to get the best pricing. Most ICOs are conducted the reverse way: cheaper tokens are offered the earlier an investor gets in. However, this proved successful as Gnosis was able to raise over $300 million in 15 minutes (*https://oreil.ly/_Cf97*) while keeping 95% of the cryptocurrency attributed to the project and its founders.

EOS

EOS.IO, brainchild of Daniel Larimer, is a blockchain protocol that aims to solve the scalability issues of blockchains by distributing computing resources equally among EOS cryptocurrency holders. The project raised over $4 billion in a year (*https://oreil.ly/79g90*), one of the biggest raises ever, by using an uncapped token sale on Ethereum. The offering was for an ERC-20 token called EOS, which was converted into the native token once their native blockchain was ready.

Are ICOs Still Possible?

ICOs have been conducted since 2013 and reached a height of popularity during the 2017 cryptocurrency boom. On December 11, 2017, the US Securities and Exchange Commission (SEC) issued a cease and desist order to California-based token project Munchee, Inc., halting an ICO intended to build a mobile restaurant review app. The SEC deemed Munchee's token to be a security. This effectively ended the US practice of offering a cryptocurrency-based token purely for speculation.

As the market prices for bitcoin and ether fell in 2018, ICOs became less popular. Regulatory pressure and lawsuits on existing projects that did not move at a pace suitable to investors also contributed to the fall in popularity. In fact, many failed to deliver at all, or offered unworkable business concepts, or simply scammed investors. North American regulators have attempted to take a hands-off approach to ICOs that court investors, but new tokens issued may require more regulatory oversight. This is evidenced in the SEC's no-action letter for TurnKey Jet, Inc. (*https://oreil.ly/h935g*), giving tacit approval for its ICO project.

Tokens on the Ethereum Platform

Creating a token allows developers to create a cryptocurrency on the Ethereum network. This enables anyone to issue an asset on a blockchain using one of the most well-known cryptocurrency protocols. The ERC-20 standard on Ethereum (*https://eips.ethereum.org/EIPS/eip-20*) is a reference implementation of blockchain assets on the network, paving the way for tokens to have properties that enable their use across many different exchanges, wallets, and other blockchain services. There *are* other blockchain platforms for issuing tokens. However, issuing an ERC-20 asset on Ethereum is one of the easiest and most secure ways to create a cryptocurrency today.

Outside of technical projects like mobile dapps, distributed computing, or payment mechanisms, tokens have the potential to disrupt existing financial services where bottlenecks still exist. Blockchain and cryptocurrency have the ability to represent something of value in the real world, as long as they can be properly pegged back to a real-world asset.

In complex real estate transactions, for example, tokens on a blockchain could enable better record keeping for owners—the state of Ohio is looking at using blockchain for this purpose (*https://oreil.ly/GEupr*). In the future, transfers of assets could be completed more quickly and easily using tokens. Other areas where tokens may prove useful to prove authenticity could include art, cars, and stocks and bonds.

Fungible and Nonfungible Tokens

Not all tokens are created equal. One of the most important differentiators when creating tokens is whether they are *fungible* or *nonfungible*. Fungible tokens all have the same value and are interchangeable with one another, whereas nonfungible tokens represent something that is unique.

Examples of fungible assets are currencies like the US dollar. One dollar is one dollar, whether it exists in a physical form as coins or a bill or digitally in a bank account or other financial service. Most cryptocurrencies, like bitcoin, ether, and ERC-20 assets, are also fungible.

Items such as cars or houses are nonfungible—each is unique and not interchangeable with any other random car or house. CryptoKitties (*https://www.cryptokitties.co*) —digital cats represented on Ethereum as ERC-721 tokens—are another example of a nonfungible asset (we discuss this example more later in this chapter).

There are implications to creating tokens. Cryptocurrency markets are highly volatile. If a token is listed on an exchange and used only for speculation, its price could become highly unstable.

Smart contract development is a nascent area of computer science. It is highly recommended that a third-party auditor (like OpenZeppelin (*https://openzeppelin.com/contracts*), which contributed background for this chapter) take a look at your code before you bring a token into the wild. Other well-known companies providing such services include Trail of Bits (*https://www.trailofbits.com*) and Chainsecurity (*https://chainsecurity.com*).

Ethereum offers many different token types that can be issued. Some popular ones include ERC-20, ERC-721, ERC-223, ERC-777, and ERC-1400. The variety enables developers to create different types of functional cryptocurrencies on top of the Ethereum blockchain.

An exhaustive list of Ethereum token standards is available on GitHub (*https://oreil.ly/zBZ5x*). Some of the tokens listed are currently functional, whereas others are merely proposed ideas.

Thanks to Ethereum's nature, new types of cryptocurrencies on the Ethereum blockchain may provide real-world benefits. ERC-846, which provides for shared ownership of a token (*https://oreil.ly/TbdBg*), is a good example of a real-world use case.

Is a Token Necessary?

One existential question developers should ask when developing blockchain-based solutions is: *Is a token necessary?* Many tokenization/ICO projects have been developed with a token for fundraising, but with no clear motivation other than to have a cryptocurrency. Although ICOs are a good method of using crypto for fundraising, regulatory pressure is pushing developers to create tokens that have a greater function within projects.

A token may not be useful for a blockchain-based project if it is only for fundraising. In addition, any project looking for stable asset value will not find a token to be a suitable solution, although assets like stablecoins may be. Any processing function that has an asset that is unstable could prove to be problematic in the future. This is an issue already experienced on the blockchain in the form of transaction fees. A fee on the Bitcoin network, for example, can change based on how much network demand there is. The greater the demand, the less space is available in the blocks, which can create a fee market where the highest bidder "wins." This supply and demand paradigm also exists in Ethereum for gas fees and token prices once they hit exchanges.

Airdrops

As we've said, the main way to distribute tokens is via an ICO or similar type of offering. Another alternative is doing an *airdrop*. Intended to leverage network effects of already existing blockchains, airdrops are free or low-cost disbursements of cryptocurrencies to a large subset of users. The idea is to rapidly give a project a user base from its inception, baking in adoption of an already existing project/cryptocurrency. The largest case so far has been the Stellar Foundation's $125 million airdrop (*https:// oreil.ly/ch3IJ*) of its XLM token via the Blockchain.info wallet.

 Airdrops may seem like a solution to nascent cryptocurrency adoption, but they're not without their drawbacks. In particular, there likely are tax implications for users to obtain a cryptocurrency-based asset at zero cost. When sold, there could be a taxable event, depending on jurisdiction. Providing a token at nearly no cost also might not bode well for future value, due to dilution of the underlying cryptocurrency being airdropped. There's no such thing as a free lunch in economics, so there could be compensating or even extra costs to airdrops.

Different Token Types

Different Ethereum tokens have different technical specifications, and they also use different nomenclature depending on how regulators around the world define them. It's important for developers to understand the various terms being floated regarding how to define tokens:

Utility
> *Utility* in the context of tokens means that a blockchain-based cryptocurrency must have some use outside of financial speculation. There are several longstanding projects attempting to do this in the blockchain world. One of the best-known is Filecoin (*https://filecoin.io*), where tokens grant users access to space on a decentralized cloud storage platform.

Security
> A *security*, as defined by the SEC, is an investment contract. Designed to provide a promise of a return, investment contracts are regulated devices used around the world for fundraising. For this reason, the tokens proposed in many ICOs could be considered securities. They are thus regulated in the jurisdiction of issuance. An example of a project that offers security tokens is bloXroute (*https://blox route.com*), a protocol that changes the way networking and routing work for

blockchain. Owning a bloXroute token means entitlement to a share in the future payout that blockchains will be making to bloXroute to use its routing protocol.

A *security token offering* (STO) is an attempt to create an ICO that fits into a regulatory framework. As ICOs mimic some of the qualities of an equity IPO, regulators around the world are increasingly trying to understand how to protect investors from fraud, excessive risk, and theft. The SEC, for example, has published a framework (*https://oreil.ly/rQOGS*) for crypto-based security offerings.

Understanding Ethereum Requests for Comment

With improving capabilities of the EVM, empowering developers to write better smart contracts, the Ethereum community began creating standards, formalized as Ethereum Requests for Comment (ERCs). These standards are important, as they ensure that apps wanting to interact with Ethereum smart contracts will know which functions and inputs to call. All proposed ERCs start as an Ethereum Improvement Proposal (EIP), which then goes through a vetting process. This is similar to the Bitcoin Improvement Process, discussed in Chapter 3.

ERC-20

The most common ERC standard for Ethereum tokens is ERC-20. Every smart contract that is compliant with the ERC-20 standard will implement the methods shown in Table 5-1.

Table 5-1. ERC-20 methods

Method	Description
`totalSupply() public view returns (uint256 totalSupply)`	Get the total token supply.
`balanceOf(address _owner) public view returns (uint256 balance)`	Get the account balance of another account with address `_owner`.
`transfer(address _to, uint256 _value) public returns (bool success)`	Send `_value` amount of tokens from address `_from` to address `_to`. Tokens are sent from the address that called the transaction.
`transferFrom(address _from, address _to, uint256 _value) public returns (bool success)`	Send `_value` amount of tokens from address `_from` to address `_to`.
`transferFrom(address _from, address _to, uint256 _value) public returns (bool success)`	Send `_value` amount of tokens from address `_from` to address `_to`.
`approve(address _spender, uint256 _value) public returns (bool success)`	Allow `_spender` to withdraw from your account, multiple times, up to `_value` amount. If this function is called again, it overwrites the current allowance with the new `_value`.

Method	Description
allowance(address _owner, address _spender) public view returns (uint256 remaining)	Return the amount which _spender is still allowed to withdraw from _owner.

Every smart contract that is compliant with the ERC-20 standard will implement the two events shown in Table 5-2. Developers can build applications that listen for these events to be triggered—for example, a cryptocurrency wallet checking to see if any of its Ethereum addresses have received tokens.

Table 5-2. Events supported by ERC-20-compliant smart contracts

Event	Description
Transfer(address indexed _from, address indexed _to, uint256 _value)	Event triggered when tokens are transferred.
Approval(address indexed _owner, address indexed _spender, uint256 _value)	Event triggered whenever approve(address _spender, uint256 _value) is called.

The following is an example of a basic ERC-20 smart contract, *Mastering_Blockchain_Token.sol* (*https://github.com/Mastering-Blockchain-Book*):

```solidity
pragma solidity ^0.4.21;

contract EIP20Interface {
    /// total amount of tokens
    uint256 public totalSupply;

    /// @param _owner The address from which the balance will be retrieved
    /// @return The balance
    function balanceOf(address _owner) public view returns (uint256 balance);

    /// @notice send `_value` tokens to `_to` from `msg.sender`
    /// @param _to The address of the recipient
    /// @param _value The amount of tokens to be transferred
    /// @return Whether the transfer was successful or not
    function transfer(address _to, uint256 _value) public returns (bool success);

    /// @notice send `_value` tokens to `_to` from `_from` on the condition
    ///  it is approved by `_from`
    /// @param _from The address of the sender
    /// @param _to The address of the recipient
    /// @param _value The amount of tokens to be transferred
    /// @return Whether the transfer was successful or not
    function transferFrom(address _from, address _to, uint256 _value) public
        returns (bool success);

    /// @notice `msg.sender` approves `_spender` to spend `_value` tokens
    /// @param _spender The address of the account able to transfer the tokens
```

```solidity
    /// @param _value The amount of tokens to be approved for transfer
    /// @return Whether the approval was successful or not
    function approve(address _spender, uint256 _value) public
      returns (bool success);

    /// @param _owner The address of the account owning tokens
    /// @param _spender The address of the account able to transfer the tokens
    /// @return Amount of remaining tokens allowed to be spent
    function allowance(address _owner, address _spender) public view
      returns (uint256 remaining);

    // solhint-disable-next-line no-simple-event-func-name
    event Transfer(address indexed _from, address indexed _to, uint256 _value);
    event Approval(address indexed _owner, address indexed _spender,
                   uint256 _value);
}

contract EIP20 is EIP20Interface {

    uint256 constant private MAX_UINT256 = 2**256 - 1;
    mapping (address => uint256) public balances;
    mapping (address => mapping (address => uint256)) public allowed;
    /*
    NOTE:
    The following variables are OPTIONAL vanities. One does not have to include
    them. They allow one to customize the token contract & in no way influence
    the core functionality. Some wallets/interfaces might not even bother to look
    at this information.
    */
    string public name;        // Token name: eg Mastering Blockchain Book
    uint8 public decimals;     // How many decimals to show. Standard is 18.
    string public symbol;      // An identifier: eg MBB

    function EIP20(
        uint256 _initialAmount,
        string _tokenName,
        uint8 _decimalUnits,
        string _tokenSymbol
    ) public {
        balances[msg.sender] = _initialAmount;  // Give creator initial tokens
        totalSupply = _initialAmount;           // Update total supply
        name = _tokenName;                      // Set name for display purposes
        decimals = _decimalUnits;   // Set number of decimals for display
        symbol = _tokenSymbol;      // Set symbol for display purposes
    }

    function transfer(address _to, uint256 _value) public returns (bool success)
    {
        require(balances[msg.sender] >= _value);
        balances[msg.sender] -= _value;
        balances[_to] += _value;
        emit Transfer(msg.sender, _to, _value);
```

```
            return true;
      }

      function transferFrom(address _from, address _to, uint256 _value) public
        returns (bool success) {
          uint256 allowance = allowed[_from][msg.sender];
          require(balances[_from] >= _value && allowance >= _value);
          balances[_to] += _value;
          balances[_from] -= _value;
          if (allowance < MAX_UINT256) {
              allowed[_from][msg.sender] -= _value;
          }
          emit Transfer(_from, _to, _value);
          return true;
      }

      function balanceOf(address _owner) public view returns (uint256 balance) {
          return balances[_owner];
      }

      function approve(address _spender, uint256 _value) public
        returns (bool success) {
          allowed[msg.sender][_spender] = _value;
          emit Approval(msg.sender, _spender, _value);
          return true;
      }

      function allowance(address _owner, address _spender) public view
        returns (uint256 remaining) {
          return allowed[_owner][_spender];
      }
  }
```

This token contract was published on the Ropsten testnet (*https://oreil.ly/X8y-v*) and has the following attributes:

- *Token name*: Mastering Blockchain Book
- *Token symbol*: MBB
- *Token supply*: 100 MBB
- *Token decimal places*: 18

To create your own custom token, you can simply copy and paste the preceding code and change these four values in the `constructor` function:

symbol
> The symbol of your token.

name
> The name of your token.

decimals
> How many decimals your token can be divided into. The standard value for most tokens is 18.

totalSupply
> How many tokens will be in existence. There is a lot of variation in supply among tokens; 1 billion is an easy round number that is common.

ERC-721

ERC-721 is a standard for nonfungible tokens. As mentioned earlier, with fungible tokens (like ERC-20 tokens), each token has the exact same attributes. With nonfungible tokens, each token can have different attributes and therefore is unique, which allows for extreme digital scarcity.

Before blockchain, most virtual items could easily be copied. Connecting a virtual good or a real-world item to an ERC-721 token is a way to create a digitally scarce item that cannot be copied or tampered with.

The most famous example of this in the blockchain world is CryptoKitties (*https:// oreil.ly/EoBEo*), virtual cats that are connected to ERC-721 tokens on the Ethereum blockchain. Figure 5-1 shows CryptoKitty #1270015.

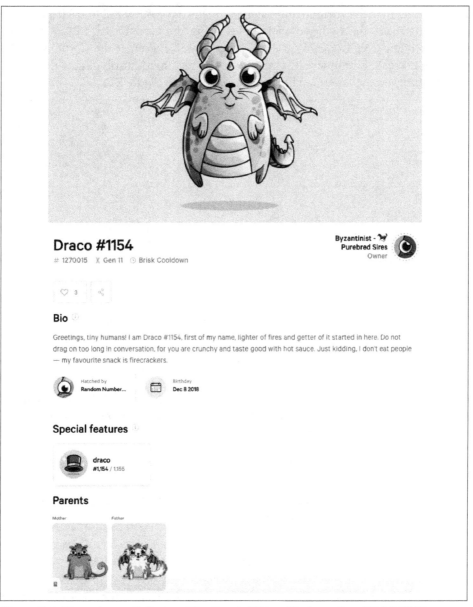

Figure 5-1. The unique attributes of the CryptoKitty with the unique ID 1270015

Instead of reading the attribute information about CryptoKitty #1270015 from a centralized database, the information is pulled from the CryptoKitty ERC-721 smart contract (*https://oreil.ly/GFQBV*). Go to function #32 and enter the CryptoKitty ID, which is 1270015. From there it is possible to see the unique attributes for this CryptoKitty stored on the Ethereum blockchain, as shown in Figure 5-2.

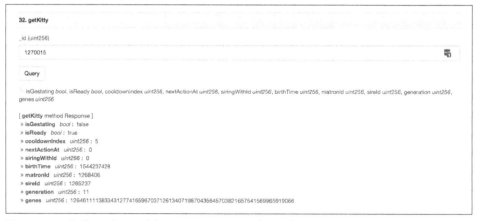

Figure 5-2. Calling the read function getKitty *from the main CryptoKitties smart contract responds with data stored in Ethereum about the specific kitty ID 1270015*

ERC-777

This proposed standard is for the next generation of fungible (ERC-20) tokens. It includes some improvements to the ERC-20 standard, the most important of which is in the way tokens are transferred.

There are two ways that users can move ERC-20 tokens from one address to another:

Push transaction

Calling the function transfer(address _to, uint256 _value) is a push transaction, where the sender initiates the transfer of tokens.

Pull transaction

The combination of the functions approve(address _spender, uint256 _value) and transferFrom(address _from, address _to, uint256 _value) is a pull transaction, where the sender gives permission to the receiver and then the receiver pulls the tokens out of the sender's account.

If a person sends tokens to a smart contract using a push transaction, then the smart contract will receive the tokens. However, the smart contract will not receive a trigger telling it that it has received the tokens and instructing it to run some code.

This is the reason for a pull transaction—the smart contract receiving the tokens initiates the transaction, and it can recognize when the tokens are received and execute additional code to react to this event. The most common use case for a smart contract receiving and sending tokens is decentralized exchanges, IDEX (*https:// idex.market/eth/idex*) being the most popular.

Pull transactions work for smart contracts receiving tokens, but their use has led to many tokens accidentally being lost. A common problem is if a user mistakenly sends tokens to a smart contract using a push transaction rather than via the correct pull method; those tokens will be burned and lost forever, because the smart contract will not recognize that it has received the tokens and therefore won't know to send them to another address at a later time.

ERC-777 proposes to fix this problem by introducing the following improvements:

`authorizeOperator(address operator)` *and* `revokeOperator(address operator)`
Allow token holders to authorize smart contracts to transfer tokens on their behalf and revoke that permission, respectively. The contracts that are authorized are known as *operators*. This is a variation of the pull transaction combination in ERC-20, but instead of authorizing the operator each time you want to transfer tokens, you only need to authorize the operator once. Then, for each additional transfer, the operator can transfer the tokens on your behalf.

`tokensReceived` *and* `tokensToSend` *hooks*
The contract receiving the tokens can include a function called `tokensReceived`. In that function, the receiving contract can identify which ERC-777 tokens the contract would like to accept and which it would like to reject (using `revert`). If an ERC-777 token is received but identified as to be rejected, the token transfer will not complete. It's like receiving a letter in the mail and sending it back. Similarly, a contract that is requesting a token transfer can receive the `tokensToSend` hook, and when that hook is called has the option to revert the transaction. It's less likely that this will happen, because this is the contract that initiated the transfer of tokens—it's like going to the post office to send a letter, but then changing your mind as you are about to hand it over.

`send(address to, uint256 amount, bytes data)`
The push transaction includes a `data` field that not only allows the sender to send tokens to a contract, but also can contain specialized logic that triggers a function in the receiving contract. This is similar to how Ethereum transactions are executed.

Although the ERC-777 standard is an improvement over ERC-20, it has not been adopted by the industry yet because there is a large switching cost for all stakeholders to move to the new standard. Many projects would have to create new token contracts, and then convince token holders to swap existing tokens for an equivalent amount using the new standard. Exchanges and some dapps would have to update their systems to support the new standard as well.

ERC-1155

This standard was designed to track virtual goods in games. For example, the default weapon in a shooting game might be a pistol, but it is possible to purchase the triple-barreled rocket-launching weapon that kills one hundred enemies in one shot.

An ideal token standard for these in-game items would have a mixture of ERC-20 and ERC-721 attributes:

- ERC-20 (fungible) so that you can attach a price to the virtual good, and users can then purchase and trade the item
- ERC-721 (nonfungible) so that the virtual good can have unique properties—for example, how many rockets it can hold, or how powerful the weapon is.

Like the ERC-777 token standard, this standard includes the concept of an *operator*, an address that has the authority to move your tokens on your behalf.

Another improvement in this standard is the ability to transfer multiple tokens in one transaction. When transferring ERC-721 tokens, you call the function `safeTransferFrom` and specify the token to be transferred by its `_tokenId`:

```
function safeTransferFrom(address _from, address _to, uint256 _tokenId, bytes data)
    external payable;
```

With ERC-1155 tokens, you can call the function `safeBatchTransferFrom` and specify an array of `_ids`:

```
function safeBatchTransferFrom(address _from, address _to, uint256[] calldata _ids,
    uint256[] calldata _values, bytes calldata _data) external;
```

The ability to do batch trades removes another layer of friction, for gamers and game publishers alike.

Enjin, the company that created this standard, is now providing a platform that makes it easy for game publishers to support virtual goods on the blockchain. One of the biggest challenges to gaining widespread adoption is that the Ethereum network is not yet fast enough to support hundreds of thousands of transactions a second, which is a common requirement in large-scale games.

At time of this writing, about 35 games have adopted this standard, and about 100,000 people hold ERC-1155 virtual goods.

Multisignature Contracts

Sending funds out of an *externally owned account* (EOA) wallet in Ethereum only requires one private key. This means if that key is compromised, there's nothing stopping funds being stolen from the account—it's a single point of failure. The purpose of a multisignature wallet is to lower the risk of unauthorized removal of funds by requiring multiple private keys to send the funds. This is a similar concept to a bank account that requires multiple signatures to authorize a payment. There isn't an ERC standard for multisignature wallet contracts, although this type of contract is widely used in the industry.

Every multisignature contract requires M of N signatures to authorize a transaction, where:

- N is the *number* of Ethereum addresses that can authorize a transaction.
- M is the *minimum* number of signatures from among those N unique addresses required for a transaction to be authorized.

Note that M must be less than N. An example would be a 2-of-3 multisignature contract, which means there are three addresses that can authorize a transaction, and only two signatures are required to complete the transaction.

It's common practice for entities that do ICOs to collect all the funds they raise into multisignature wallets. These ICOs also make their multisignature wallet code transparent and publicly share which addresses can sign a transaction. This transparency increases trust from investors, because at any time investors can audit the funds.

If you audit the multisignature wallet (*https://oreil.ly/mkRsK*) of a well-known company that raised \$33 million in its ICO, you can see all the funds that have come in and been sent out. You can also audit the wallet's M of N:

1. Calling the function `getOwners` shows which addresses can authorize transactions. These addresses are called *owners*. In this case, there are five of them:
   - 0x197a3d8fea67ee3b5a8436c5d9b4a794a196006b (*https://oreil.ly/woTp1*)
   - 0x0063af5125737564407a4081f017c34d647dad4f (*https://oreil.ly/s5BHD*)
   - 0x00c947cdb9112086d203843be8132bc992737f69 (*https://oreil.ly/X3yob*)
   - 0x003cb639f3c0120051abf4f927c2414d56ac766c (*https://oreil.ly/7DgeO*)
   - 0x00cb0d8171a9fa71e71fbf3f9cc17c6442755c29 (*https://oreil.ly/7ZSg3*)

2. Reading the current value of the variable `required` shows how many signatures are required to execute a transaction. This wallet requires three signatures to execute a transaction.

This wallet that is being audited here is thus a 3-of-5 multisignature wallet.

As you can see in Figure 5-3, you can also audit which addresses signed all the transactions that this wallet has executed.

	Txn Hash	Method	☰ Event Logs
3b	0xbfc42626b0e720... #7468500 ⏳ 103 days 14 hrs ago	0xc01a8c84 confirmTransaction (uint256)	> Execution (index_topic_1 uint256 transactionId) [topic0] 0x33e13ecb54c3976d8e8bb8c2881800a4d972b792045ffae98fdf46df365fed75 ⏳ [topic1] 0x0000000000000000000000000000000000000000000000000000000000000039
3a	0xbfc42626b0e720... #7468500 ⏳ 103 days 14 hrs ago	0xc01a8c84 confirmTransaction (uint256)	> Confirmation (index_topic_1 address sender, index_topic_2 uint256 transactionId) [topic0] 0x4a504a94899432a9846e1aa406dceb1bcfd538bb839071d49d1e5a23f5be30ef ⏳ [topic1] 0x00000000000000000000000003cb639f3c0120051abf4f927c2414d56ac766c [topic2] 0x0000000000000000000000000000000000000000000000000000000000000039
2	0x7a1e7e12c58a53... #7331154 ⏳ 103 days 10 hrs ago	0xc01a8c84 confirmTransaction (uint256)	> Confirmation (index_topic_1 address sender, index_topic_2 uint256 transactionId) [topic0] 0x4a504a94899432a9846e1aa406dceb1bcfd538bb839071d49d1e5a23f5be30ef ⏳ [topic1] 0x000000000000000000000000063af5125737564407a4081f017c34d647dad4f [topic2] 0x0000000000000000000000000000000000000000000000000000000000000039
1b	0xd53dc941983f02... #7331149 ⏳ 123 days 10 hrs ago	0xc8427474 submitTransaction (address,uint256,bytes)	> Confirmation (index_topic_1 address sender, index_topic_2 uint256 transactionId) [topic0] 0x4a504a94899432a9846e1aa406dceb1bcfd538bb839071d49d1e5a23f5be30ef ⏳ [topic1] 0x000000000000000000000000c947cdb9112086d203843be8132bc992737f69 [topic2] 0x0000000000000000000000000000000000000000000000000000000000000039
1a	0xd53dc941983f02... #7331149 ⏳ 123 days 10 hrs ago	0xc8427474 submitTransaction (address,uint256,bytes)	> Submission (index_topic_1 uint256 transactionId) [topic0] 0xc0ba8fe4b176c1714197d43b9cc6bcf797a4a7461c5fe8d0ef6e184ae7601a51 ⏳ [topic1] 0x0000000000000000000000000000000000000000000000000000000000000039

Figure 5-3. Example of the series of events (https://oreil.ly/bvK_8) that took place to set up and execute a multisignature transaction

As this figure shows, the process for executing a multisignature transaction is as follows:

1. One of the owner addresses (0x00c9…7f69 (*https://oreil.ly/qATRF*)) that is authorized to perform a multisignature transaction calls the submitTransaction function to submit the transaction details. The submitTransaction call performs two events:

   a. It stores the details of the requested transaction.

   b. It adds 0x00c9…7f69 to the list of addresses that confirm the transaction. This address therefore both initiates the transaction and confirms the transaction.

   The submitTransaction call (*https://oreil.ly/OyENJ*) occurs in block #7331149.

2. A second owner (0x0063…ad4f (*https://oreil.ly/Ofyns*)) calls the function confirmTransaction to give the second of the three required signatures. This confirmTransaction call (*https://oreil.ly/N63a8*) occurs in block #7331154.

3. A third owner (0x003c…766c (*https://oreil.ly/nTVqu*)) calls the function confirmTransaction to give the third signature. This call leads to two events:

   a. The third owner confirms the transaction.

   b. The contract recognizes that all required signatures have been given and then executes the transaction using the details that were submitted in step 1.

This `confirmTransaction` call (*https://oreil.ly/OXyFD*) occurs in block #7458500.

Decentralized Exchange Contracts

Before Ethereum, every cryptocurrency exchange had to be controlled and managed by a company—a centralized authority. Centralized exchanges still exist, with popular examples including Coinbase, Bitstamp, and Gemini. The purpose of an exchange is to act as a trusted platform where two parties can exchange cryptocurrencies securely. To accomplish this, an exchange must do the following for its customers:

- Provide a secure place to deposit/withdraw crypto, and hold the funds in escrow.
- Provide an order book, so that two parties can agree on a price to trade the crypto at.
- Swap the cryptocurrencies between the two parties.

A smart contract has the capability to perform the following three actions:

- Send/receive and hold ETH and ERC-20 tokens.
- Record price requests from EOA accounts.
- If two price requests match, change ownership of the corresponding cryptocurrencies.

A good example of a *decentralized* exchange on Ethereum is IDEX (*https:// idex.market/eth/idex*). Even though the IDEX website looks similar to a centralized exchange, there are significant differences between the two types of exchanges.

All of the code running a centralized exchange is deployed to a web hosting provider —for example, AWS or Azure. Frontend code running on a decentralized exchange is also deployed to a web hosting provider, but the backend code is written into a smart contract and deployed to the Ethereum network. The database is just the Ethereum or some other smart contract blockchain, as illustrated in Figure 5-4.

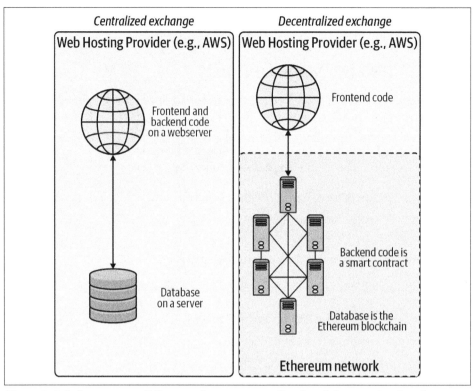

Figure 5-4. Infrastructure differences between centralized and decentralized exchanges

Advantages of a decentralized exchange include:

Greater transparency
Because the backend code is in a smart contract, anyone can audit it before using the exchange. The code in a centralized exchange is private. This type of transparency increases trust in the decentralized exchange.

Reduced counterparty risk
When you deposit cryptocurrency in a centralized exchange, it maintains custody of your funds, and customers expect that at any point in time they can get those funds back. However, there have been many cases where exchanges have lost all of their customers' funds. In a decentralized exchange, the smart contract maintains custody of the cryptocurrency, and if an audit of the smart contract shows that the contract is safe to use, then it's impossible for the exchange to lose your funds.

Decentralized exchanges also have a few downsides, though. Notably, they are:

Very slow
> On a centralized exchange, users expect that if they execute a trade it will be completed instantly. On a decentralized exchange, in order for a trade to execute, a user must wait for their transaction to be included in a block, which often takes at least 10 seconds, or even a minute. By the time the user's trade executes, the opportunity could be gone.

Expensive
> Decentralized exchanges require users to generate a new transaction every time they want to perform an action, including adding an order and cancelling an order. Exchange users frequently make multiple orders and changes to those orders in a short period of time. On a centralized exchange, these order changes are free, but on a decentralized exchange, you have to pay gas to the network for each action, which makes it much more expensive to use.

Difficult for nontechnical users
> Since users must sign a transaction every time they complete an action, nontechnical users may find using a decentralized exchange is too complicated and requires too much effort.

One other big difference between the two is that there is no need to ask anyone's permission to add an ERC-20 token to a decentralized exchange. As soon as an ERC-20 token is created, it can instantly be traded on a decentralized exchange. Depending on whom you speak to, this can be considered a pro or a con. We'll talk more about decentralized exchanges and how they're used in Chapter 7.

> You can view all the ERC standards (*http://eips.ethereum.org/erc*) online, and OpenZeppelin provides a great library of ERC-compliant smart contracts (*https://oreil.ly/LOwnY*).

Summary

Ethereum is by far the largest blockchain for tokenization today. In a short time frame, any developer can create their own blockchain-based asset. A lot of work has been done to give programmers a framework within Ethereum to operate in, with the different ERC standards providing a plethora of options. Ethereum-based tokenization has enabled the creation of a number of innovative new blockchain-based applications, and there surely will be many more as this technology continues to mature.

CHAPTER 6

Market Infrastructure

Bitcoin, ether, and many other cryptocurrencies are openly traded on various markets around the world. Speculation is estimated to account for 60–80% of all blockchain transactions (*https://oreil.ly/JdV3i*), which makes examining this component of blockchain important.

In the early days, a lack of infrastructure made the blockchain ecosystem highly volatile and risky. Although things have improved, the cryptocurrency market infrastructure is still far from perfect. A lot of structural scaffolding has been built, but there are still critical issues with the way these markets function. They're not fully regulated, and manipulation exists. This chapter is in no way an endorsement of speculation in cryptocurrency. To put it plainly, it's possible to lose a lot of money trading cryptocurrency.

Evolution of the Price of Bitcoin

Bitcoin is the bellwether of the entire cryptocurrency economy. This means the prices of other cryptocurrencies generally follow the trend of BTC—and it's important to understand that peaks and valleys in price are the norm for this, the world's most popular digital asset (Figure 6-1).

There have been many bitcoin bubbles, each one resulting in a higher price than the last, as more and more players entered the ecosystem for various reasons. Here are some of the bubbles that have led to all-time highs for BTC:

- *2010 (1):* Price goes from $0.008 in October to $0.08 in November, 900% increase
- *2010 (2):* Price rises to $0.50 by end of November, 525% increase
- *2011:* Price jumps to $31.91 in June, 6,282% increase over previous high
- *2013 (1):* Price climbs to $266.00 in March, 734% increase over previous high

- *2013 (2):* Price rises to $1,154.93 in December, 334% increase over previous high
- *2017:* Price reaches $17,900.00 by December, 1,450% increase over previous high

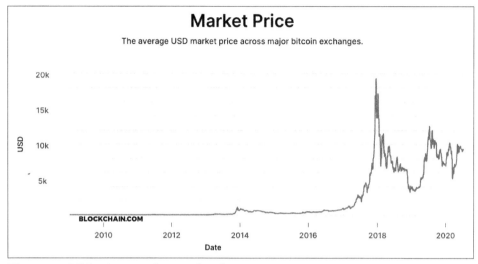

Figure 6-1. BTC price over the past decade

Over the course of cryptocurrency's history, there have been a number of ways to buy and sell it:

Person-to-person
Buying and selling cryptocurrency is done in face-to-face transactions.

Buying or selling products/services
A person acquires or spends cryptocurrency in exchange for something.

Cryptocurrency ATMs
Kiosks dispense cryptocurrency for cash. They can also accept crypto for fiat.

Mining
By contributing computing power to a network, miners are rewarded with transaction fees as well as newly minted cryptocurrency.

Exchanges
Crypto is traded on purpose-built websites that act similarly to stock exchanges, with a few nuances.

All of these methods have pros and cons. Person-to-person trading might be a safe option if the two parties are known to each other, but it could be problematic if one person is trying to cheat the other. Buying or selling products or services was once thought to be the pathway to mass adoption of cryptocurrency. However, high transaction fees, slow confirmation times, and network scalability issues have poured cold water on the idea of crypto becoming a popular payment mechanism anytime soon.

Cryptocurrency ATMs, many of which are listed on the Coin ATM Radar website (*https://coinatmradar.com*), are a convenient way to buy/sell from a physical location. But they are expensive in terms of the transaction fees applied and aren't always as easy to use as traditional ATMs. Cryptocurrency mining was discussed in Chapter 2, but as you saw, for most, mining is no longer a hobbyist activity and has become an enterprise data center–centric effort.

Exchanges have emerged as the main way to trade cryptocurrency.

The Role of Exchanges

Cryptocurrency exchanges have become the dominant force within the cryptocurrency market. To understand the market, you have to know about these platforms.

There are several different types of cryptocurrency exchange, so let's first look at the differences between them. Users can use all of them to send and receive cryptocurrency transactions, but the exchanges have differences in terms of security, speed, and interface.

Here are the basic types of exchanges:

Centralized exchanges
> These are run by a company that collects fees from trading, usually in the form of a percentage.

Decentralized exchanges
> Rather than being run by a company, decentralized exchanges are sites where *order books* (see the next section) operate using smart contracts, which were discussed in Chapter 5. Decentralized exchanges are crypto-only; we'll talk more about these in the next chapter.

Spot exchanges
> These exchanges trade cryptocurrencies. The trader owns the assets, and if it is a centralized exchange, the exchange usually holds the assets in the trader's account. If it is a decentralized exchange, the assets are self-custodied.

Derivatives exchanges
> These are entities that enable traders to use more complex trading tools such as highly leveraged products, options, swaps, and futures.

Cryptocurrency exchanges have pretty basic order types, which are similar to those in stock trading. Here are some terms you'll encounter:

Market
> An order to be executed immediately at current market prices. This is the fastest way to buy or sell.

Limit
> An order where a price is specified. It will not fill until the market matches the buy or sell price.

Expires
> With limit orders, some exchanges allow an expiration—days, weeks, months, or *good til canceled* are usually the parameters.

Maker/taker
> Almost all cryptocurrency exchanges use a maker/taker model to charge fees. This means that a trader providing liquidity (called the *maker*) does not pay a fee, while a trader doing market trades on an order book (the *taker*) pays the exchange for the ability to do so.

Bid
> The maximum price a buyer is willing to pay for a market order.

Ask
> The minimum price a seller is willing to receive for a market order.

The remainder of this section introduces various concepts you should be aware of when trading cryptocurrencies.

Order Books

An *order book* is a visual representation of outstanding orders for a cryptocurrency on an exchange. Although interfaces can vary, all order books generally do the same thing: they allow traders to see bids (buys) and asks (sells) that have been placed to be filled. Figure 6-2 shows an example of an order book.

The *market size* is the amount of cryptocurrency being placed in the order. Unlike traditional stocks, cryptocurrencies are divisional, many down to the eighth decimal place. For bitcoin, exchanges like Coinbase Pro use four decimals for trading. Traders looking to sell are indicated in red, and buys are in green.

Order Book	
Market Size	Price (USD)
0.0600	7332.02
1.0000	7331.94
0.0400	7331.79
0.3000	7331.14
1.1386	7331.10
0.3000	7330.65
5.2977	7329.54
2.0000	7329.47
0.4086	7329.31
2.4917	7328.13
USD Spread	0.01
0.6417	7328.12
0.3988	7327.85
0.9100	7327.84
0.3000	7327.80
0.0266	7326.66
0.6000	7325.95
0.8000	7324.79
1.0526	7324.78
0.0038	7324.63
6.0000	7324.58

Figure 6-2. A typical order book

Slippage

The difference between the expected price of a trade and its execution price, *slippage* is a major issue in cryptocurrency trading. Because order books on most exchanges are *thin*, meaning they lack substantial orders, larger orders "slip" through the order book at less-than-ideal prices.

Say a trader wants to sell $60,000 worth of bitcoin on a cryptocurrency exchange. Most order books could not handle that type of pricing because there aren't that many offers to buy. Figure 6-3 shows a sample view of the Coinbase Pro order book.

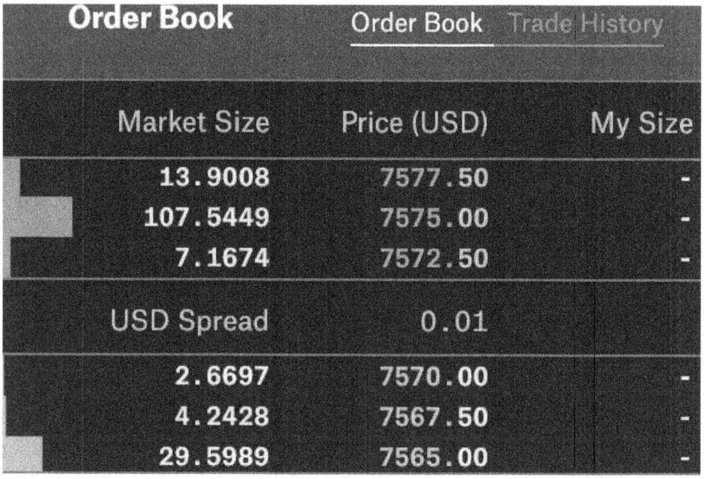

Figure 6-3. Coinbase Pro order book showing slippage

The amount of sells in this instance is much higher than buys. $40,000 worth of BTC isn't available at one buy price; therefore, a sell order executed would *slip through* to $7,565.

Traders do have options—they can break up the orders into smaller increments or go into the *over-the-counter* (OTC) market to fill the sell at one price. However, this example of exchange slippage shows how small cryptocurrency order books typically are. They operate on a much different scale than mature markets; large platforms like the NYSE and the NASDAQ can easily fill orders of this size.

Miners must convert their block rewards and transaction fees gained into fiat currency to pay for overhead, so mining impacts market data. This overhead may include mining equipment, energy costs, and data center operations, among other things, creating constant selling pressure. However, most miners use OTC providers to sell cryptocurrency, and OTC has less of an impact on cryptocurrency slippage as there is not a transparent order book.

Depth Charts

An order book visualization tool, *depth charts* allow traders to see how deep buys and sells are for a particular cryptocurrency, as shown in Figure 6-4. They display the real-time relationship between supply and demand in the market.

Figure 6-4. Depth chart

In Figure 6-4, bids (buys) are in green (the lefthand curve), and asks (sells) are in red (on the right). In the middle of the chart where the curves meet is what the market price for the asset is, with the lowest bids on the left and highest asks on the right. The rise on each side represents the steps in price on the order book, where the asks are in a converse relationship with price (meaning technically they should be trending down). In Figure 6-4, there is a deeper book of asks on the market than buys.

These depth charts are usually interactive on exchanges. This means a trader can place a cursor at any point on the line and determine the pricing it will take to move through the order book with some simple math. Depth charts are a useful tool for spotting abnormalities in the market, especially determining which side has a stronger order book for trading. They are also useful to determine, given a certain market order at a certain price, how much an individual person selling at a certain price could push the price of the market.

Jurisdiction

Most assets in the traditional financial world are traded on centralized exchanges that are highly regulated. For example, Apple stock is traded on the NASDAQ, and the price of Apple stock is dictated by the trading activity on that one market.

By contrast, cryptocurrency trading is done on *thousands* of markets on *hundreds* of exchanges. These operate in different jurisdictions and therefore must comply with different levels of regulatory oversight. Figure 6-5 illustrates.

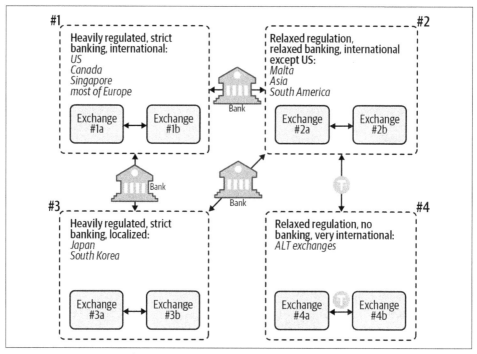

Figure 6-5. Four types of cryptocurrency exchanges

Cryptocurrency exchanges are bound by the laws of the jurisdictions they operate in. Figure 6-5 shows four categories that exchanges may fall into:

1. *International exchanges under heavy regulation.* These have strict Know Your Customer rules to maintain banking, meaning they have identifying customer information. They mostly reside in the US, Canada, Singapore, and Europe.

2. *Exchanges under relaxed regulation.* These have relaxed customer rules to maintain banking and service international customers outside the US, sometimes meaning having less identifying customer information. Most of these exchanges reside in Asia and South America.

3. *Localized exchanges under heavy regulation.* These have strict Know Your Customer rules for banking, but they only service customers located in their country. These exchanges are mostly located in Japan and South Korea, with a few in other places.

4. *Exchanges that do not have any banking and therefore have relaxed regulation.* These do not comply with regulations to keep bank accounts. They service international customers and mostly reside in Asia and South America.

Since exchanges in the first three categories offer bank accounts, it is possible to *arbitrage*—purchase an asset in one market at one price and sell the same asset in another market at a higher price—through the traditional banking network. Arbitrage keeps prices relatively close between these exchanges. Unregulated exchanges (category 4) do not have banking and use stablecoins such as USDT (tether) to arbitrage between exchanges to maintain relatively similar prices (see "Arbitrage" on page 135).

Wash Trading

Wash trading is a form of market manipulation prevalent in cryptocurrency markets. This is where traders are concurrently buying and selling a cryptocurrency in order to produce an artificial market, which is illegal in highly regulated jurisdictions. Wash trading in cryptocurrency markets is conducted by bad actors trying to do one or more of the following:

- Prop up the trading volume of a cryptocurrency in an attempt to increase its price (also known as *spoofing*).
- Hide nefarious activity, such as massive selling (or *dumping*) of a particular cryptocurrency.
- Increase the trading fees an exchange reaps by inflating the volume of trades.

The Commodity Exchange Act (CEA), passed in 1936, made wash trading illegal in the United States. Other countries have similar laws, but many jurisdictions and therefore exchanges have lax policies regarding wash trading.

Whales

As the largest holders of crypto, *whales* can have an unpredictable impact on the market. Whales are different from institutional investors in the cryptocurrency world. Unlike asset managers like Fidelity, whales can move funds on a whim. Traditional asset managers operate in a highly regulated environment and have many restrictions they need to follow before moving funds. Crypto whales just need a private key, a computer, and the internet. These movements are easily seen on the blockchain and can result in price changes as traders attempt to decipher what they mean.

Exchanges, custody providers, and even Satoshi Nakamoto can be considered whales because the holdings these entities have are so significant. Movement of funds by whales can signal market changes. For example, movement of old coins (*https://oreil.ly/urBKz*) has in the past caused market movements.

Whales also have the ability to control cryptocurrencies with a low *market capitalization*, which is the price of an asset times its outstanding supply. A whale that owns a large amount of a particular cryptocurrency with a small capitalization is able to control the price. This is done by creating buy and sell "walls" on exchanges (see Figure 6-6).

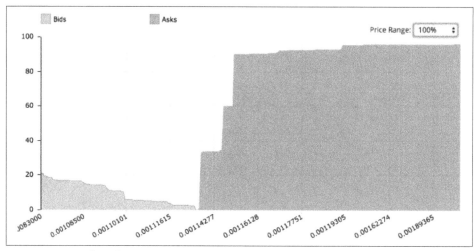

Figure 6-6. A sell wall on a cryptocurrency depth chart

These walls are caused by large numbers of bids or asks, to prevent a certain asset from moving one way or another. However, when there is interest in a particular cryptocurrency, they can be broken. These walls, caused by coordinated buying and selling by a group of participants to manipulate prices, are often what create huge price gains or losses that occur in some smaller cryptocurrencies.

Bitcoin Halving

Bitcoin *halving* is a once-every-four-years event that reduces the supply of new bitcoin (see Table 6-1). In the past it has created bull runs in the market, which many believe is due to supply decreasing while demand stays constant. However, that may not always be the case—past performance does not always predict future results. Figure 6-7 illustrates.

Table 6-1. Bitcoin supply schedule

Year	Coinbase transaction[a]	Hourly supply	Daily supply	Monthly supply	Annual supply
2009	50	300	7,200	216,000	2,628,000
2012	25	150	3,600	108,000	1,314,000
2016	12.5	75	1,800	54,000	657,000
2020	6.25	38	900	27,000	328,500

[a] A coinbase transaction is produced every 10 minutes or so, so these numbers are estimates.

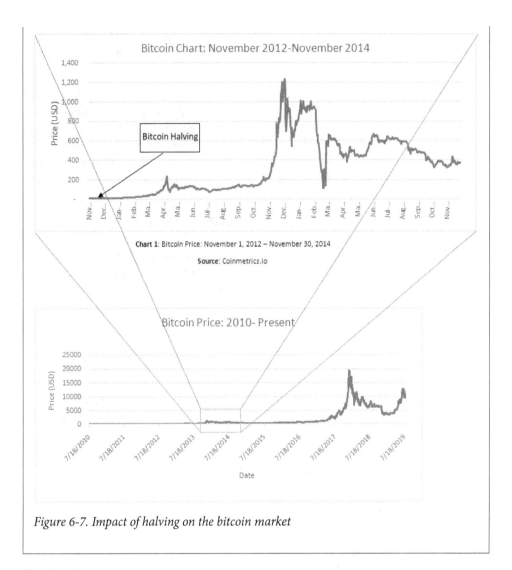

Figure 6-7. Impact of halving on the bitcoin market

Derivatives

As financial products that allow investors access to the underlying value of cryptocurrency, *derivatives* are increasingly becoming an important part of the ecosystem. Here is a summary of some of the important terms used in discussing derivatives:

Options

Contracts give traders the right but not the obligation to profit from a rise in the price of the asset (*call*) or profit from a decrease in the price of the asset (*put*). In the case of cryptocurrencies, options allow traders to better manage risks in the market. The options landscape in cryptocurrency markets is still nascent due to regulatory reasons but is expected to grow over the next few years.

Futures

Bitcoin futures allow businesses that receive their income in bitcoin to lock in the price of the cryptocurrency at some future time. In this way, these businesses will not be subjected to volatile price movement that might affect their revenue. Common users of futures contracts include bitcoin miners, who may use them to protect their revenue, and speculators. The major providers of bitcoin futures include commodities stalwart Chicago Mercantile Exchange (CME) and Bakkt.

ETFs

Exchange traded funds, or ETFs, are products that give investors access to an asset or mix of assets managed by another party for a fee. For cryptocurrencies, this would mean a fund manages the cryptocurrency for the investor. In the US, there has not yet been approval for these types of investment vehicles, although in places like Europe there are similar structures available (known there as *exchange traded notes*, or ETNs).

Margin/leveraged products

Many exchanges allow traders to trade *on margin,* where credit is provided to an investor for putting up some amount of value, known as *collateral.* On regulated exchanges, this is usually between 5 and 10 times a trader's balance. However, some exchanges allow for up to 100 times margin. This can be dangerous, as very small price swings can result in autoliquidation. Similar to a margin call, an *auto-liquidation* will quickly wipe out a trader's balance.

 Be *very* careful using margin. It may not provide much leverage in trades, and it can prove a quick way to get totally liquidated in the crypto market.

Cryptocurrency Market Structure

As a whole, the cryptocurrency market lacks the *market depth,* or the ability to absorb large orders, that is seen in traditional markets. There are several reasons for this. One is the relatively small number of traders compared to other markets. Another is that regulatory issues surrounding cryptocurrency make it difficult to trade against fiat currencies.

Arbitrage

As mentioned previously, *arbitrage* is the act of purchasing an asset in one market at one price and selling the same asset in another market at a higher price, thus exploiting the difference in prices between markets. This is a common occurrence in cryptocurrency trading.

Arbitrageurs serve an important purpose in the trading community. They help remove price differences and increase *liquidity*, or volume of activity, making the ecosystem less volatile. For example, imagine the price of bitcoin ranges from $9,800–$10,000 across one hundred exchanges. How do you know what the actual price of bitcoin is? Arbitrageurs help reduce that variance in price.

Arbitrage is often an appealing trading strategy because of its relatively low risk profile. In arbitrage, there is no risk involved in estimating what cryptocurrency prices will be in the future. Traders only take action based on what the price is right now. The biggest downside to arbitraging is that the barrier to entry is fairly low. If opportunities exist, you will find competition with many other traders, which can lower margins.

We'll discuss arbitrage trading in a little more detail later in this chapter.

Counterparty Risk

Arbitrage requires leaving large amounts of capital on one or more exchanges. The larger the scale of revenues gained from arbitrage, the more capital is required. One of the biggest risks in arbitrage is trusting your capital to the exchanges that maintain custody of those funds. To quote a phrase popularized by early cryptocurrency proponent and *Mastering Bitcoin* author Andreas Antonopoulos, "Not your keys, not your money."

 Since 2010, a steady stream of exchanges have been hacked or have shut down and lost customer funds, making this risk fairly high. See Chapter 9 for more on this.

Building an exchange custody infrastructure that is highly secure from hacks requires the following:

- A lot of technical resources
- Auditing by multiple security groups
- Well-defined and well-thought-out corporate governance processes

Many well-established exchanges—for example, Coinbase Pro (*https://pro.coin base.com*)—have had the time and resources to build robust solutions. They are still around today because they have kept their customers' funds secure. Newer exchanges following proper security practices should cut no corners when it comes to custody solutions. Using well-established custody services like BitGo (*https://www.bitgo.com*) can help. These *custody providers* can help with key management, educate the exchange on proper security practices, and even provide an insurance policy for funds that are in their custody.

Each exchange has a different custody setup. Figure 6-8 shows a standard arrangement.

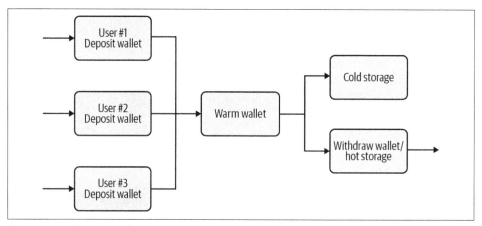

Figure 6-8. How custody might work on an exchange

Let's walk through how this works, and go over some of the key terms.

When an exchange user wants to deposit funds into an account, they send the funds to a *deposit address*. An exchange gives a separate deposit address to each user. This lets the exchange know which user to credit funds to as they come in.

As funds are deposited into an exchange through user deposit addresses, they are automatically swept to the *warm wallet*, which can only send funds to whitelisted, or predetermined, addresses. The warm wallet then distributes the incoming funds to either the *hot storage wallet* or *cold storage wallet*, depending on the exchange's need to top up the withdrawal wallet with more funds.

Cold storage refers to storing cryptocurrency holdings and private keys offline, in a location that is not connected to the internet. For example, the private keys might be printed on a piece of laminated paper sitting in a bank vault. The process to generate the signature that authorizes funds to be sent from an address whose private key is in cold storage is also completed offline, using an *airgapped* computer—that is, a computer that has never been connected to the internet. Once the signature is generated, it is manually entered onto a machine that is connected to the internet, which broad-casts the transaction request to the blockchain network. This can be done in two ways:

- On an airgapped computer, save the signature into a text file, then copy the text file onto a formatted and cleaned USB stick. Then put the USB stick into an internet-connected computer, and broadcast out the transaction with the signa-ture from that computer. Wipe the USB stick.
- Write down the signature on a piece of paper, then manually type it in on an internet-connected computer. Destroy the paper.

Keeping the private keys disconnected from the internet means a person has to be physically present to access them. This makes it impossible for the private keys to be copied by a hacker over the internet, or compromised through a virus, malware, key-logger, or other exploit. There are still ways to break in, but they involve physical theft.

The downside to cold storage is that because human intervention is required, a trans-action can take on average 24–48 hours. But when an exchange user withdraws cryp-tocurrency funds from their account, they normally expect those funds to be withdrawn within minutes. That means exchanges need to have funds sitting in a *hot storage* wallet, or *withdrawal wallet*, that allows for instant withdrawals. The advan-tage of hot storage is that blockchain transactions can be initiated instantly by a machine, without requiring human intervention.

Hot storage is the cryptocurrency equivalent of a bank branch keeping stacks of cash locked away in a back room—an amount that should be enough to satisfy daily cus-tomer demand for cash. The disadvantage, of course, is that the private keys are sit-ting on a machine that is connected to the internet, and that makes it possible for hackers to compromise them (like gaining access to the back room). Exchanges must therefore take extreme care to ensure the security of these keys.

Here are some other concepts to be aware of:

Less than 5% rule
Common practice is for exchanges to keep over 95% of customer funds in cold storage, and under 5% of funds in hot storage. That way, if hackers compromise an exchange, they will only be able to steal the funds sitting in hot storage. Losing that amount will likely hurt the exchange's bottom line, but is unlikely to force it to totally shut down.

Whitelisting addresses
It is important that exchanges configure all incoming wallets to only be allowed to send funds to the warm wallet. This practice is known as *whitelisting*. This is so if a deposit wallet is compromised, the hacker can only send funds to that address

(or any others on a predetermined set of whitelisted addresses), which is problematic for an attacker.

Signs of illiquidity

One warning sign that could signal that an exchange is in trouble and might shut down is when users consistently see long delays in withdrawing funds. Delays *could* be caused by a technical issue, but they are often a symptom of an exchange that is close to default (the inability to issue funds on demand). For example, during the years when Mt. Gox operated, most users did not complain about slowness in withdrawing funds. But during the weeks leading up to the exchange shutting down (*https://oreil.ly/HShKJ*), user withdrawal requests began taking significantly longer to process, sometimes requiring days to fulfill. Delays in honoring customer requests for withdrawals is a symptom that the exchange is *illiquid* and does not have custody of users' funds anymore. This is a problem that is difficult for an exchange to hide from users.

Market Data

Accurate data can be hard to come by. Different sources may provide different data, for example, on cryptocurrency market capitalizations and prices. Two sources may even be in stark contrast, with a differential of billions of dollars. That's why it's vital to be familiar with different cryptocurrency market data sources.

There are tons of general sources for market information today. Here are a few of the most well-known data sources:

- CoinDesk (*https://coindesk.com*)
- Skew (*https://skew.com*)
- Glassnode (*https://glassnode.com*)
- TradingView (*https://www.tradingview.com*)

Each offers different datasets and tools.

There are also specialized cryptocurrency information sources that it's good to know about, such as block explorers and transaction flow tracking systems.

Block explorers

A *block explorer* enables the user to see all on-blockchain transactions by examining the contents of each block in the chain. Users look up the details of any recent or historical transaction on a blockchain using its transaction ID and view all the transactions made by a particular address. Block explorers also link addresses to other transactions; by viewing one address, it is possible to see transactions made by another address. In the cryptocurrency world, a block explorer can let you peer into the blockchain transactions to see what is (and has been) taking place.

 For bitcoin transactions, *Blockchain.com* is the most popular block explorer. For Ethereum and ERC-20 tokens, *Etherscan.io* (*https:// etherscan.io*) is the predominant explorer.

Using block explorers can help identify cryptocurrency movements. However, many exchanges do not record transactions between internal wallets on-chain, and therefore, fund flows are often hidden until a transaction with an external party (an outside exchange or wallet) is completed.

Transaction flows

The ability to track transaction flows on the blockchain can help when analyzing trading patterns. Tracking the movement of cryptocurrency can be much easier than tracking fiat currency. This is especially true when transfers are happening between wallets, exchanges, and other services because these transactions occur on-chain.

GraphSense (*https://graphsense.info*) is an open source tool by the Austrian Institute of Technology that enables cross-ledger analytics on blockchain flows, with support for Bitcoin, Bitcoin Cash, Litecoin, Zcash, and more. Whale Alert (*https://whale-alert.io*) offers a free basic API to track many different cryptocurrencies, including the top 100 ERC-20 tokens. It also has a Twitter account, @Whale_Alert, that tweets large transactions.

Analysis

In cryptocurrency markets, traders use several methods of market analysis in order to try to make money. The two major types of analysis used to make decisions are *technical analysis* and *fundamental analysis*. Some traders use both kinds, whereas others are ardent supporters of just one.

Briefly, fundamental analysis involves measuring a cryptocurrency's value by examining related economic and financial factors. It takes in all the available information about the cryptocurrency, including news, foundation reports, technical roadmaps, and extrapolations like expected user or network growth.

Technical analysis involves a chart-focused approach to measuring a cryptocurrency's value. It's based on market data and specific indicators related to how a cryptocurrency trades and its past performance.

Let's take a closer look at the two different approaches.

Fundamental Cryptocurrency Analysis

Monitoring cryptocurrency foundation reports that steer development, user adoption figures, and news about regulatory developments helps with fundamental analysis in the short term. For the long term, two comparisons can be made: are cryptocurrencies Tulip Mania or the internet? The argument references two very different points in the history of financial markets.

Tulip Mania or the internet?

In the seventeenth century, Holland was in what was called its Golden Age, a time when the country ranked among the best in the world in the sciences, trade, and art. During that time, a speculative rush on tulip bulbs occurred, mainly due to the scarcity and rarity of certain flowers' colors. There were many varieties of tulips available on the market, and in some months their prices appreciated over 1,100%. This created a huge run-up in the market, followed by a total bottoming out that led to gigantic losses for some investors. Figure 6-9 shows the rise and fall of tulip prices during what became known as Tulip Mania.

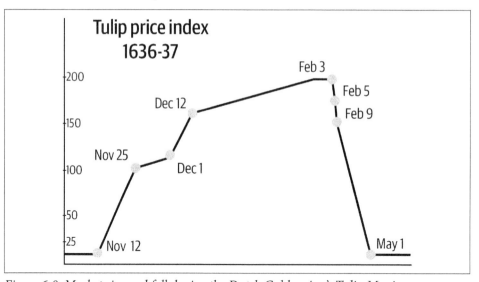

Figure 6-9. Market rise and fall during the Dutch Golden Age's Tulip Mania

In the 1990s, people invested fortunes in seemingly any publicly traded company with ".com" in its name. This investment was fueled by low interest rates, which encouraged people to borrow and spend. Prices went up and up, eventually leading to the so-called *dot-com crash* (*https://oreil.ly/8xfAU*), where the bottom fell out of the market and many companies were wiped out (see Figure 6-10). While there were gigantic losses for many investors, some of these dot-com companies did survive and thrive—

most notably Amazon, which transformed itself from an online bookseller into a retail and computing infrastructure behemoth.

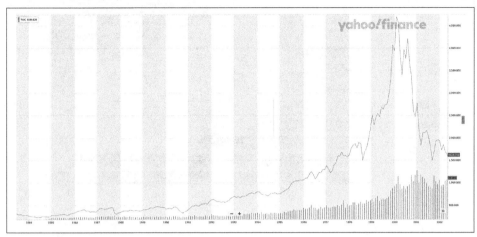

Figure 6-10. Graphs of the NASDAQ dot-com crash

Why are we bringing up these two seemingly unrelated events? A fundamental argument held by many investors in the cryptocurrency market revolves around these two crashes. Whereas the tulip market never flourished like that again, the internet came back, fueled by emerging technologies that did not exist in the 1990s, such as the dynamic web, smartphones, and social media.

The question is: does cryptocurrency have a long-term future? A number of economists don't believe the cryptocurrency market is as unbridled as some may think—including Cornell's Joseph Stiglitz, who believes government will heavily regulate cryptocurrency (*https://oreil.ly/9tInN*). The reality today is that the main use case for cryptocurrency is speculation, which is why an examination of markets is important.

Tools for fundamental analysis

Fundamental analysis requires reviewing news and analysis sources. There are a number of established outlets in the traditional media that do a good job of reporting on cryptocurrency. Others are a good deal shadier, and feature news stories that are slanted toward advertisers.

"Pay-to-play"—paying a significant fee to be featured in a seemingly unbiased news story—is rampant in the cryptocurrency industry. One reporter reached out to cryptocurrency news sites and found many of them were willing to take money in return for favorable coverage. Sometimes these news outlets would request thousands of dollars for a positive story, which shows the kind of shadow market for disinformation (*https://oreil.ly/nU0FL*) that exists in the industry. Figure 6-11 shows the prices some outlets wanted to charge for a favorable story.

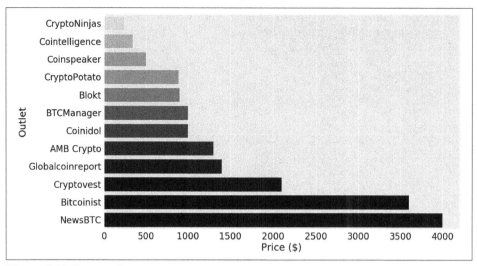

Figure 6-11. Pay-to-play

Social media can be a tool for news gathering, but it should be taken with a grain of salt. On Twitter, there are entire campaigns meant to influence thinking on bitcoin, XRP (*https://oreil.ly/UrwyX*), and many other smaller cryptocurrencies.

Some crypto communities on Reddit are censored to remove any critical information. It's important to keep this in mind when looking for accurate fundamental information regarding various cryptocurrency projects. Very few information sources are immune to this issue, which requires traders to be vigilant about verifying data!

Technical Cryptocurrency Analysis

Cryptocurrencies have pricing datasets that can be extrapolated into charts. These charts allow traders to analyze past history in order to determine future prices. As mentioned in the previous section, in the cryptocurrency world it can be hard to find reliable sources of information for fundamental analysis. Therefore, the use of technical analysis is helpful for many to properly evaluate the movements of the cryptocurrency markets, which can be quite volatile at times. There is even a subset of traders that can detect where asset prices will move using only charts, avoiding any fundamental analysis.

Charts for technical analysis

The best tools for technical analysis are chart-based. TradingView (*http://www.tradingview.com*), a charting tool that is also used by stock market chartists, has done a good job of integrating a variety of cryptocurrency exchange data sources. It also has a number of tools that technical analysts use, including moving averages, volume indicators, and various oscillators. TradingView is free, and with an email signup allows users to save charts.

Hunting for Bart

Technical analysis requires looking at patterns, and there are some unique ones when it comes to cryptocurrency. The most famous is the Bart pattern (*https://oreil.ly/ G4S8C*), which bears a striking similarity to the top of Bart Simpson's head, as shown in Figure 6-12.

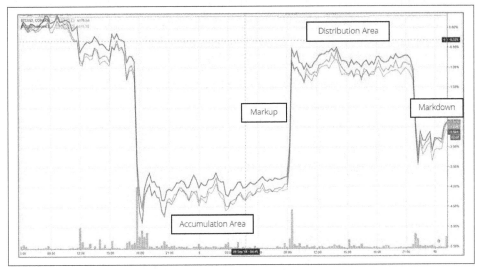

Figure 6-12. The famous Bart pattern

Technical analysts will say that this process of analysis is more art than science. While it cannot predict the future, it is sometimes able to provide indicators to help traders make decisions. A number of factors go into making these decisions, and it's up to traders themselves to figure out how to act.

The Bart pattern in cryptocurrency offers an instructive lesson about the nature of this market. Cryptocurrencies are still quite new, and there aren't as many market participants as many would believe. Because of this, the *depth*, or amount of liquidity in the market, is low, also known as *thin*. Crypto is thus said to be a *thinly traded* market. This lack of liquidity contributes to Bart patterns; because the order books on cryptocurrency exchanges are not as deep as in traditional markets, prices can move quickly.

Arbitrage Trading

We mentioned arbitrage earlier in the chapter. Here we'll take a deeper look, with a few examples of how it works.

A *basic arbitrage* is buying and selling an asset using two different markets. For example, if there was a 1% arbitrage spread between the bitcoin buy price on Coinbase Pro and sell price on Gemini, a trader might:

1. Buy 1 bitcoin from the USD/BTC market on Coinbase Pro for $10,000 USD.
2. Immediately sell 1 bitcoin on the USD/BTC market on Gemini for $10,100 USD.

This would lead to revenue gain of $100, minus fees.

A *triangular arbitrage* involves buying and selling the asset using three or more different markets. For example:

1. Buy 1 bitcoin from the USD/BTC market on Coinbase Pro for $10,000 USD.
2. Trade 1 bitcoin for 70 ether on Coinbase Pro.
3. Sell 70 ether on Gemini for $10,200 USD.

This would lead to revenue gain of $200, less fees.

Timing and Managing Float

In order to execute arbitrage strategies, a *float,* or liquid pool of funds ready to trade, is required. This float sits on various exchanges and is used at the moment an arbitrage opportunity is presented.

When an arbitrage opportunity arrives, it is imperative to complete all of the steps in the arbitrage as quickly as possible, for two main reasons:

1. Pricing on exchanges may change quickly.
2. Others may take advantage of the opportunity, driving spreads down.

Generally, the more float that is reserved for arbitrage, the faster the execution. However, there is an opportunity cost (and risk) to just leaving capital sitting around waiting for a potential future opportunity. It is important to identify which markets and arbitrage paths to target because there will always be a limit to the amounts of funds, or float, available on hand at any given time.

The next subsections look at a few possible configurations to setting up the float for arbitrage.

Float Configuration 1

Configuration 1 reserves $50,000 USD to sit on Coinbase Pro and 5 BTC to sit on Gemini. When an arbitrage opportunity between these two markets becomes available, this configuration allows for instant execution. This is because the float means the arbitrageur can purchase the bitcoin instantly on Coinbase Pro and sell it instantly on Gemini. However, the speed of arbitrage execution is completely dependent on the exchange receiving and fulfilling trade API calls.

After arbitrage is executed, there is a change of balance for all exchange accounts. If there is continuously an arbitrage opportunity going in this same direction (for example, a lower buy price on Coinbase Pro and a higher sell price on Gemini), then eventually there will be an imbalance of float, where one exchange has more funds than the other. This imbalance means the trader will be unable to purchase bitcoin on Coinbase Pro, or sell bitcoin on Gemini. Therefore, some decisions must be made to continue using the float for arbitrage. A trader could do the following:

- Rebalance the float by transferring 5 BTC from Coinbase Pro to Gemini, and transferring $50,000 USD from Gemini to Coinbase Pro. Transferring 5 BTC between exchanges is simple and takes about an hour to complete. Transferring $50,000 USD between exchanges happens through the banking network and therefore requires a bank account. Some banks have the ability to transfer easily between exchanges. Research the available options.

- Wait for an arbitrage opportunity in the opposite direction. This means buying bitcoin at a low price on Gemini and selling it at a higher price on Coinbase Pro.

Float Configuration 2

Configuration 2 reserves $50,000 USD to sit on Coinbase Pro and does not require any float to be sitting on Gemini. Since there is no float sitting on Gemini, when an arbitrage opportunity becomes available between these two exchanges, an extra step is required: a transfer of funds from Coinbase Pro to Gemini must be executed.

In this example, when an opportunity becomes available, the arbitrageur does the following:

1. Purchase 1 BTC on Coinbase Pro.

2. Transfer the 1 BTC from Coinbase Pro to Gemini.

3. Sell the 1 BTC on Gemini at a price 1% higher than it was purchased for on Coinbase Pro.

The biggest risk in configuration 2 is that transferring the BTC to Gemini takes about an hour to complete. During that window of time, the sell price of BTC on Gemini will likely change, and it's possible the trader may be forced to sell that 1 BTC at a loss.

Even though configuration 2 requires much less capital to execute, in the case of bitcoin the lack of a float introduces a significant delay, increasing the risk of losing money. One way to mitigate this risk is by arbitraging other cryptocurrencies. Here are a few examples of time delays you might encounter:

- Bitcoin block times on average are 10 minutes, and exchanges often require 6 confirmations to credit funds, totaling 60 minutes to transfer funds.
- Ethereum block times on average are 15 seconds, and exchanges often require 30 confirmations to credit funds, totaling 7.5 minutes to transfer funds.
- Ripple block times on average are 4 seconds, and exchanges often credit funds as soon as their system sees the transaction processed. Depending on the exchange, the transfer time is often 30–60 seconds.

Float Configuration 3

The most effective way to mitigate the risk of time lost moving funds between exchanges is by completing the entire arbitrage on one exchange. This can be done using triangular arbitrage on an exchange with multiple markets, assuming that the buy and sell rates at each step are favorable.

Here the arbitrage is executed using only markets that are on Coinbase Pro:

1. USD/BTC market: Buy 1 BTC for $10,000 USD.
2. BTC/ETH market: Trade 1 BTC for 70 ETH.
3. ETH/USD market: Sell 70 ETH for $10,200 USD.

This would eventually lead to a $200 USD gain, minus fees, after completing all of the steps in the arbitrage.

In 2012, when the industry was in its infancy, arbitrage opportunities for bitcoin went as high as 30% spread across some exchanges. In 2020, there are many more arbitrageurs, and hidden behind the opportunities are various challenges (outlined in the next section). Often the cost of overcoming these challenges is higher than the reward of the arbitrage opportunity, which is likely to fall into the range of 0.1% to, at most, 10%—still, even today opportunities do exist.

Regulatory Challenges

Exchanges that are compliant with regulations follow the laws of the country they operate out of, and laws differ between countries. For example, most exchanges around the world can service customers who reside in other countries. However, exchanges in South Korea, for example, can only service customers who reside in that country. The South Korean government has banned exchanges from servicing foreigners. In addition, South Korea has capital controls that limit the amount of funds that can leave the country.

During bitcoin's bull run in 2017, these factors led to a long-sustained "Kimchi Premium" (*https://oreil.ly/nHAS5*) in South Korean exchanges, which often saw selling prices 5–10% higher than exchanges in other countries.

Banking Risk

When performing arbitrage that involves fiat, a bank account is required to shift the funds between exchanges. Internationally, there has been a trend by regulators and banks to impose stricter Anti-Money Laundering (AML) and Know Your Customer (KYC) rules, which are further discussed in Chapter 9. These rules significantly increase the barriers for new cryptocurrency businesses to open a bank account. For example, in Canada only two of the big five banks will even consider opening a new account for a money services business. In the US, only a handful of firms will open bank accounts for cryptocurrency businesses.

When banks audit transactions, they consider the following properties as indicative of increased risk of fraud:

Funds being sent to/received from another country
> There are international organizations like the Financial Action Task Force (FATF) that provide a risk ranking for each country. For example, Syria has seen sanctions and a heavy presence of ISIS; it would thus be considered a high-risk country.

High-volume transactions
> One of the biggest fears a bank has is being mentioned in the news for facilitating fraudulent activity, but the risk of this is low if the scale of funds moved is low. In addition, it is mandatory for banks in most countries to submit suspicious activity reports to the government for any transaction above a certain threshold. In the US, any transaction over $10,000 USD must be reported to the Financial Crimes Enforcement Network (FinCEN).

Anything related to cryptocurrency
> The banking view of cryptocurrency is still that it is often used for nefarious purposes. Many international news stories about cryptocurrency are related to unscrupulous or illegal activities. These activities may include selling drugs, forcing ransomware payments in crypto, and North Korea evading sanctions.

Arbitraging fiat, at scale, between cryptocurrency exchanges in different countries can raise all three of those flags. Using a bank not friendly to cryptocurrency involves risks. Anytime, without notice and for reasons outside your control, the bank could freeze your funds or reverse your transactions.

Exchange Risk

A lot of trust is placed in the exchanges to conduct arbitrage. To execute arbitrage steps quickly, the reliability of exchange APIs and *trading engines,* the software that powers exchanges between buyers and sellers, is key. Here are some issues you may encounter:

- Bugs in an exchange's API
- Unregulated exchanges running trading bots to prioritize their trades
- Exchanges deploying *rate limiting*, which limits arbitrage API calls
- An exchange server having connectivity problems, causing API calls to be delayed

Basic Mistakes

Basic arbitrage mistakes include:

- Forgetting to include trading fees and taxes in arbitrage calculations
- Only looking at the ticker price when calculating arbitrage opportunities

It's not enough to consider the difference in price when calculating opportunities; it's also important to consider the *market depth* by looking at the volume of funds sitting on the order book at each price, to ensure slippage does not negate your profits or turn them into losses.

Exchange APIs and Trading Bots

A large amount of crypto trading is executed by trading bots. But no matter how good a trading bot is, its performance relies heavily on the exchange APIs that it integrates with.

Every exchange began as a small startup and tried to build a high-quality API, though good documentation is usually not a priority. Banking, regulation, wallet custody, and getting liquidity usually *are* high priorities. After an exchange reaches a certain point in its business, when it is flush with cash, it can hire the right technical talent, and the quality of its API will improve dramatically.

The best exchanges build their websites and mobile apps using the same APIs they provide for third-party developers. Not all exchanges are created equal, however, and it's important to test basic API functions prior to real-time trading.

Characteristics of a high-quality API include the following:

- Runs on powerful servers with fast network connectivity
- API calls are designed to accommodate many different trading strategies
- Support for both REST (pull) and WebSockets (push)
- High rate limits
- Follows industry-standard security schemes, such as OAuth 2, popularized by Facebook, or HMAC, which uses hash computation
- Documentation is presented in a clear, concise, and consistent manner with examples for each API call
- Provides a test/staging environment
- Provides libraries for many different coding platforms
- Real-time communication on the status of the platform, and transparency with regard to incident management

Two examples of exchanges that have gained enough resources to build a high-quality API are Coinbase Pro and Kraken.

One of the first things a developer will try when evaluating an API is to perform a basic call that requires the least amount of effort possible. For example, looking up the current BTC/USD ticker price doesn't require any setup, as that data is public.

On Coinbase Pro, the BTC/USD ticker API call looks like this:

```
Request:
    GET - https://api.pro.coinbase.com/products/BTC-USD

Response:
{
    "id": "BTC-USD",
    "base_currency": "BTC",
    "quote_currency": "USD",
    "base_min_size": "0.00100000",
    "base_max_size": "280.00000000",
    "quote_increment": "0.01000000",
    "base_increment": "0.00000001",
    "display_name": "BTC/USD",
    "min_market_funds": "5",
    "max_market_funds": "1000000",
    "margin_enabled": false,
    "post_only": false,
    "limit_only": false,
```

```
        "cancel_only": false,
        "trading_disabled": false,
        "status": "online",
        "status_message": ""
    }
```

On Gemini, the BTC/USD ticker API call looks like this:

```
Request:
    GET - https://api.gemini.com/v2/ticker/btcusd

Response:
{
    "symbol": "BTCUSD",
    "open": "9179.77",
    "high": "9298",
    "low": "9050",
    "close": "9195",
    "changes": [
        "9219.54",
        "9211",
        "9211.71",
        "9243.67",
        "9243.71",
        "9250",
        "9249.03",
        "9235.41",
        "9237.69",
        "9244.22",
        "9244.68",
        "9240.38",
        "9248",
        "9263.61",
        "9289.8",
        "9291.62",
        "9269.68",
        "9222.01",
        "9210.09",
        "9160.63",
        "9165.4",
        "9152.46",
        "9164.7",
        "9173.33"
    ],
    "bid": "9195.00",
    "ask": "9195.01"
}
```

Even with something as simple as a ticker API call, you can see big differences in the response data. Amongst these, Coinbase Pro's API includes a status field that allows the bot to recognize when the market is unavailable for trading and adjust accordingly, while Gemini's API includes changes, an array showing the previous prices for this trading pair. This can allow a trading bot to recognize a trend in the price.

These are two exchanges in the US with significant resources, and as you can see, their APIs are quite different. There are hundreds of exchanges all over the world with even greater variance in their API schemes and quality. Developing a trading bot that integrates into multiple exchanges therefore requires a lot of time and effort.

The remainder of this section introduces some of the things to keep in mind when using trading bots and dealing with APIs.

Open Source Trading Tech

It's a lot faster for a developer to integrate with an exchange's API using an existing library that they can include into their code. In this way, they can adopt existing code that already integrates with all the exchange's API calls and navigates the API's security. Without such a library, the developer is required to write up and test a lot of extra code themselves.

There are some open source projects with trading tech that are helpful to get started trading with APIs. One of the most popular projects is the CryptoCurrency eXchange Trading Library (*https://github.com/ccxt/ccxt*) (CCXT), which enables developers to integrate with over 125 cryptocurrency exchanges. Using this library means a developer does not have to learn the nuances of each exchange's API, or write custom code for each exchange. Rather, the library provides one unified set of calls to integrate with many exchanges.

All *public* calls do not require the developer to have an account on the exchange. Public calls enable the reading of public information, such as the market price for BTC/USD. All *private* calls do require that the developer provide an API key from the exchange, which requires account setup. Private calls allow the reading/writing of private information. Examples of private calls include getting an exchange user's open limit orders or initiating a market order.

Some important API calls to get started include the following:

- Retrieving ticker prices (public)
- Retrieving order book data (public)
- Retrieving account trade history (private)
- Transferring funds between trading accounts (private)
- Creating, executing, and cancelling orders (private)

Rate Limiting

Every exchange API will have a limit to the number of requests that can be made from an external server. Each call made to the API server uses up server resources, and the rate limit forces external servers to not abuse API access. It also provides a layer of protection from DDoS attacks, which are very common in this industry.

For example, Coinbase imposes a limit of three requests per second for some API endpoints, or communications channels, and five requests per second for other endpoints. The external server will get a 429 error when it makes a request that has exceeded the limit.

REST Versus WebSocket

Speed is an important factor in building a high-quality trading bot, so that the bot can read the market and execute trades before others can. With a REST API, the trading bot must continuously poll the API to view the latest state of the market, which often leads to gaps of time between a change occurring in the market and the trading bot seeing that change. These gaps increase significantly when the trading bot is rate-limited and has to wait a split second until it can make a valid request.

A faster way for a trading bot to view the current state of the market is by subscribing to a WebSocket. With this setup, as soon as a change occurs in the market, the exchange's server pushes a notification to all subscribers of the WebSocket. Then all trading bots subscribing to the WebSocket will receive the same information at the same time, and they do not need to make additional API requests that will fill their rate limit quotas.

> It can be helpful for traders to find out the exact location where the exchange hosts its API server, and host their trading bot in the same location. For example, if the exchange's API server is hosted on AWS in the Northern Virginia region, a trader could host their bot with AWS in the same region to ensure faster communication.

Testing in a Sandbox

When developers are testing various features of a trading bot, ideally they should do the testing in a *sandbox* environment using fake money. If an exchange's API does not have a sandbox environment, developers are forced to test out functionality using real money, which often limits the testing capacity of a trading bot. It's usually too risky to test out new features using real dollars that could easily be lost to a bug.

Market Aggregators

There are some services, like CoinMarketCap (*http://www.coinmarketcap.com*) and CoinGecko (*http://www.coingecko.com*), that aggregate market pricing from hundreds of exchanges and package out this data to an API. The advantage of such an API is that it makes it easy for a trading bot to get a high-level view of the market. The downside is that relying on a third party to aggregate the data causes a delay in the aggregator's pricing data—plus there is a risk that there could be mistakes in the aggregator's API, and it will send incorrect data.

Summary

The cryptocurrency markets are a fascinating window into what happens in a nascent ecosystem when regulatory structures have to catch up. The opportunities that exist in this space are what bring a lot of new entrants into the blockchain world. Speculation due to these markets being in their infancy draws the interest of many people, as price remains a singular motivator.

These markets are subject to quick changes. Still, the information covered in this chapter should help developers and traders alike with lots of ideas on how to get started.

CHAPTER 7

Decentralizing Finance and the Web

The growing popularity of cryptocurrency, blockchain, and smart contracts has ushered in a number of new use cases that provide specialized functionality, from increased privacy to the creation of a stable payments system to entirely new types of blockchain-based applications. This chapter explores the exciting possibilities being revealed in the realms of *decentralized finance* (DeFi) and *decentralized apps* (dapps).

Redistribution of Trust

Although they are trying to innovate, banks today are still slow and expensive (*https://oreil.ly/G7ixe*). Sending money across borders takes more than a day. And for those who don't have a bank account, sending money to family or friends living in other countries is costly. With a payment layer that uses cryptocurrency, blockchain can remove intermediaries. Over time, it may also allow users to own their data instead of that data being owned by big technology companies.

Identity and the Dangers of Hacking

Why is it important for users to have ownership of their data? Large companies in the technology and finance space have not been great stewards of data. They have repeatedly been breached, hacked, and otherwise compromised. In many cases they have then attempted to downplay or conceal these breaches, though they have often been caught (and fined) later. For example:

- Yahoo! disclosed 3 billion accounts had been compromised in 2013. It didn't release information regarding the hack until 2017 and eventually reached a settlement to pay $117.5 million in compensation.

- Facebook saw 50 million user accounts compromised in 2018. The US Federal Trade Commission (FTC) fined the company $5 billion for mishandling user data.

- Equifax disclosed that the personal information of 143 million of its customers had been compromised in 2017. The company reached a deal with regulators to pay $700 million in fines and compensation.

- eBay suffered an attack in 2014 that exposed the personal information (including passwords) of over 145 million users.

- Uber's servers were breached in 2016, after two hackers were able to retrieve password information from GitHub. The hackers then accessed the personal information of 57 million riders and 600,000 drivers. Uber hid the breach for over a year and was ultimately fined $148 million.

And these are just technology companies. Well-known hacks at Target, Marriott, Home Depot, and JPMorgan, among others, have taken user data and put it in the hands of those who try to use that information for nefarious purposes.

Blockchain technology is promising in that it has the ability to disintermediate various industries, many perhaps quite quickly. Some experimentation has already begun. Industries including technology, finance, jobs, and gaming are ripe for disruption. The technical "scaffolding" is being built today for users to have more control over their data.

The ultimate realization of this idea is the concept of self-sovereign identity, where individuals generate their own unique identifiers and store and control access to their own personal information, using public/private key pairs. The idea of an identity that is owned by a user instead of large companies and government bureaucracies is something blockchain developers are enthusiastic about, and it could remove the danger of future hacks and thefts that put people's identities at risk.

A central issue will be how to balance complexity with ease of use. Private key management and transaction broadcasting may be difficult to teach or too cumbersome for mainstream users. However, some early platforms are trying to tackle this problem, as you'll see in this section.

Wallets

In order to use a number of DeFi services, users must become familiar with wallets. Fortunately, a number of good options are available today. MetaMask (*https://meta mask.io*) is a software wallet that currently works inside the Chrome, Firefox, and Opera browsers. It is also available for Brave, a new type of browser discussed later in this chapter. Hardware wallets like Ledger (*https://www.ledger.com*) are another alternative, and Coinbase (*https://www.coinbase.com*) also offers support for those who don't want to concern themselves with key storage.

 Remember: if you don't own the keys, you don't own the asset.

Private Keys

The MetaMask and Ledger wallets require users to know and carefully store their private keys. The loss of a password, or *seed*—a list of words that store all the information needed to recover a wallet—can equal the loss of a private key. Because of this, new services that help users maintain identity while securing private keys are important. Coinbase already does this for cryptocurrency wallets. Identification services like Keybase (*https://keybase.io*) and Blockstack (*https://www.blockstack.org*) make it easier for users to maintain private keys for different types of Web 3.0 services, covered later in this chapter.

Naming Services

Public keys are much more difficult to use than email addresses, usernames, or other identifiers, yet they are very important to decentralized services. Figure 7-1 shows examples (*https://oreil.ly/A_JbA*) of public and private keys. The QR codes are representations of the keys.

Figure 7-1. Public and private keys

Naming services allow users to have *names* that are much more easily read and typed than complex public keys are. An example is the Ethereum Naming Service (*https://ens.domains*), which allows people to use a *<username>.eth* naming convention that translates to a public key. The drawback is that using these names can allow analytics to track transactions on the blockchain, which risks revealing identity information (*https://oreil.ly/htxHK*).

Decentralizing Finance

The ecosystem of financial services without intermediaries is growing quickly. This is a fascinating area of blockchain that is attracting a lot of attention from developers, and a number of platforms are now working to provide decentralized finance.

DeFi services use smart contracts, cryptocurrency, and blockchain to replace some of the services that banking has traditionally provided (*https://oreil.ly/DrR7o*). Figure 7-2 illustrates.

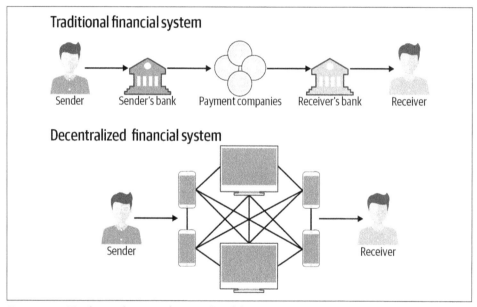

Figure 7-2. Traditional versus decentralized finance

DeFi has a lot of moving parts, many of which rely on Ethereum and ERC-20 assets. The flexibility of ERC-20 on Ethereum is what makes DeFi possible, since pools of liquidity can be expanded or reduced depending on market conditions.

Important Definitions

Smart contracts are essential to the DeFi model. Many cryptocurrencies are valuable because of the existence of a fixed supply of assets in circulation. However, many DeFi tokens have an *elastic* supply to make them inflationary or deflationary, depending on the design of the system. This is where some new terminology needs to be defined:

Minting

Used to increase a cryptocurrency supply, *minting* involves the creation of new assets. This is done with the creation of new blocks as rewards are generated for *stakers*, or users who pool assets for incentives. Minting must be properly controlled in order to limit inflation via some system of governance. Otherwise, the value of a cryptocurrency may fall in relation to other assets, diminishing its purchasing power and store of value properties. Minting is *algorithmically fixed*, or relegated to authorities within a system.

Burning

Used to decrease a cryptocurrency supply, *burning* involves the destruction of assets. This destruction is done by system authorities. By reducing circulation and lessening supply, this can cause the price of a cryptocurrency to go up. However, the asset could become *deflationary* via this process—while the value goes up, prices of other assets may go down. Burning could be a one-time event, or a staggered event triggered by revenue/earnings. Burning is also a way to distribute profits back to token holders by reducing the supply in hopes demand and prices rise.

Wrapped tokens

The Ethereum platform was not designed with the ERC-20 standard in mind. Neither were Bitcoin or any other cryptocurrencies outside of the Ethereum ecosystem. Because of users wanting to trade various cryptocurrencies with ERC-20s in smart contracts, *wrapped tokens* have become a solution. The original asset is "wrapped," meaning provably held on-chain as collateral. A smart contract facilitates the processes of *depositing* (minting) and *withdrawing* (burning) for these ERC-20 representatives of their external cryptocurrency counterparts. Some level of trust is required to assure that the external tokens remain in custody for the holder of the wrapped token balance. Typically, a multisignature scheme is implemented among disinterested custodians who mutually sign off on withdrawal requests.

DAOs

Decentralized autonomous organizations (DAOs) are projects organized via code, mostly through Ethereum smart contracts. Not controlled by a central authority, DAOs have token holders to provide governance. Because DAOs utilize blockchain-based smart contracts, there are transparent records of transactions and the rules governing a DAO. Although their legal and regulatory status isn't clear, DAOs have already been used for finance, gaming, and social media.

Oracles

Because blockchains don't interface well with data sources, such as relational databases, *oracles* are required to provide outside information. Real-world events that are recorded in centralized databases are still needed for these systems to function, and oracles serve that purpose. Oracles bring off-chain data on-chain (*https://oreil.ly/nRW1o*), as illustrated in Figure 7-3.

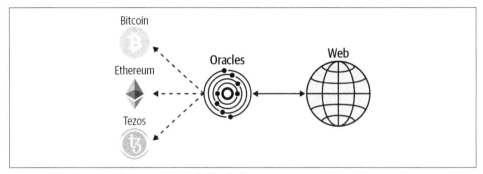

Figure 7-3. How oracles interact with blockchains

 Oracles play an important role in the blockchain ecosystem because they provide data smart contracts use to execute code. Any wrong or manipulated feed from an oracle could trigger a smart contract execution that could mean an irretrievable loss of funds. A smart contract might be fully secured and audited, but if the oracle is being manipulated, it would also serve as a weak entry point for hackers to exploit. This is why trust in an oracle system is paramount.

Stablecoins

As blockchain-based assets that peg to the US dollar and other fiat currencies, *stablecoins* underpin services that don't require banking intermediaries. Many stablecoins do have some regulatory risk (discussed in Chapter 6). In addition, there are various levels of governance and centralization between different projects. Nevertheless, interesting experiments are being done with stablecoins. We'll briefly look at a few of them here.

DAI

In the volatile world of cryptocurrencies, DeFi requires a stable asset in order to properly service users. The major stablecoin cryptocurrency used for this today is the Maker project's DAI (*https://makerdao.com/en*). DAI, launched in 2018, was originally a "single-collateral token" backed by Ethereum's ETH. Now DAI is a *multicollateral token* backed by several cryptocurrencies, including ETH and BAT (Basic Attention Token, the Ethereum token that powers the Brave browser) and others.

However, the cryptocurrencies that back the DAI stablecoin are inherently volatile. So how does Maker create a stable asset from volatile markets? By locking in assets. Here's how it works:

1. A user deposits ETH into the Maker smart contract, called a *vault*.

2. Maker then allows the user to withdraw DAI. The amount that can be withdrawn must be collateralized 150%. That means a user who deposits $150 worth of ETH can withdraw up to $100 worth of DAI. This DAI is backed by the ETH a user deposits.

3. If ETH begins to drop against the value deposited, in this example below $150, the system will begin to close out the position. If, for example, the user only withdraws $50 worth of DAI, the system will not close out until ETH drops to $75, which is the 150% collateralization threshold. The position will close unless the user deposits ETH or DAI to make up for the collateral requirement.

4. A *stability fee* is charged to return DAI in order to retrieve ETH or another cryptocurrency used for collateral. Currently the fee is 3%, but it's subject to change. When DAI is returned to the system, it is *burned* or destroyed because it is no longer backed by collateral. The stability fee is used by Maker to fund the system's development.

Maker is a DAO, and it also offers an investment token, MKR. MKR is the cryptocurrency that determines elements inside the MakerDAO system. Those who hold MKR have influence over the system. This includes providing input on collateralization requirements, stability fees, how the stability fees are spent, and the emergency shutdown protocol in the event of a price crash.

For every dollar that is paid in stability fees, the equivalent is bought and removed from the MKR market. In addition, for liquidations that cannot be rectified by a standard collateral auction, a debt auction occurs where the equivalent amount of MKR is also bought and removed from the market.

Because the Maker system is smart contract–based, it does not require users to submit personal Know Your Customer (KYC) information to participate. The only thing required to interact with it is a private key and access to some ether.

USDC

An ERC-20 stablecoin, USD Coin (USDC) (*https://www.centre.io/usdc*) is supported by two of the largest and best-known companies in cryptocurrency: Coinbase and Circle (*https://www.circle.com*). USDC is part of a larger consortium called Centre, whose members collaborate on the stablecoin's governance and use cases. Grant Thorton, LLP, is the auditor for USDC. The firm provides monthly attestations that there are enough reserves to back the USDC stablecoin. The system requires users acquiring or redeeming USDC from the issuer to submit personal information for KYC checks.

TrueUSD

Backed by a US-based company called TrustToken, TrueUSD (TUSD) (*https://www.trusttoken.com/trueusd*) is a dollar-based stablecoin that uses the ERC-20 protocol. TrustToken also has stablecoins backed by the Canadian dollar, the British pound, the Australian dollar, and the Hong Kong dollar. TrustToken uses the auditing firm Cohen & Cohen to provide monthly attestations that it has sufficient bank-held reserves to back its crypto assets. This system requires users to submit personal KYC information in order to acquire or redeem TUSD.

KYC and pseudonymity

As mentioned in the previous sections, although DAI does not require KYC information from users, TUSD and USDC do. Because of banking relationships, TUSD and USDC require users to provide personal information to redeem their stablecoins for fiat. However, inside the blockchain ecosystem, the stablecoins can be used pseudonymously (*https://oreil.ly/Cb6zm*), changing hands while leaving a blockchain record, as Figure 7-4 illustrates.

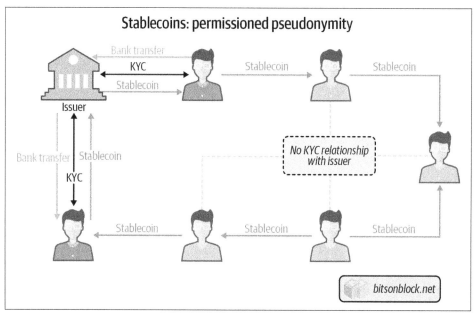

Figure 7-4. How stablecoins can be used pseudonymously

Although DAI is the most used stablecoin in DeFi applications, bank-backed solutions are competitors. The main difference is that TUSD and USDC are backed by fiat, whereas DAI is currently backed by cryptocurrencies.

DeFi Services

With increased stablecoin liquidity, financial services are being built on top of crypto. The website DeFi Pulse (*https://defipulse.com*) is a good barometer for projects that are getting traction. By looking at the number of ETH locked up in smart contracts, it's easy to tell from DeFi Pulse which projects are gaining users. This is a good way to see what these services are being used for in this nascent market, which is growing every day.

Lending

There is a market for users who want to borrow fiat and keep crypto. DeFi loans generally have a very specific purpose. Many cryptocurrency holders don't want to sell crypto, whether for speculative reasons, because they believe in the long-term value of cryptocurrency, or because they don't want to pay taxes upon converting to fiat. They don't want to give up their assets, and will pay for the privilege.

One way to accomplish this is to use a service such as Compound (*https:// compound.finance*), one of the largest decentralized lending platforms today. Compound allows users to borrow against cryptocurrency holdings. The amount borrowed is overcollateralized, and issued in DAI. This DAI, because it is pegged to the dollar, can be sold on the market for fiat or used to invest in other cryptocurrencies.

Savings

DeFi savings involves users locking cryptocurrency, usually stablecoin, into a smart contract. The contract then provides a yield in the native cryptocurrency. The concept is similar to staking (discussed in Chapter 2), except there are no transactions being validated as a result of the cryptocurrency being locked up in a smart contract.

Maker has savings rates for DAI (*https://oreil.ly/46dpI*) locked up in what is called a *DAI Savings Rate* (DSR) contract. The interest paid comes from the stability fees that vault owners pay to borrow DAI against cryptocurrencies like ETH. The rate is variable, determined by the MKR token holders. Unlike when borrowing DAI, there is no penalty to take out saved DAI or the interest paid. Compound also has a DeFi savings program.

Derivatives

In DeFi, *derivatives* are used as collateral for *synthetic assets*. For example, you might use ETH to get an asset like BTC or gold on the ERC-20 network. Exchanges are emerging that offer a number of derivative assets, enabling traders to frictionlessly move between these assets in ways that were not possible in the past. Previously, this would have required access to several different trading markets.

Synthetix (*https://oreil.ly/cNgm1*) is currently the leading DeFi platform for derivative assets. Users must hold SNX tokens, and stake them in order to access the derivative assets. Synthetix currently supports ERC-20 versions of ETH, BTC, USD, MKR, gold, EUR, and BNB (Binance Coin). The SNX collateralization is 750%, which users can maintain by burning or minting SNX tokens.

Decentralized Exchanges

Most cryptocurrency exchanges are centralized, hosting wallets and taking fees for every trade. With smart contracts, developers can build decentralized exchanges, also known as *DEXes*. A DEX allows traders to hold their own private keys and swap cryptocurrencies (usually in the form of wrapped tokens).

Uniswap (*https://docs.uniswap.io*) is one of the most popular DEXes available today. It has many smart contracts that facilitate ETH/ERC-20 exchange. The platform charges 0.3% for each trade, which is placed into a liquidity reserve. This reserve is used to incentivize liquidity providers to maintain a pool of assets for trading. Unlike centralized exchanges that use databases for trading, all trades on DEXes like Uniswap occur on-chain, with no middlemen.

Decentralized Versus Centralized Exchanges

DEXes are designed to work in a very different way than a centralized exchange. The goal of a DEX is that it can provide users with 100% functionality without depending on one centralized authority to power any part of the exchange. This can lead to a more transparent, secure, and trustworthy service that allows users to maintain custody of their funds at all times. The downside of a DEX is that its speed and scalability are limited by the blockchain it runs on. This is because users maintain custody of funds, which adds complexity to the overall experience.

Infrastructure

In a centralized exchange, all of the infrastructure is controlled by a single entity, usually a company, and is delivered to the user through a website. In contrast, all parts of the Uniswap DEX are run by the community, as illustrated in Figure 7-5.

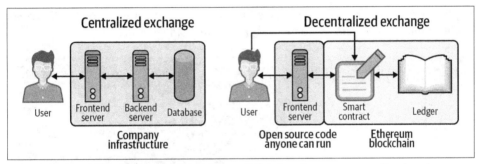

Figure 7-5. High-level view of infrastructure differences between centralized exchanges and DEXes

Table 7-1 compares the frontend code for a centralized and decentralized exchange (in this case, Uniswap).

Table 7-1. Frontend differences between centralized exchanges and Uniswap

Type	Centralized exchange	Uniswap
Distribution & transparency	The frontend code is kept private by the exchange and runs on infrastructure the exchange controls.	The frontend code is shared in the Uniswap GitHub repository.
Control	The frontend runs on infrastructure the exchange and its hosting provider control.	Anyone in the community can launch their own website that interacts with the Uniswap DEX.
Functionality	The frontend receives data from the backend, for example to get the exchange rate for the market USD/ETH. The frontend code also sends instructions to the backend, for example to execute a trade.	The frontend code only receives data from the DEX smart contract. It does not send instructions to the backend. Instead, the user sends instructions to the smart contract directly from their client device using an Ethereum wallet like MetaMask. The frontend code makes this process more user-friendly by setting up the transaction for the user.
Transaction authorization	The transaction authorization is performed in the frontend code, usually with a cookie or an access token stored in the browser.	The user authorizes the transaction by generating a transaction signature using their private key, stored in MetaMask. MetaMask then pushes the transaction to the smart contract.

Figure 7-6 is a screenshot of a user executing a trade on Uniswap. Note that *the transaction authorization occurs in MetaMask, not in the frontend code.*

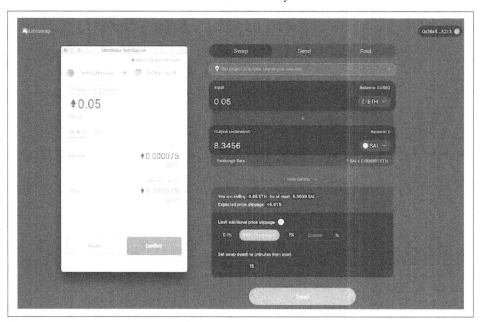

Figure 7-6. A user executing a trade on Uniswap

Table 7-2 outlines the differences between a centralized exchange and a DEX with regard to the backend and database.

Table 7-2. Backend/database differences between centralized exchanges and Uniswap

Type	Centralized exchange	Uniswap
Distribution & transparency	The backend and database are kept private by the exchange. The public is unable to audit the exchange's code.	The backend logic runs in a smart contract. The code in Uniswap smart contracts can be viewed publicly, so potential users can audit the code before using the DEX. All Uniswap transactions are recorded on the Ethereum blockchain, which is also publicly viewable.
Control	The backend runs on infrastructure the exchange and its hosting provider control. The exchange can make changes to the backend server or database at any time. In addition, the exchange or hosting provider can shut down the backend or database at any time.	Uniswap smart contracts and transactions are powered by and recorded by thousands of miners. The smart contracts and transactions are immutable and can never be changed. The only way to shut down the smart contract or stop transactions from completing is by shutting down the Ethereum network.
Authorizing code execution	Before executing any business logic, the backend authorizes API requests using security standards like JWT or OAuth.	Smart contract code is run on the Ethereum Virtual Machine (EVM). The smart contract runs on the node of the miner producing the block and everyone in the network running a full node validating the chain.

Figure 7-7 shows part of the Uniswap V1 Exchange Template smart contract, viewable on the blockchain (*https://oreil.ly/T5ruS*).

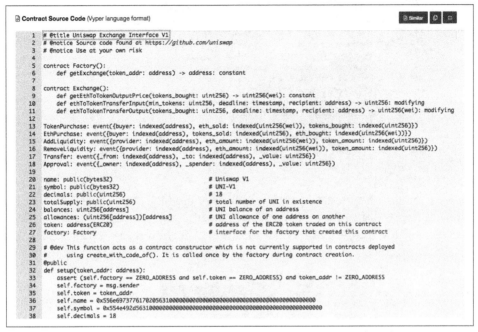

```
Contract Source Code (Vyper language format)                                    Similar

1   # @title Uniswap Exchange Interface V1
2   # @notice Source code found at https://github.com/uniswap
3   # @notice Use at your own risk
4
5   contract Factory():
6       def getExchange(token_addr: address) -> address: constant
7
8   contract Exchange():
9       def getEthToTokenOutputPrice(tokens_bought: uint256) -> uint256(wei): constant
10      def ethToTokenTransferInput(min_tokens: uint256, deadline: timestamp, recipient: address) -> uint256: modifying
11      def ethToTokenTransferOutput(tokens_bought: uint256, deadline: timestamp, recipient: address) -> uint256(wei): modifying
12
13  TokenPurchase: event({buyer: indexed(address), eth_sold: indexed(uint256(wei)), tokens_bought: indexed(uint256)})
14  EthPurchase: event({buyer: indexed(address), tokens_sold: indexed(uint256), eth_bought: indexed(uint256(wei))})
15  AddLiquidity: event({provider: indexed(address), eth_amount: indexed(uint256(wei)), token_amount: indexed(uint256)})
16  RemoveLiquidity: event({provider: indexed(address), eth_amount: indexed(uint256(wei)), token_amount: indexed(uint256)})
17  Transfer: event({_from: indexed(address), _to: indexed(address), _value: uint256})
18  Approval: event({_owner: indexed(address), _spender: indexed(address), _value: uint256})
19
20  name: public(bytes32)                        # Uniswap V1
21  symbol: public(bytes32)                      # UNI-V1
22  decimals: public(uint256)                    # 18
23  totalSupply: public(uint256)                 # total number of UNI in existence
24  balances: uint256[address]                   # UNI balance of an address
25  allowances: (uint256[address])[address]      # UNI allowance of one address on another
26  token: address(ERC20)                        # address of the ERC20 token traded on this contract
27  factory: Factory                             # interface for the factory that created this contract
28
29  # @dev This function acts as a contract constructor which is not currently supported in contracts deployed
30  #      using create_with_code_of(). It is called once by the factory during contract creation.
31  @public
32  def setup(token_addr: address):
33      assert (self.factory == ZERO_ADDRESS and self.token == ZERO_ADDRESS) and token_addr != ZERO_ADDRESS
34      self.factory = msg.sender
35      self.token = token_addr
36      self.name = 0x556e6973776170205631000000000000000000000000000000000000000000
37      self.symbol = 0x554e492d5631000000000000000000000000000000000000000000000000
38      self.decimals = 18
```

Figure 7-7. One of Uniswap's smart contracts, publicly viewable on the Ethereum blockchain

Token listing

When the makers of a token want a centralized exchange to list their token, there is often a long delay while both parties attempt to negotiate the terms of this business transaction. Often, the token company has to pay a listing fee and provide legal documents and legal opinions to reduce the exchange's liability.

Since a DEX is not controlled by anyone, the makers of a token can list their token on their own—no permission required.

If someone wants to list an ERC-20 token on Uniswap, all they have to do is call the createExchange method in the Uniswap Token Factory smart contract (*0xc0a47dFe034B400B47bDaD5FecDa2621de6c4d95*), shown in Figure 7-8.

```
18  @public
19  def createExchange(token: address) -> address:
20      assert token != ZERO_ADDRESS
21      assert self.exchangeTemplate != ZERO_ADDRESS
22      assert self.token_to_exchange[token] == ZERO_ADDRESS
23      exchange: address = create_with_code_of(self.exchangeTemplate)
24      Exchange(exchange).setup(token)
25      self.token_to_exchange[token] = exchange
26      self.exchange_to_token[exchange] = token
27      token_id: uint256 = self.tokenCount + 1
28      self.tokenCount = token_id
29      self.id_to_token[token_id] = token
30      log.NewExchange(token, exchange)
31      return exchange
```

Figure 7-8. Uniswap Token Factory method that allows anyone to list an ERC-20 token on the Uniswap DEX

As an argument, they need to pass the address of the ERC-20 token smart contract. For example, if you wanted to add the SAI ERC-20 token (*0x89d24A6b4CcB1B6fAA2625fE562bDD9a23260359*), you would execute the crea teExchange method and pass the following argument:

Argument name	Value
token	0x89d24A6b4CcB1B6fAA2625fE562bDD9a23260359

The Uniswap Token Factory would then generate a new smart contract that allows anyone to trade ETH for SAI and vice versa.

Custody and counterparty risk

Users of a centralized exchange have to deposit cryptocurrency to begin trading, and the exchange takes custody of their funds. Since the exchange controls users' funds, there is exposure to *counterparty risk*. That is, if the exchange gets hacked or shuts down, there is a risk that its users' funds may be lost.

When someone uses a DEX, the smart contracts manage deposits, withdrawals, trades, and maintaining custody of user funds. Before sending funds to the DEX, users can audit the smart contract code to know how their funds will be used.

Here are the important things to look for in the smart contract:

- What smart contract methods can move the user's funds?
- Who can call those methods to move the user's funds?
- Where can those funds be moved to?

To clarify how Uniswap manages user funds, we executed a small trade on the DEX and then audited the transaction, as shown in Figure 7-9.

Transaction Hash:	0xa7f991b86f20909617fa436e1f16ab7ec995d1c488454d0a95b09b6a2c76dba0 🗐
Status:	✓ Success
Block:	9331285 5875 Block Confirmations
Timestamp:	⏱ 21 hrs 33 mins ago (Jan-22-2020 12:06:31 PM +UTC)
From:	0x76e55ab64c5e2415a8a6375fef216977de7ea213 🗐
To:	Contract 0x09cabec1ead1c0ba254b09efb3ee13841712be14 (Uniswap: SAI) ✓ 🗐
Tokens Transferred:	▸ From 0x09cabec1ead1c0... To 0x76e55ab64c5e24... For 8.342650846452389346 ($8.47) ◈ Sai Stableco... (SAI)
Value:	0.05 Ether ($8.16)
Transaction Fee:	0.000067689 Ether ($0.01)
Gas Limit:	75,221
Gas Used by Transaction:	67,689 (89.99%)
Gas Price:	0.000000001 Ether (1 Gwei)
Nonce Position	6 63
Input Data:	Function: ethToTokenSwapInput(uint256 min_tokens, uint256 deadline) MethodID: 0xf39b5b9b [0]: 0000000000000000000000000000000000000000000000007349d8cdf224ded3 [1]: 00000000000000000000000000000000000000000000000000000005e283df6

Figure 7-9. Publicly viewable record of a method call to a Uniswap smart contract

As you can see, we traded 0.05 ETH for 8.34 SAI tokens, worth about $8 USD.

In the transaction record, the input data field contains this value:

```
0xf39b5b9b0000000000000000000000000000000000000000000000007349d8cdf224ded30000000
00000000000000000000000000000000000000000000000000000005e283df6
```

Breaking down the input data shows which smart contract function is called and the arguments passed.

The first 10 characters of the input data field specify the function being called. In this transaction, the first 10 characters are 0xf39b5b9b. Using an online directory (*https://www.4byte.directory*), you can learn that the function being called is ethToTokenSwapInput(uint256,uint256). The remaining characters in the input data field are the values of the arguments passed into the function:

```
00000000000000000000000000000000000000000000000007349d8cdf224ded3
```

```
00000000000000000000000000000000000000000000000000000005e283df6
```

Auditing this transaction, we see that the following steps took place:

1. The transaction sent 0.05 ETH from our address (*0x76e55ab64c5e2415a8a6375fef216977de7ea213*) to the Uniswap SAI smart contract (*0x09cabec1ead1c0ba254b09efb3ee13841712be14*). Those funds will remain in the smart contract to be used as liquidity for future trades. It's similar to a bank account: when a user puts funds in, they still own the funds and can pull them out at any time; however, while the funds are sitting there, the bank can use them too.

2. The transaction called the function `ethToTokenSwapInput` in the Uniswap SAI smart contract (0x09ca…be14) with these input values:

Argument name	Value
min_tokens	00000000000000000000000000000000000000000000000007349d8cdf224ded3
deadline	00000000000000000000000000000000000000000000000000000005e283df6

These arguments are in hex format because smart contracts are compiled into bytecode. Decoding them into human-readable values gives us this:

Argument name	Value	Type
min_tokens	8307409366703988435	uint256
deadline	1579695606	uint256

> When calling a smart contract, users must send values in hex as arguments. There are tools available online, such as Moesif's binary encoder/decoder (*https://oreil.ly/FO2Qv*), to help create the input data to be sent with a transaction.

Let's take a closer look at the `ethToTokenSwapInput` function defined in the Uniswap V1 Exchange Template smart contract (*https://oreil.ly/EJTca*) mentioned earlier (Figure 7-10).

```
151  def ethToTokenSwapInput(min_tokens: uint256, deadline: timestamp) -> uint256:
152      return self.ethToTokenInput(msg.value, min_tokens, deadline, msg.sender, msg.sender)
```

Figure 7-10. The ethToTokenSwapInput function from the Uniswap template code

Looking at the method definition, you can see that it calls another method, ethToTokenInput. As Figure 7-11 shows, this method is where the real logic of this transaction takes place.

```
127  def ethToTokenInput(eth_sold: uint256(wei), min_tokens: uint256, deadline: timestamp, buyer: address, recipient: address) -> uint256:
128      assert deadline >= block.timestamp and (eth_sold > 0 and min_tokens > 0)
129      token_reserve: uint256 = self.token.balanceOf(self)
130      tokens_bought: uint256 = self.getInputPrice(as_unitless_number(eth_sold), as_unitless_number(self.balance - eth_sold), token_reserve)
131      assert tokens_bought >= min_tokens
132      assert self.token.transfer(recipient, tokens_bought)
133      log.TokenPurchase(buyer, eth_sold, tokens_bought)
134      return tokens_bought
```

Figure 7-11. Transaction logic

Line 128 in Figure 7-11 checks to make sure that the following are true:

- The deadline given is equal to or later than the timestamp of the block in which this transaction is being included.

- The amount of eth_sold is greater than 0.

- The number of min_tokens expected is greater than 0.

Line 129 gets the quantity of tokens that the smart contract is currently holding.

Line 130 gets the number of tokens that the user should receive in the trade. This is an important line because it shows how the exchange rate for the trade is calculated. It calls the function getInputPrice, which determines the exchange rate based on the ratio of ETH to SAI currently sitting in the smart contract.

Line 131 checks to make sure the value of tokens_bought is greater than or equal to the min_tokens value, which is the minimum number of tokens the user is willing to receive.

If all the previous checks were valid, line 132 is executed. This line transfers the tokens from the smart contract to the recipient's address. More technically, it calls the method transfer in the SAI smart contract (0x89d2…0359) with the following arguments:

Argument name	Value	Type
dst	0x76e55ab64c5e2415a8a6375fef216977de7ea213	address
wad	8342650846452389346	uint

Line 133 broadcasts out to all listeners of the event TokenPurchase that this trade has been executed.

Finally, line 134 returns the value token_bought, which is how many tokens the user received.

Here are the input values passed to the `ethToTokenInput` method in our example transaction, resulting in the trade of 0.05 ETH for 8.34 SAI tokens:

Argument name	Value	Type	Description
eth_sold	50000000000000000	uit256(wei)[a]	msg.value is passed for this argument, which refers to the amount of ETH that was sent in the transaction (0.05 ETH). The type is uint256(wei), where 1 ETH = 10^{18} wei, so we multiply 0.05 by 10^{18}.
min_tokens	8307409366703988435	uint256	This value was passed from the original transaction. It specifies the minimum number of tokens that we are willing to receive before executing the transaction.
deadline	1579695606	timestamp	This value was passed from the original transaction. It represents the latest possible date that we are OK with for executing the transaction.
buyer	0x76e55ab64c5e2415a 8a6375fef216977de7ea213	address	msg.sender was passed for this argument, which refers to the address that executed the transaction. That was our address.
recipient	0x76e55ab64c5e2415a 8a6375fef216977de7ea213	address	Same as previous.

[a] Wei is the smallest denomination of ether. 1 ether = 1,000,000,000,000,000,000 wei. When interacting with the Ethereum blockchain, numbers are in terms of wei.

Exchange rate

On a centralized exchange, the exchange rate in a market trade is set to a price that both a buyer and seller agree to. That logic is programmed into the backend server of the exchange. On a DEX, the exchange rate is programmed into the smart contract that executes the trade, and can be audited.

Know your customer

Every centralized exchange has a signup process where users must share identifying information such as an email address, phone number, or government-issued ID. Depending on its jurisdiction, the exchange must collect a certain amount of identifying information before allowing someone to use its service. This is an important way that governments prevent financial institutions like exchanges from facilitating money laundering and terrorist financing. However, with a DEX, anyone can use the exchange without sharing any identity information. The only information shared is a cryptocurrency address.

The advantage is that anyone with cryptocurrency can use the DEX without asking permission. The disadvantage is that DEXes only allow for the trading of cryptocurrencies, and do not support fiat currencies like USD or EUR. This is because all fiat currencies are tied to the traditional banking system, which uses all central authorities like banks and financial institutions.

Scalability

A centralized exchange can run its infrastructure on well-established technology that can easily perform millions of operations per second. Therefore, it can provide a fast trading experience even if it's serving millions of users.

Since a DEX runs entirely on a public blockchain, the DEX's transaction throughput is limited by the blockchain's maximum transaction speed. As of 2020, Ethereum's maximum transaction rate was less than 20 transactions per second. By comparison, as mentioned earlier in the book, Visa's payments network can handle up to 65,000 transactions per second (*https://oreil.ly/85rhO*).

Flash Loans

Most standard loans have a process for evaluating who can qualify for a loan and the maximum amount they can borrow. Some loans may require the borrower to provide collateral to guarantee a loan. Lenders create and follow these processes to protect themselves from the risk that the borrower may not return the funds, and that risk increases the longer the borrower holds onto the funds.

A *flash loan*, on the other hand, allows an Ethereum smart contract to borrow a lender's funds without collateral under the condition that the smart contract return the funds plus a fee within the same Ethereum transaction. This is useful to a smart contract borrowing funds because it can execute multiple calls to other smart contracts within one Ethereum transaction, and therefore can make use of the borrowed funds while still returning the funds at the same instant.

Figure 7-12 illustrates what is possible for a smart contract to do within one transaction.

Figure 7-12. Example flash loan

If the smart contract does not properly return the funds plus the fee (step 3), the DeFi lending platform can produce an error in step 1, because steps 1 and 3 occur in the same transaction. Therefore, the lending platform is not at risk of the loan defaulting. Since there is no risk to the lender, the lender can loan out to smart contracts all the funds it has available in its lending pool.

Smart contracts hold, receive, and send funds. They also keep a record of balances. Essentially, the smart contract and community incentives replace the centralized authority in a traditional financial product.

Creating a Flash Loan Contract

Let's look at an example of how to perform a flash loan. In this example we will do the following:

1. Create a smart contract that can execute flash loans.
2. Execute a simple flash loan.

The flash loan contract will borrow 1 DAI (ERC-20 token) from the Aave (DeFi service) lending pool, and then return 1.0009 DAI. The amount returned is higher because it includes the flash loan fee.

The code for the Flashloan smart contract is as follows:

```
pragma solidity ^0.6.6;
// Import Aave flashloan code. By importing you are saving resources from
// having to write out this code.
import "https://github.com/aave/flashloan-
  box/blob/Remix/contracts/aave/FlashLoanReceiverBase.sol";
import "https://github.com/aave/flashloan-
  box/blob/Remix/contracts/aave/ILendingPoolAddressesProvider.sol";
import "https://github.com/aave/flashloan-
  box/blob/Remix/contracts/aave/ILendingPool.sol";

contract Flashloan is FlashLoanReceiverBase {

/**
The following constructor method is run when you create this flashloan smart
contract. Make sure to specify the address of the Aave LendingPoolAddressProvider
contract. This argument is different based on the environment you are working in.
Visit the Aave docs to get this address.
*/

    constructor(address _addressProvider) FlashLoanReceiverBase(_addressProvider)
        public {}
```

```
/**
The following function is called by Aave to the flashloan contract after the
contract has received the flash-loaned amount:
 */

function executeOperation(
    address _reserve,
    uint256 _amount,
    uint256 _fee,
    bytes calldata _params
)
    external
    override
{
    require(_amount <= getBalanceInternal(address(this), _reserve),
            "Invalid balance, was the flashloan successful?");

    // Your logic goes here.
    // !! Ensure that *this contract* has enough `_reserve` funds to
    // pay back the `_fee` !!

    uint totalDebt = _amount.add(_fee);
    transferFundsBackToPoolInternal(_reserve, totalDebt);
}

/**
Call the following function when you want to execute a flash loan. The
parameter _asset is the address of the token you want to borrow in the
flash loan. In our example the token we will borrow is DAI.
 */

function flashloan(address _asset) public onlyOwner {
    bytes memory data = "";
    uint amount = 1 ether;

    ILendingPool lendingPool =
      ILendingPool(addressesProvider.getLendingPool());
    lendingPool.flashLoan(address(this), _asset, amount, data);
}
}
```

Deploying the Contract

You can use Remix (*https://remix.ethereum.org*) and MetaMask to deploy this smart contract, as shown in Figure 7-13.

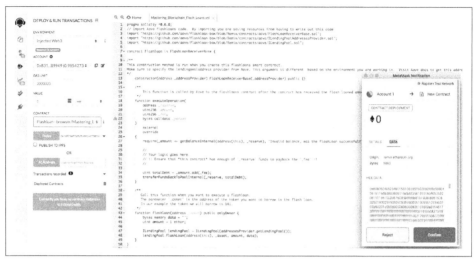

Figure 7-13. Deploying the Flashloan contract

Here are the steps required to publish the Flashloan smart contract to the Ropsten network:

1. Copy the smart contract code (you can find it on GitHub (*https://github.com/Mastering-Blockchain-Book*)) and paste it into Remix.

2. Compile the code using compiler version 0.6.6+commit.6c089d02 (to check the compiler version, click the third button from the top on the lefthand side of the Remix IDE).

3. Publish the code to the Ropsten environment. Be sure to enter the address of the Aave LendingPoolAddressProvider contract in the field next to the Deploy button. This argument is passed to the constructor method when creating the Flashloan contract; it essentially tells the Flashloan contract how to communicate with Aave when borrowing funds.

4. Click Deploy in Remix, then confirm the deployment in MetaMask.

The Flashloan smart contract now has the following address:

```
0x978e5f2149024D5742476Bc2d3b5B820926537A2
```

Executing a Flash Loan

To execute a flash loan, perform an Ethereum transaction that calls the function `flashloan(address _asset)`.

In this example, we want to execute a flash loan that borrows 1 DAI. The Flashloan contract is in the Ropsten environment, so the argument we need to pass is the address of the DAI token contract on Ropsten. That address is:

```
0xf80a32a835f79d7787e8a8ee5721d0feafd78108
```

Remember that Aave charges a fee, and if the Flashloan contract is unable to pay that fee, it will get an error. To ensure you can pay this fee, make sure the Flashloan contract holds at least 0.0009 DAI. You can use the smart contract tools on Etherscan to mint and then transfer funds to the contract.

Once you've identified the DAI token contract address and loaded the Flashloan contract with DAI to pay the fee, the contract is ready to execute a flash loan.

It's important to set a very high gas limit because a flash loan will perform multiple transactions, using up large amounts of gas—if the gas limit is too low, it will get an "out of gas" error.

In this example, we will send the following transaction to the flash loan contract:

- *Amount*: 0 ETH
- *Gas limit*: 300,000
- *Data*: 0x36c40477000000000000000000000000f80a32a835f79d7787e8a8ee5721d0 feafd78108

The data field contains two pieces of information:

Data value	Description
0x36c40477	Instruction to call the function `flashloan(address _asset)`.
000000000000000000000000f80a32a8 35f79d7787e8a8ee5721d0feafd78108	The _asset argument being passed into the function. In this example, it is the address of the DAI token contract.

Figure 7-14 shows the transaction to be sent to the Flashloan contract, including the input data.

Figure 7-14. Flashloan contract transaction in MetaMask wallet

You can see a successfully executed transaction of the flash loan online (*https:// oreil.ly/3Azdz*). A lot of activity happened in the one transaction (0xc779...1f23), including function calls and token transfers.

Auditing the token transfers in the sample flash loan transaction reveals that three token transactions occurred in the one flash loan (see Table 7-3).

Table 7-3. List of funds transferred in the flash loan transaction

Transaction #	Sender	Receiver	Amount
1	Aave lending pool (0x4295...9472)	Flashloan contract (0x978e...37A2)	1 DAI
2	Flashloan contract (0x978e...37A2)	Aave lending pool (0x4295...9472)	1.0009 DAI
3	Aave lending pool (0x4295...9472)	Aave fee collector (0xeBA2...fC9C)	0.00027 DAI

Auditing the function calls made in the flash loan transaction reveals a total of 24 function calls made involving 10 different smart contracts and one user account, as shown in Figure 7-15.

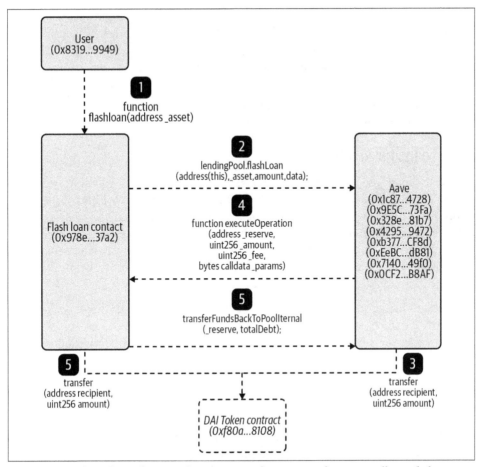

Figure 7-15. Flow chart showing the sequence of important function calls made between different smart contracts

The important function calls made in the flash loan transaction are as follows:

1. *Initiate flash loan*: The flash loan is initiated using the same user account (0x8319...9949) that created the flash loan contract. This user account calls the function `flashloan(address _asset)` on the flash loan contract (0x978e...37a2), with sufficient gas.

2. *Request to borrow*: The flash loan contract (0x978e...37a2) sends a request for a flash loan from one of the Aave contracts.

3. *Process and send funds*: The Aave contract runs through a series of calls and eventually calls the DAI token contract (0xf80a...8108) to transfer 1 DAI to the Flash-loan contract (0x978e...37a2). This 1 DAI is the amount borrowed.

4. *Notify funds sent*: After the 1 DAI is sent to the flash loan contract (0x987e…
37a2), one of Aave's contracts calls it to notify it that the funds have been sent. At
this point, the flash loan contract can use the 1 DAI for any purpose. In this
example, the token does not get used, for simplicity.

5. *Repay funds with fee*: The flash loan contract (0x987e…37a2) then returns the
funds by calling one of Aave's contracts, which leads it to call the DAI token contract (0xf80a…8108) to transfer 1.0009 DAI to an Aave contract.

Flash Loans for Arbitrage

One of the main use cases for flash loans is to arbitrage between multiple DeFi platforms. The biggest advantage of using a flash loan to execute an arbitrage is that liquidity is no longer required to sit on the exchanges involved in the arbitrage. The
requirement for liquidity between crypto exchanges introduces counterparty risk,
limits the amount that can be arbitraged, and introduces a large barrier to entry to
begin arbitraging. However, arbitraging with a flash loan provides real-time access to
multiple large liquidity pools without the need to ask permission.

The lender gives permission for funds to be borrowed when funds are deposited into
the smart contract. At any time they can look at the contract balances and see what
percentage of the funds have been loaned out. If a transaction stops midloan, the
transaction does not complete, and therefore the funds were never lent out. The cost
for performing a flash loan is simply the gas required to execute it.

The Fulcrum Exploit

Flash loans have also been used by bad actors to exploit vulnerabilities in DeFi platforms. A well-known example occurred on February 15, 2020, when an attacker used
a flash loan to perform an oracle manipulation attack on the Fulcrum (*https://
fulcrum.trade*) margin trading platform.

An oracle provides smart contracts with a trusted view of the outside world. For
example, a DeFi smart contract will use an oracle to know what the BTC/USD
exchange rate is. On the day of the attack, the Fulcrum platform was listening to multiple oracles for exchange rate data, including Kyber and Uniswap. One reason Fulcrum gathers exchange rate data from these DEXes is that it accesses their liquidity
pools to provide margin trades for Fulcrum's users.

The flash loan contract that performed the oracle manipulation attack has the transaction ID:

```
0xb5c8bd9430b6cc87a0e2fe110ece6bf527fa4f170a4bc8cd032f768fc5219838
```

The transaction details can be viewed online (*https://oreil.ly/e8EMp*). In total, 13
smart contract function calls were made.

In an exploit such as this, the attacking flash loan contract borrows, trades, and repays wrapped tokens. These are ERC-20 tokens that represent the value of a different cryptocurrency. For example, 1 wBTC is a wrapped bitcoin that represents 1 BTC and in theory is worth 1 BTC, but is in the form of an ERC-20 token.

Wrapped tokens allow DeFi platforms to trade cryptocurrencies that are not originally in the form of an ERC-20 token. For simplicity, anytime you see 1 wETH in this discussion, you can assume that it is the equivalent of 1 ETH; the same goes for wBTC and BTC.

We can break down the process of the attack into five distinct steps, which are illustrated in Figure 7-16.

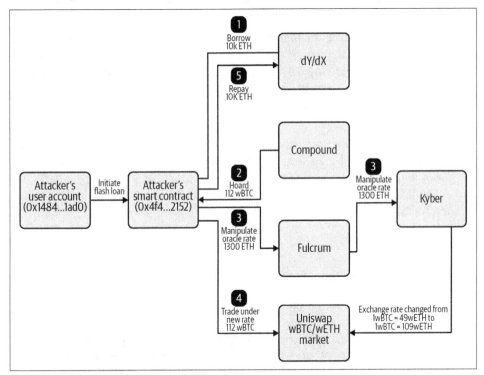

Figure 7-16. Walkthrough of the Fulcrum attack

The steps can be summarized as follows:

1. *Borrow*: The attacking flash loan contract borrows 10,000 ETH ($2.81M USD) from the dYdX decentralized trading platform. This action is only valid if it repays the loan plus a fee at the end of this Ethereum transaction.

2. *Hoard*: It then borrows 112 wBTC ($1.15M USD) from DeFi lending platform Compound. To secure these funds, it provides 5,500 ETH ($1.5M USD) as collateral. The 112 wBTC will later be dumped onto another market in order to manipulate the oracle rate.

3. *Manipulate oracle rate*: Next, it deposits 1,300 ETH onto the Fulcrum margin trading platform and opens a short trading position, which is a bet the price will fall, on the wETH/wBTC market with 5x leverage. This short position creates a domino effect. In order for Fulcrum to service the short position, it swaps 5,637 ETH ($1.58M USD) for 51.34 wBTC ($525,000 USD) from Kyber. Kyber sources the 51.34 wBTC from Uniswap. Significant slippage—when a price moves substantially because of a lack of sufficient liquidity—occurs when Kyber pulls this large amount of wBTC from Uniswap. This changes the exchange rate of wETH/wBTC on Uniswap from 1wBTC = 49 wETH, which is the rate given by Compound in the hoarding stage, to 1wBTC = 109.8 wETH.

4. *Trade under new rate*: Now that the wETH/wBTC exchange rate on Uniswap has been pumped, the attacking flash loan contract dumps its 112 wBTC onto the Uniswap market, receiving 6,871 ETH ($1.93M USD) in this trade. In this action, it receives an exchange rate of 1wBTC = 61.3 wETH. This is about 25% higher than the original rate it received on Compound, leading to a profit of 1,371 ETH ($385,000 USD).

5. *Repay loan*: After the profit has been gained, the flash loan contract repays the original 10,000 ETH loan from dYdX. This is required, or else an error will be raised and the transaction will not complete. In total, the attacker spent 0.03 ETH ($7.47 USD) to execute the transaction and gained about $385,000 USD worth of cryptocurrency. It then paid back the Compound loan.

Every time there is a big innovation in financial technology, there are always bad actors who look for new ways to exploit the technological shift. For example, in the early days of PayPal, hackers started automatically generating fake PayPal accounts to perform large-scale credit card fraud. Eventually PayPal created an early version of CAPTCHA, a computing test to distinguish human users from machines, to help contain this threat. DeFi is no exception. It's a fundamental shift in how financial services are provided, and this fluid situation leads to attackers constantly searching for exploits to profit from.

Privacy

Public blockchains like Bitcoin and Ethereum are not great when it comes to privacy. When thinking about decentralizing finance and the web, information security must be carefully considered. To conceal identity, a number of solutions are available. Different implementations will make different uses of these solutions, as privacy is an experimental (yet growing) area of blockchain technology.

With Bitcoin and Ethereum, all transaction information is visible in the public blockchain, including the transaction amount and addresses of the sender and receiver. There are use cases where blockchain transaction information must remain private, however, and different privacy-focused blockchains, such as Zcash and Monero, have been launched to satisfy this need. There are also private blockchain networks such as Corda and Quorum that require either an invitation or automatic vetting before an organization is allowed to participate. This section considers a few aspects of privacy, and we'll come back to this topic in Chapter 9.

Zero-Knowledge Proof

A *zero-knowledge proof* is a cryptographic method or protocol where party A (the prover) proves to party B (the verifier) that a statement is true without revealing any information other than that the statement is true.

Suppose a prover needs to prove to the verifier that they found Waldo in a *Where's Waldo?* drawing. The easiest approach would be for the prover to point to Waldo, but doing so reveals the secret of where Waldo is, when the point is merely to prove that the prover *knows* where Waldo is. A zero-knowledge approach might be for the prover to get a large piece of paper, significantly bigger than the Waldo drawing, and cut a hole the shape of Waldo in the center. Out of sight of the verifier, the prover covers the drawing so that only Waldo is visible through the hole in the paper. The prover has demonstrated that they found Waldo without revealing any information that could help the verifier find Waldo.

Let's consider another example. Say the prover wants to prove to the verifier that they know the correct password for logging in to a website. The current method many websites use is to store a hash of the user's password in their database. When the user wants to log in, the following sequence takes place:

1. The user sends the password as plain text to the server.
2. The server encrypts the password using a standard encryption algorithm, such as MD5.
3. If the newly generated MD5 hash matches the hash stored in the database, then the password entered is valid.

However, this method makes the user's password vulnerable to the following:

Man in the middle attacks

If a hacker compromises the communication between the user and the server, it is possible to intercept the plain-text password.

Brute force and dictionary attacks

If a website's database is breached, a hacker can potentially decrypt the user's password through various methods, including brute force using trial and error or dictionary attacks using a list of words or phrases.

In a zero-knowledge approach, a user can prove they have a valid password without the need to reveal what it is—the server does not store any variation of the password, not even a hash. This can be done by implementing the Thinbus Secure Remote Password protocol (SRP) (*https://oreil.ly/djyVy*):

1. The server stores a randomly generated *salt,* or random data that is used as an additional input, and a *verifier* that cannot be decrypted into the password.

2. When the user logs in to the website, they send a one-time value used only for that particular login. Future messages will look very different. The server receives this one-time value, and through the SRP can verify whether the message received was sent by a user with a valid password. Figure 7-17 illustrates.

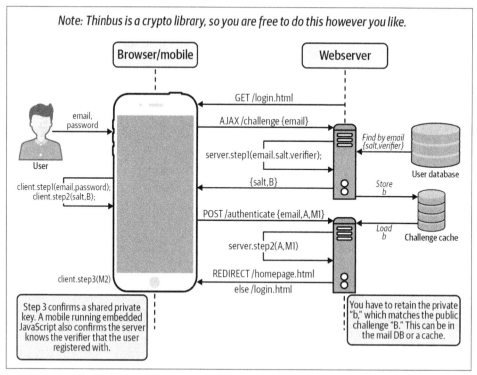

Figure 7-17. Flow of actions in the registration action of the SRP

Implementation of a zero-knowledge proof significantly improves the privacy and security of many systems. However, it introduces additional costs in processing power and hard drive space. Another downside is that it requires the two parties (prover and verifier) to interact directly with each other.

These downsides would not matter in the case of a website, but implementing zero-knowledge proofs in a blockchain would have a significant impact, for a few reasons:

- Blockchain miners maintain a copy of the entire blockchain history, which gets big very fast as network usage scales. Adding more data makes this problem even worse.

- In a blockchain network, the sender of a transaction wants to prove that the transaction is valid, and the miners each verify that validity. The problem is that the sender does not communicate directly with every miner. Rather, the sender broadcasts out transaction details and miners verify the transaction—a process that does not involve direct, one-to-one interaction.

So, in order for a blockchain to adopt a zero-knowledge proof method, it must be *succinct*, to allow for better scalability, and *noninteractive*, so that nodes in the network can verify zero-knowledge statements from nodes they are not communicating with directly. With this method, the sender (prover) of the transaction can broadcast out one piece of data and the miners (verifiers) can verify the transaction's validity without any additional interaction with the sender. The data that the transaction sender broadcasts to the network must be very small in size, because that data will be stored on the blockchain.

Zero-knowledge proofs are used in enterprise blockchain applications where mining is not used. More on this in Chapter 9.

zk-SNARKs

One form of zero-knowledge proof is *Zero-Knowledge Succinct Non-Interactive Arguments of Knowledge* (zk-SNARKs), a privacy technology already used in cryptocurrencies like Zcash. In Ethereum, it can be used to enhance privacy in smart contracts.

Though it's expected to be integrated at some point, zk-SNARKs for now requires *precompiling*, or processing input data to produce an output, on networks like Ethereum because of the extensive gas costs required. For the time being, running code outside of the EVM is the best way to precompile, using Rust or JavaScript. Aztec (*https://www.aztecprotocol.com*) is an early mainnet, or production environment, tech for Ethereum that successfully integrates zk-SNARKs for enhanced privacy.

Zcash

Zcash (*https://z.cash*) is a privacy-focused blockchain that provides senders of a transaction the option to make transaction information public or private. Private Zcash transactions use zk-SNARKs. Zcash's implementation of zk-SNARKs has provided the community with evidence of how useful this can be to public blockchains. Notably, it:

- Allows for private transactions to be done on a public blockchain like Bitcoin or Ethereum
- Allows for private execution of smart contract code on a public blockchain

Ring Signatures

With ring signatures, anyone from a predefined group can sign transactions, increasing the difficulty of determining the identity of the actual signer. Any one of the group members could be sending the transaction, concealing the sender and increasing privacy. The larger the ring, the higher the chances of concealment. The Monero cryptocurrency currently uses this technology, in addition to using decoy outputs to hide UXTOs.

Web 3.0

Blockchain and cryptocurrency with proper levels of privacy could create new platforms for the web, incentivizing new types of development and moving users away from the oligarchical model that has come to dominate (*https://oreil.ly/YAge3*) over the last decade.

It's become common to talk about different stages in the evolution of the World Wide Web. Web 1.0 consisted of static pages, form fields, and passive content. Web 2.0 introduced dynamic pages, interactive fields, and user-generated content. Web 3.0 is the next iteration, whereby the data generated from the previous two generations is returned, monetized, and controlled by the user. What that will look like in totality is unclear, but some characteristics are emerging, and scaffolding for Web 3.0 technology is being built today.

Users give away a lot of data, often without realizing it, and much of this occurs within web browsers. Brave (*https://brave.com*) is a Chromium-based browser focused on privacy. Although other web browsers make various claims about their privacy features too, Brave is the first to implement blockchain technology. It has built-in ad blockers, replacing advertising with cryptocurrency. The Basic Attention Token (BAT), its ERC-20 cryptocurrency, is used to compensate website owners and content creators in lieu of ad platforms.

Paying independent developers to work on open source code can be a complex process. Cryptocurrency and blockchain are leading to exciting changes in software development. Sites like Gitcoin (*https://gitcoin.co*) are embracing and supporting this movement: it pairs developers looking for projects to work on with funders looking for people to implement a bug fix or feature request or do some other work on a project, and all the payments are made in crypto.

File storage is an important part of web-based applications, and decentralizing this aspect is key. Storing and sharing data is what allows many technology providers to take liberties with user information via their terms of service. The Interplanetary File System (IPFS) (*https://ipfs.io*) is a persistent network that enables distributed storage of files as long as a single node keeps running; its aim is to.... Its design is modular, allowing it to be used for a variety of use cases.

Building decentralized web frameworks is a huge task. It requires melding identity, distributed systems, and blockchain into a scaffolding developers can use to create increasingly decentralized applications. Blockstack (*https://www.blockstack.org*), which started with identity and then moved into distributed systems, is one of these early frameworks. It uses REST calls to create dapps in a framework similar to what developers have used in the past.

Then there's gambling. Since the value is being transferred via smart contract in Web 3.0, it is easier to audit whether the rules are fair. In traditional gambling, the house usually has the advantage in terms of odds. In this new framework, newer kinds of games are being invented—for example, *no-loss gambling*. One example is a DAO pool in which everyone puts in stablecoin, which earns returns. The pool goes through a randomized selection process to pick the winner; the winner gets all the interest earned from the pool, and the losers get back their original amount of stablecoin.

Summary

Web 3.0 technology is based on a disruption of the traditional centralized services model. That model, though it has been successful for some time, is beginning to weaken as numbers of cyberattacks increase. New ideas are being injected into finance and the web, with developers exploring the use of blockchain, cryptocurrencies, and smart contracts to protect user privacy and put control over personal information back in the hands of users.

CHAPTER 8

Catch Me If You Can

Blockchain and cryptocurrencies offer a lot of promise. However, the path to success is littered with ruts and pitfalls. Ever since it was first implemented, there have been various scandals, hacks, and thefts involving Bitcoin.

It's important to know about and understand these events, because the past is capable of repeating itself if history is not used as a guide. Although the issues we describe in this chapter may seem severe, in the long run they will be seen as mere bumps in the road leading to a world of opportunity.

Probably the most famous nefarious example was Silk Road, an anonymous, illicit marketplace on the dark web that used Bitcoin as a payment mechanism. Users would log in to Silk Road using Tor (*https://www.torproject.org*), an anonymous virtual private networking (VPN) software. Tor uses a global network of computers to route internet traffic so it is almost impossible to trace. This allows users to remain anonymous by obscuring identifying information like IP addresses.

In October 2013, after a long investigation, the FBI arrested Ross Ulbricht for his role as the operator of Silk Road. They were able to catch Ulbricht by grabbing his encrypted laptop while it was open as he was working at a public library in San Francisco, California. The authorities were able to access everything on his computer, including incriminating information regarding the operations of the site. Ulbricht is now serving a double life sentence for operating what was at the time one of the largest marketplaces for illegal drugs, guns, and other contraband.

In the early days of Bitcoin, many users believed transactions on the blockchain would likewise be hard to track. However, over time a number of crypto-focused researchers and businesses discovered ways to link addresses to each other using metadata from exchanges, wallet providers, and other stakeholders in the ecosystem.

The Evolution of Crypto Laundering

Before 2014, when most people still thought bitcoin transactions were anonymous, many criminals assumed that moving dirty funds through crypto would keep their tracks hidden.

From 2011–2013, Silk Road was successfully using Bitcoin for payment. When funds were stolen from exchanges during this time, the common thinking was that there was no recourse. After the collapse of the Japanese exchange Mt. Gox in early 2014 (see "Mt. Gox" on page 203), followed by ultimately successful efforts by investigating authorities to trace the missing funds, many people began to realize that bitcoin transactions are not completely anonymous.

At that time, the only visibility people had into bitcoin transactions was using a blockchain explorer such as Blockchain.info (now *Blockchain.com*), as shown in Figure 8-1.

Hash	f4184fc596403b9d638783cf57adfe4c75c605f6356fbc913385...			2009-01-12 11:30
	12cbQLTFMXRnSzktFkuoG3eHoMeFtpTu3S	50.00000000 BTC	1Q2TWHE3GMdB6BZKafqwxXtWAWgFt5Jvm3	10.00000000 BTC
			12cbQLTFMXRnSzktFkuoG3eHoMeFtpTu3S	40.00000000 BTC
Fee	0.00000000 BTC			
	(0.000 sat/B - 0.000 sat/WU - 275 bytes)			50.00000000 BTC

Figure 8-1. The first bitcoin transaction sent between two addresses, viewed in a public blockchain explorer

Many crypto exchanges did not perform KYC checks on customers, but authorities had yet not begun penalizing these exchanges for not doing so, making it easy for criminals to use them to convert funds from crypto to fiat.

KYC is a common term in regulation and compliance; it means *Know Your Customer* and refers to a process for verifying the identity of a user looking to open an account at a financial institution.

Around 2014, a few blockchain analytics companies began helping authorities follow the trail of funds relating to criminal investigations. People began to realize bitcoin was actually only *pseudo*-anonymous—an identity can be associated with a Bitcoin address. And since all bitcoin transactions are public, there is an entire transaction history, so it's possible to determine relationships between different addresses.

There are many different ways to associate a Bitcoin address with an identity, including the following:

- People may publicly identify themselves as the owner of a Bitcoin address. For example, some charities (and even WikiLeaks (*https://wikileaks.org*)) post their crypto addresses for people to send donations to. Another example is Hal Finney, who posted (*https://oreil.ly/Mq4Dk*) on an online forum about how he had participated in the first bitcoin transaction, receiving 10 BTC from Satoshi Nakamoto. Studying this transaction reveals further information about Satoshi's relationships, as shown in Figure 8-2.

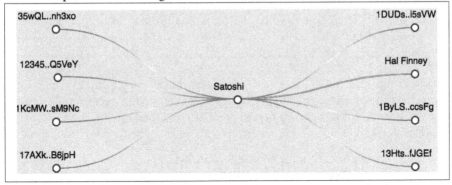

Figure 8-2. Screenshot from the blockchain analytics tool Breadcrumbs (https://www.breadcrumbs.app) showing the other Bitcoin addresses Satoshi has a relationship with, including Hal Finney

- Participants in a bitcoin transaction usually know the identity of the other party.

- Many Bitcoin addresses are owned and managed by crypto-related businesses, including wallets and exchanges. Exchanges generate a unique Bitcoin address for each of their users and will usually have identity information for that user.

- Evidence gathered from criminal investigations can sometimes connect a Bitcoin address to an identity. For example, after the authorities confiscated the Silk Road servers, they had all the bitcoin transaction information. They were able to trace the transactions to the Silk Road operator, but not necessarily all the participants.

Privacy advocates in the crypto community soon recognized that Bitcoin is not anonymous enough. This is why there are privacy-focused blockchains today that hide transaction details from the public. Monero (*https://www.getmonero.org*) is the most popular privacy blockchain.

From a criminal's point of view, holding dirty funds is not ideal. Cleaning the funds and then spending them is the goal. There are three well-known stages of money laundering: placement, layering, and integration. Here, briefly, is how funds are laundered through cryptocurrency:

1. *Placement*: This stage is when the dirty funds are placed into a cryptocurrency. If the funds are in cash, the criminal must use some type of on/off-ramp to convert the cash into crypto. Many criminals can skip this step because the funds are

already in crypto. For example, a merchant selling drugs on the dark web will receive payment in crypto.

2. *Layering*: This stage is when the funds are cleaned. In crypto, the most effective ways to do this are by moving the funds through either a *tumbler/mixing* service or a privacy blockchain like Monero.

3. *Integration*: This stage is when the funds are brought back into fiat and can be spent by the criminal. After cleaning the funds, the criminal must use an on/off-ramp to convert the funds back into fiat.

The layering stage can be done in a fully decentralized way, without depending on a central authority. However, the placement and integration stages require an on/off-ramp to convert funds between crypto and fiat. This is where the real battle in money laundering takes place.

There are many different types of crypto on/off-ramps, domiciled in many different jurisdictions, and they vary in how strict their KYC rules are.

Sophisticated money launderers will use fake or stolen KYC documents when signing up to a cryptocurrency exchange. Depending on how diligent an exchange's compliance processes and employees are, some launderers succeed in misrepresenting their identity. Using false KYC documents protects the launderer from being identified in the event the exchange discovers that illicit funds are being laundered. However, the success of this approach depends on the processes the financial institution puts in place to prevent money laundering and terrorist financing. Many good operators will cross-reference document ID. Some will manually check the KYC docs, while others use tools like Acuant (*https://oreil.ly/Qn5Zl*) to check their validity.

FinCEN Guidance and the Beginning of Regulation

In terms of regulations and crime, 2013 was a pivotal year for blockchain networks. In addition to Silk Road being shut down, the Financial Crimes Enforcement Network (FinCEN), a US agency under the purview of the Treasury Department, issued its first *convertible virtual currency* (CVC) guidance. It states: "A user who obtains convertible virtual currency and uses it to purchase real or virtual goods or services is not an MSB (Money Services Business) under FinCEN's regulations."

However, it also states: "An administrator or exchanger that (1) accepts and transmits a convertible virtual currency or (2) buys or sells convertible virtual currency for any reason is a money transmitter under FinCEN's regulations, unless a limitation to or exemption from the definition applies to the person."

In other words, those who transmit money on behalf of others are required to obtain MSB licensing. FinCEN lists those types of businesses that are MSBs as follows:

- Currency dealer or exchanger
- Check casher
- Issuer of traveler's checks, money orders, or stored value
- Seller or redeemer of traveler's checks, money orders, or stored value
- Money transmitter
- US Postal Service

With the 2013 CVC guidance, this list also encompassed virtual currency operators, which may include exchanges, wallets, and other platforms that facilitate virtual currency transactions for users or customers.

When it comes to figuring out which bodies require compliance for what, the array of regulatory regimes can be confusing. A number of US agencies and regulatory bodies have laid claim on regulating cryptocurrencies. Here are the three major ones that have made clear some of the rules of the game:

CFTC

The Commodity Futures Trading Commission is in charge of regulating commodities, futures, and derivatives markets. The Commissioner of the CTFC has advocated a "do no harm" (*https://oreil.ly/uLauI*) stance toward cryptocurrencies, noting the internet was able to flourish with a light regulatory touch. However, it is clear from CTFC statements that it will go after market manipulation and fraud. So far, the CFTC has claimed jurisdiction over Bitcoin and Ethereum and subsequent derivative instruments. The CFTC has an innovation unit to look at new technologies and meet with entrepreneurs, called CFTCLab.

SEC

The Securities and Exchange Commission has regulatory authority over securities. A security is defined as an investment contract, and a number of blockchain-based tokens that have been used to raise money may fall under that definition. In fact, the SEC has issued guidance on investment contracts for digital assets (*https://oreil.ly/-9ES6*). It also has been open to providing no action letters for projects it deems suitable for avoiding the Howey test, a measure of whether an asset is a security or not. This is a process whereby a project or company will reach out to legislators to obtain a letter promising not to enforce rules retroactively. The SEC also has an innovation unit called FinHub to review blockchain and other financial technologies.

NYDFS

The New York Department of Financial Services regulates financial activities in the state. New York is the financial capital of the US, and the NYDFS is responsible for financial services and products there. In 2015, the NYDFS started requiring virtual currency operators to obtain a "BitLicense" to do business in the state. This includes exchanges, wallets, and other products/services that incorporate cryptocurrencies. Obtaining the license involves a 30-page application and a $5,000 fee, and putting together all the necessary information can cost upward of $100,000. Only about 25 companies (*https://oreil.ly/xPCui*) operating in New York have a BitLicense.

The FATF and the Travel Rule

A new stipulation brought by the Financial Action Task Force (FATF), the *Travel Rule* requires more data sharing between cryptocurrency operators. The FATF is a Group of Seven (G7) intergovernmental group that includes the US, Canada, France, Germany, the UK, Italy, and Japan.

The standards require *virtual asset service providers* (VASPs) to provide user data when transactions occur, including moving funds from service providers such as exchanges. This data can include the following:

- The sending customer's name
- The sender's cryptocurrency address used to process a transaction
- The sender's physical identity number as a unique identifier
- The receiving customer's name
- The receiver's cryptocurrency address used to process a transaction

These rules may be new for cryptocurrency and blockchain companies, but they are not new for banking. They have been in place for banks to combat money laundering, terrorist financing, and other financial crimes for many years.

Any service provider in the cryptocurrency world that already has to submit to Money Services Business (MSB) standards is likely to have to do the same for the Travel Rule. A review of these standards is expected in 2020.

Skirting the Laws

Cryptocurrency and blockchain technology are interesting in that they intertwine with money, and this intertwining has caused a number of early adopters to have run-ins with regulators and law enforcement. It has definitely been shown that just because blockchain is a new paradigm doesn't mean it is above the law. This section lists a few examples of people or groups that have been penalized by US enforcement agencies:

Trendon Shavers

Created Bitcoin Savings & Trust, a scheme that took in over 764,000 BTC by promising investors a 7% return per week via arbitrage trading. Shavers was sentenced to one and a half years in prison and ordered to pay $1.23 million in restitution in 2015. This is widely known as the first Ponzi scheme conviction and first US criminal securities fraud case in cryptocurrency.

Charlie Shrem

Facilitated bitcoin transactions as an unlicensed money transmitting business. Using his company BitInstant, Shrem helped a broker provide bitcoin without KYC/AML to users of Silk Road. Over $1 million in bitcoin transactions were conducted. In 2014, Shrem was sentenced to two years in federal prison and ordered to forfeit $950,000.

Erik Voorhees

Sold unregistered securities in two companies, FeedZeBirds and SatoshiDICE, in exchange for bitcoin. In 2014, the SEC settled with Voorhees for full disgorgement of the $15,843.98 raised (i.e., returning the funds to the harmed parties), and a $35,000 fine. Voorhees also agreed not to participate in any more unregistered securities sales using bitcoin or any other virtual currency.

Carl Force

Former Drug Enforcement Agency (DEA) agent; seized bitcoin under misrepresented DEA authority during the Silk Road investigation. Force also attempted to launder funds via Bitstamp and Venmo. Payment services froze his accounts, which he then attempted to get released using his DEA stature. He was sentenced to six and a half years in prison for money laundering, obstruction of justice, and extortion in 2015.

Zachary Coburn

Operated EtherDelta, an unregistered national securities exchange. EtherDelta was a smart contract–based platform that allowed users to trade Ethereum ERC-20 tokens. It was labeled a decentralized exchange, where no KYC/AML was required. Coburn paid $300,000 disgorgement, $13,000 in interest, and a $75,000 penalty to the SEC in 2018.

Reggie Middleton

Led Veritaseum's ICO, which was investigated by the SEC as being an unregistered securities offering. Veritaseum raised $14.8 million from investors, purporting to offer a markets platform that didn't require intermediaries. Middleton's assets were seized during the investigation. His 2019 settlement included disgorgement plus interest of $8.47 million and a civil penalty of $1 million.

Homero Joshua Garza

Operated GAW Miners, a cryptocurrency mining firm that sold more units than it possessed in inventory. In this way, the operation acted like a Ponzi scheme. GAW Miners also sold customers "virtual miners," or "Hashlets," for future mining profits, which to the SEC appeared like securities. In 2018, Garza was sentenced to 21 months in prison for wire fraud.

Mark Scott

Acted as an attorney for OneCoin, a Ponzi scheme that generated billions in revenue. Scott was responsible for laundering $400 million of revenue through tax havens. OneCoin was a multilevel marketing operation that has seen prosecutions globally over false claims of its private blockchain-based cryptocurrency. Sentencing is still ongoing.

Block.One

Operated an unregistered securities offering via an ICO from June 2017 to June 2018. During that time the SEC released its DAO report, which covered a previous unregistered security offering in the cryptocurrency space as guidance for operators. The company was required to pay a $24 million settlement to the SEC.

Enigma

Operated an unregistered securities offering via an ICO in the summer and fall of 2017. Initially an MIT project that launched in 2015, Enigma raised $45 million selling ENG tokens. Enigma's settlement with the SEC involved a fine of $500,000, registration of its token as a security, and the establishment of a claims process for harmed investors.

Avoiding Scrutiny: Regulatory Arbitrage

Regulatory arbitrage is a term for measures taken to avoid compliance scrutiny in heavily regulated jurisdictions like the US. This can be done in a number of ways, such as by falsifying the nature of transactions or switching geographical areas. It has long been a common practice in finance, and the blockchain industry has followed this trend by moving to various jurisdictions, including the ones discussed here.

Malta

In 2018, Malta enacted several laws aimed at fostering digital currency regulation. These include the Malta Digital Innovation Authority Act (MDIA), the Innovative Technology Arrangements and Services Act (ITAS), and the Virtual Financial Assets Act (VFAA). These rules put in place specific operating procedures for cryptocurrency businesses. As a result, a number of cryptocurrency and blockchain companies have incorporated in Malta.

An archipelago in the central Mediterranean Sea, Malta is not without controversy. Although it is a member of the EU, a number of scandals have engulfed the island state. Corruption, tax evasion, and fraud are common problems. The new regime installed in 2020 as a result of previous government misconduct may help to stem some of these systemic problems and foster cryptocurrency innovation in the country.

Singapore

Cryptocurrencies are treated as goods in Singapore, whether used for the purposes of trading, ICOs, or general sales. This is beneficial from a tax perspective, as Singapore's Goods and Services tax is similar to the Value Added Tax (VAT) many other countries apply to saleable items.

Singapore has been forward-thinking and clear on its laws around cryptocurrency and blockchain. In 2020, the Monetary Authority of Singapore issued rules requiring AML and KYC laws be put in place for cryptocurrency companies (*https://oreil.ly/ dMyPA*). Concerns around money laundering, terrorist financing, and other criminal activity seem to have precipitated this, with the growth of ICOs as a financing method serving as a possible trigger point.

Hong Kong

Like Singapore, Hong Kong is a financial hub in Asia. One of the attractions of Hong Kong is the region's tax policy. There are no capital gains taxes in Hong Kong, only a standard income tax rate. Cryptocurrencies are labeled "virtual commodities." The leading financial regulator, the Securities & Futures Commission (SFC), has taken a hands-off approach to regulation, inviting some cryptocurrency companies to a "sandbox" program as a test.

The SFC has issued regulations for cryptocurrency exchanges that require a license. However, these requirements are for securities and other advanced products such as futures and derivatives. Regular cryptocurrency exchanges that trade assets like bitcoin are not expected to apply for such a license. This is because the registration is for professional investor exchanges, not retail. However, Hong Kong's status as a separately governed entity from China may be in doubt, so this could change in the future.

Bahamas

Long known as a jurisdiction open to financial companies, the Bahamas is working to enact rules to enable cryptocurrency projects to domicile there. This includes the Digital Assets and Registered Exchanges (DARE) bill, introduced in early 2019. The bill is being constructed with feedback from cryptocurrency and blockchain companies prior to being passed into law.

In addition, the Bahamas has given out no action letters to various cryptocurrency projects. Although manipulation, tax evasion, and money laundering are still prohibited, the Bahamas is taking a forward-looking approach to cryptocurrency in order to foster innovation.

Who Is Satoshi Nakamoto?

The original Bitcoin whitepaper was released pseudonymously, and a number of people have made claims about who its author, Satoshi Nakamoto, might really be. However, there is little evidence to suggest any of these claims are true. Two of the most popular guesses are:

Dorian Nakamoto
> In 2014, *Newsweek* published an investigation piece identifying this person as the creator of bitcoin. The article pointed to a man living in Southern California with the name "Dorian Prentice Satoshi Nakamoto." Although Dorian Nakamoto does have a computer science background, he himself denied his involvement in bitcoin. In addition, no hard evidence could link him to the actual inventor of bitcoin.

Craig S. Wright
> An Australian computer scientist, Wright was identified in the media as someone who could possibly be Satoshi Nakamoto. After promising publicly to provide concrete evidence that he was indeed the inventor of bitcoin, Wright has repeatedly failed to do so. One way Wright could do so would be to prove control of the keys to the bitcoin Satoshi originally mined, which has not occurred so far.

However, those are just two high-profile examples. Others have also claimed to be (or denied being) Satoshi, and to date there has not been enough evidence to reveal their true identity.

There has also been speculation about the number of bitcoin Satoshi allegedly owns. One thing that's for sure is that Satoshi mined the Genesis block (*https://oreil.ly/Jsa5q*) of Bitcoin, so in theory the easiest proof would be to uncover evidence of the identity behind that address.

Crypto-Based Stablecoins

In the previous chapter, we discussed a few examples of stablecoins, which use block-chain technology to peg a cryptocurrency to another, more stable asset. For the most part, stablecoins are pegged to the US dollar, since it is known as a global reserve currency, but other assets have been used too, including gold, agricultural commodities, and the euro.

Many stablecoins are unregulated in the cryptocurrency world, although there are several stablecoin projects that are working with regulators and banks to foster a future where stablecoin assets are a large part of the ecosystem. While stablecoins attempt to stay pegged to their linked real-world assets, it is questionable whether they all have the requisite backing or liquidity to remain stable long-term. This has led to some of them running into difficulties in the past, and others becoming mired in legal problems. This section discusses a few examples.

NuBits

Introduced in 2014, NuBits was a stablecoin pegged to the US dollar. It used fractional bitcoin reserves, similar to how a bank keeps only a percentage of account balances, to "back" the stability of its token. Those reserves theoretically would allow it to absorb changes in the value of bitcoin. From 2014 to mid-2016, the price of bitcoin remained relatively stable. However, in 2016, as the price of bitcoin rose, NuBits lost its dollar-based peg for over three months.

At the end of 2017, NuBits then rose to a value higher than the dollar. This happened during a bull cycle in cryptocurrency, as enthusiasts were trading out of bitcoin, the project's reserve, and into other assets, creating volatility. The lack of stability essentially caused many to jump ship, and its value has not recovered.

Digix

Known as a "gold token," Digix was launched in 2014 to peg gold to a unit of cryptocurrency. The concept was to allow investors to own fractional or small amounts of gold, derived from London Bullion Market Association refiners, with one Digix token (DGX) worth one gram of gold. Digix is registered in Singapore and has been able to maintain a relatively stable peg to one gram of gold, although it doesn't have a lot of liquidity, signaling a lack of demand. The Digix token is not listed on regulated cryptocurrency exchanges.

Digix was one of the first projects to launch on Ethereum, using a DAO smart contract structure with a token called DigixDAO (DGD) to raise funds, mostly in ether, for the project. In 2020, the DAO was shut down after a community vote, returning DGD to investors for ether. One of the problems with Digix is that the price of gold fluctuates in dollar value, a peg cryptocurrency traders prefer. However, it is an interesting example of tying a cryptocurrency to a real-world asset.

Basis

An ambitious project that sparked fervent interest within Silicon Valley, Basis raised $133 million in 2018 from prominent venture capitalists. Its aim was to create a decentralized token by creating incentives for traders to buy and sell what were referred to as *bond* and *share* tokens. This would then provide a stable asset for the market that could be utilized globally for a number of use cases, including applications in the developing world, crowdfunding, and exchange trading.

After the large fundraise, Basis started to confront the legal realities of being a US-based company launching a stablecoin. This included the bond and share tokens being recognized as securities by the SEC. In addition, KYC rules would have required Basis to keep a whitelist of users with authority to make transfers. After looking at several options, including centralizing the system, the project shut down and returned funding to its investors. It's a common mentality in Silicon Valley that it's better to ask for forgiveness than ask for permission, and Basis is an example of this.

Tether

Originally launched on the Omni protocol built on top of Bitcoin, discussed in Chapter 3, Tether (USDT) now reaches across several blockchains, including Ethereum, TRON, EOS, Liquid, and Algorand. Tether is nominally pegged to the US dollar and is by far the largest stablecoin in the cryptocurrency ecosystem, with over $15 billion in market capitalization in 2020. As a result of its prevalence across blockchains and exchanges, it is the most popular trading pair for moving into and out of more volatile cryptocurrencies (for example, ETH/USDT or BTC/USDT).

Tether is considered controversial, however. It is centrally controlled by Bitfinex, an offshore exchange. While supposedly backed by equivalent assets, there has never been a professional audit of its reserves. Tether has also been the subject of legal issues, including an investigation by the New York attorney general for the loss of an $850 million undocumented loan. Tether's own attorney has also attested in court documents that one tether hasn't always equaled one dollar of its own reserves, creating counterparty risk for those who trade USDT.

Initial Coin Offerings

As discussed in earlier chapters, ICOs are a way for founders to raise money for cryptocurrency projects. The process is fairly straightforward: an issuer looking to raise money for a blockchain-based project accepts one cryptocurrency, usually bitcoin or ether, and in exchange provides tokens representing a new cryptocurrency created as part of the project.

> *ICO* is a popular term for these projects, but other vocabulary is also used. *Security token offering*, *token generation event*, *token offering*, and *token sale* are other common names.

On July 25, 2017, the SEC released a report (*https://oreil.ly/4DN5n*) on the findings of its investigation into the ICO of The DAO, a project running on the Ethereum blockchain. As detailed in Chapter 4, The DAO was a smart contract–based decentralized autonomous organization created to raise money from cryptocurrency investors. A voting mechanism was put into place so that investors could then decide on various projects for The DAO to invest in, mostly revolving around blockchain or cryptocurrencies.

The DAO report concluded that this activity—the sale of tokens to investors—constituted the issuance of securities. It also indicated that US securities laws could apply to blockchains and cryptocurrencies in many instances. ICOs were an example of regulatory arbitrage in that ICO issuers were often ahead of the regulators. Despite this, as a result of The DAO investigation, out-of-court settlements in the ICO space have become common.

There have been thousands of ICOs launched since 2016, and they have significantly varied in quality. As Figure 8-3 illustrates, they range from well intentioned and viable to entirely fraudulent.

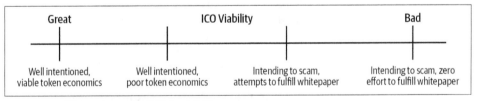

Figure 8-3. The spectrum of ICO viability

There are three main factors to consider regarding the long-term viability of an ICO: founder intentions, token economics, and the amount of effort put in to fulfill the promises made in its whitepaper.

Founder Intentions

The more passionate a project's founder is about the problem a token is intended to solve, the greater the chances are that they will be very excited to spend the next 5 to 10 years solving it. Startups are tough. It takes a very high level of motivation and a talented team to get through the challenges involved. If the intention of the founder is to simply raise funds, then the project will focus on sales tactics. Usually once the sales goals have been met, time and resources will no longer be put into the token, leaving it to die.

Token Economics

Investors in a startup purchase equity in a business with the hope that the company's value will increase and they can sell that equity later at a higher price. Generally, the value of a startup goes up over time if the business is able to grow. In an ICO, investors purchase a *token* with the hope that the token value will increase and they can sell that token later at a higher price; often it has nothing to do with business prospects.

Generally speaking, there are two types of tokens:

Security tokens
> Similar to equity in a business, these tokens entitle the investor to part ownership in the business. Sales of security tokens fall under securities laws for the jurisdictions that both the buyer and seller are in, and have decreased in popularity as of 2020. Some of this has to do with the lack of security token exchanges and low liquidity on said exchanges.

Utility tokens
> Utility tokens offer access to a product or service. When an investor purchases a utility token, it's with the hope that demand for the product or service proposed by the project will increase significantly in the future. For example, if the project is an arcade, then the tokens might be the coins that game players need in order to play the arcade games. Investors will purchase these tokens in the hopes that demand for playing games at the arcade will increase and they will be able to sell the tokens later at a higher price.

Whitepaper

A *whitepaper* is a cryptocurrency project's equivalent of a business plan. Some project founders will spend some investor funds to build a team and attempt to fulfill the promises made in the whitepaper. Projects with long-term viable token economies are usually able to articulately answer the following questions: *Why does this product/ service have to be on a blockchain? Why can't you provide the same thing through a centralized database?*

Most token projects cannot answer this question well and therefore have poor token economics. An example of a product/service that has to be on a blockchain is the Augur token (REP). Augur is a prediction market that requires regulatory scrutiny in many jurisdictions. If Augur were run on a centralized server, there would be increased capability to shut down the service by seizing the server.

Motivations for those running an ICO are often not the same as for those running or investing in a venture capital–backed startup company. With a startup, the earlier an investor puts money into the company, the more equity they receive. Liquidating this equity is not possible until the company becomes so valuable that others want to purchase the equity, either through a merger, an acquisition, or a stock offering. This aligns the motivations of the founders (who have equity) and the investors who have purchased equity: to increase the value of the company. Token projects often receive millions of dollars of investment with minimal effort on the part of the founders, who also have the possibility of complete absolution from any liability. Because of this, with ICOs it can be extremely tempting for some founders to just take money for themselves and exit the company, either immediately or a little way down the road.

Exchange Hacks

As you know by now, "Not your keys, not your coins" is a popular saying in the cryptocurrency world. Centralized exchanges, which store private keys on users' behalf, have often had troubles with security in the blockchain world. Exchanges offer a centralized attack vector that attracts thieves, and therefore exchanges are under constant assault. The story of Mt. Gox and what was discovered in the aftermath of its implosion is the best cautionary tale, but there have been a few other notable examples too. We'll walk through a few of them here.

Mt. Gox

In early 2014, it was revealed that over 850,000 bitcoin had been stolen from Mt. Gox, a centralized exchange based in Tokyo. The theft was only discovered after it had been going on for several years, when the exchange was on the brink of collapse and was desperately trying to find investors for a bailout. Ultimately it did implode, although authorities in Japan have been able to organize a recovery effort to attempt to return funds to Mt. Gox users.

Launched in 2010, Mt. Gox was the first large cryptocurrency exchange. Over its lifetime it was victimized by multiple attacks, leading to thousands of people losing their funds. The following were the major incidents:

1. *January 27, 2011*: Hackers performed an XML injection that exploited a bug in the Mt. Gox payments platform. A now-defunct company called Liberty Reserve was facilitating customer withdrawals from Mt. Gox. When a customer requested a withdrawal on Mt. Gox's website, the Mt. Gox servers made an API call to Liberty Reserve, and the bug was able to capture this information. A total of $50,000 was stolen through this exploit before the bug was fixed.

2. *January 30, 2011*: Shortly after the previous incident, a hacker tried performing a withdrawal of $2,147,483 through Liberty Reserve, and was accidentally credited $2,147,483 to their Mt. Gox account. The bug was fixed and the funds frozen before any funds were moved.

3. *March 1, 2011*: Just before ownership of Mt. Gox was transferred from founder Jed McCaleb to new owner Mark Karpelès, a hacker made a copy of the Mt. Gox hot wallet's *wallet.dat* file and stole 80,000 BTC (*wallet.dat* files contain the private keys for a bitcoin wallet). As of 2020, the funds are still in the same Bitcoin address: 1FeexV6bAHb8ybZjqQMjJrcCrHGW9sb6uF.

4. *May 22, 2011*: Owner Mark Karpelès was in the process of figuring out where to securely store the Mt. Gox private keys, and his unsecured personal computer had temporary access to the files. Someone was able to access his computer, and stole 300,000 BTC. The thief gave back the stolen funds in exchange for keeping a 3,000 BTC fee.

5. *June 19, 2011*: A hacker gained access to an admin account for the exchange. They changed multiple account balances and crashed the market. During this time, they stole 2,000 BTC.

6. *September 2011*: A hacker gained read/write access to Mt. Gox's database and proceeded to inflate their account balances, then withdraw funds. In total, they stole 77,500 BTC.

7. *September 11, 2011*: A hacker again managed to gain access to the Mt. Gox hot wallet's *wallet.dat* file. This security breach went completely unnoticed, and from October 1, 2011 until mid-2013, the hacker continued to steal funds—a total of 630,000 BTC—from the exchange. Funds were occasionally credited to random Mt. Gox users, even though those users had never actually made a deposit. This led to the loss of an additional 30,000 BTC, as those users withdrew the funds.

8. *October 28, 2011*: Mark Karpelès had created new software to manage Mt. Gox wallets, but the code had bugs. When performing a withdrawal from the exchange, instead of putting the destination address bitcoin was supposed to be sent to, the new code would put a NULL or 0 in the destination field. This led to a number of withdrawals from Mt. Gox going to addresses that no one had a private key to, meaning lost bitcoin. A total of 2,609 BTC was lost this way.

The biggest problem with these incidents was that they were mostly kept secret from the public, including customers and investors. At the time of its collapse, Mt. Gox was supposed to have generated 100,000 BTC of revenue and to have 950,000 bitcoin of customer funds in custody. But when the exchange shut down in February 2014, it only had 200,000 BTC in custody, and a total of 850,000 BTC—worth around $425 million at the time and much, much more today—was unaccounted for.

Efforts to track down the 630,000 BTC lost during incident 7 turned up the following:

- The same addresses used to launder the stolen Mt. Gox funds were also used to launder funds from two other hacks targeting the exchanges Bitcoinica and Bitfloor (see Figure 8-4).
- Most of the stolen funds were deposited into the now defunct exchange BTC-e, which was located in Russia.
- The suspected operator of the BTC-e exchange was Alexander Vinnik. In July 2017, he was arrested in Greece over allegations that he had helped launder over $4 billion in funds through the BTC-e exchange. Court cases are still ongoing in 2020.

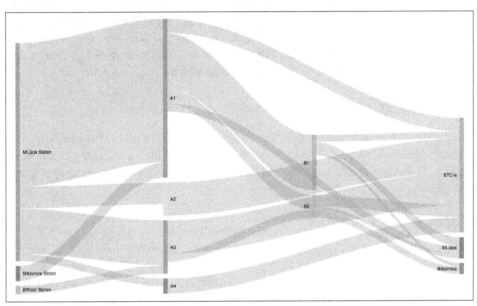

Figure 8-4. Flow of stolen funds through exchanges

Bitfinex

Nearly 120,000 BTC (worth about $72 million at the time) was stolen from Bitfinex, a centralized exchange based in Hong Kong, in 2016. Although Bitfinex used multi-signature technology provided by the security company BitGo, the system was apparently compromised. In 2019, some of the funds from the hack began to move on the blockchain (*https://oreil.ly/X_PKc*) after remaining dormant for three years. The same year, two Israeli nationals were arrested for involvement in the hack and other schemes; they were accused of having stolen a total of $100 million worth of cryptocurrency.

Coincheck

In 2018, more than $500 million was stolen from this Japanese-based exchange, mostly in the NEM cryptocurrency. Coincheck did not utilize the basic security mechanisms that most exchanges used during this time, including keeping most customer funds in a cold wallet and implementing multisignature key technology. The exchange did take steps to label which tokens on the NEM blockchain were stolen to make it harder for the theft's perpetrators to spend the funds.

NiceHash

A marketplace for miners to rent out hashing power, NiceHash was hacked in late 2017. Users started reporting that their cryptocurrency wallets were being emptied on the NiceHash website. A wallet address (*https://oreil.ly/w5k9E*) was identified as the location for the stolen funds, which totaled over 4,700 BTC (worth around $64 million), but they were not recovered. NiceHash resumed operations within weeks and promised to return the funds to customers via reimbursements on a monthly basis.

Other Hacks

Besides attacking exchanges, there have been a number of other creative ways cryptocurrencies have been parted from their owners. The following are some of the best-known. Hopefully these examples will help impart how important security is when owning crypto.

Bloomberg TV BTC Stolen

In 2013, Bloomberg TV reporter Matt Miller demonstrated some basics of bitcoin on-air. He gave other hosts $20 worth of bitcoin in paper wallets. One of the hosts, Adam Johnson, proceeded to open the paper wallet on live television, displaying its private key for about 10 seconds. A viewer named "milkywaymasta" was able to scan the private key's QR code and stole the funds. As a lesson in key security, milkywaymasta promised to return the $20 if Johnson created a new wallet, since the old one could be "swept" because the private key had been shared publicly.

EtherDelta Redirection

In 2017, hackers were able to obtain personal information on the dark web about decentralized exchange EtherDelta's operator, Zachary Coburn. The thieves were then able to set up call forwarding from Coburn's cell phone, ensuring that all calls would be directed to a different number. After changing Coburn's DNS settings and putting up a clone EtherDelta site, the hackers were able to steal at least $800,000 worth of cryptocurrency from one user.

CryptoLocker and Ransomware

CryptoLocker was an early and well-known variant of what is known as *ransomware*. Launched in 2013, this attack targeted Windows computers and spread via email attachments. It contained a Trojan virus that would lock up the user's files using cryptography. In order to release the files, CryptoLocker demanded payment via vouchers or bitcoin. It infected over 250,000 computers (*https://oreil.ly/vTU3s*) and demanded an average payout of $300. Tracing Bitcoin addresses shows that CryptoLocker has been able to obtain millions from locked-out users. Ransomware has spread and proliferated since.

SIM Swapping

Michael Terpin operates a PR firm in the cryptocurrency industry. This made him a target of hackers, who took over $24 million in various cryptocurrencies in his possession. Nefarious actors were able to get Terpin's wireless carrier to "swap SIMs," transferring his phone number to a SIM card they controlled. The access they gained then allowed them to reset his exchange/wallet passwords. Terpin won a $75.8 million settlement in a civil judgment against 21-year-old Nicholas Truglia for the loss of funds.

Hackers often target well-known people in the blockchain industry with this hack because there is a high chance that those people hold a large amount of cryptocurrency. Most people who own cryptocurrency are not security experts and trust large companies to manage the deeply complex security steps required to protect their funds.

When a hacker targets someone to steal their crypto, they aim to break into their email. This is because an email account contains a significant amount of sensitive information and empowers the hacker to access many of the target's internet accounts.

Here are the typical steps in a SIM swapping hack:

1. Find out the target's phone number. It is common for people to include their phone numbers in an email signature or on a business card. Hackers may also be able to find a target's phone number by purchasing it on the dark web if the individual's personal information has already been compromised.

2. In the US, telecom carriers offer customers the ability to port their phone number to a different SIM card. This is extremely convenient when a telecom customer loses their phone, and wants to maintain the same phone number. Once a hacker knows the phone number of their target, they need to convince the telecom carrier to port over the target's phone number. This can be done either through

social engineering (by pretending to be the target requesting the phone port), by bribing a telecom employee, or through other creative methods.

After a SIM swap occurs, the hacker receives all of the target's SMS messages. It's very common for people to set their phone number as one of the recovery options for their Gmail account—it's part of the sign-up process, as Figure 8-5 shows.

Figure 8-5. Gmail password recovery options include a phone number

Using SMS messages, a hacker can successfully complete the recovery process for an email account and gain access.

Once the hacker has control of a target's email account, they can do all of the following:

- Find out on which crypto exchanges the target has accounts, and reset the passwords. This is fairly simple with access to the email account. Many crypto exchanges send an SMS as the second-factor authentication (2FA), but the hacker has already compromised the user's phone.

- Access all documents in Google Drive. This might include private keys and sensitive business documents.

- Access all photos in Google Photos. This might include QR codes of private keys, Google Authenticator keys, or even compromising photos that could be used for extortion.

- Access the target's passwords via *chrome://settings/passwords*, if the target is using Chrome's built-in password manager.

- Get the target's entire contact list, which likely includes the phone numbers of many others in the blockchain industry.

As you can see, the list of damaging data a hacker gains access to is long. It may even include the target's current location and schedule, via Google Calendar.

Armed with all this information, the hackers can break into crypto exchange accounts and withdraw all of the target's crypto holdings. Since blockchain transactions are immutable, the target and the exchange have no ability to recover the stolen funds.

Consumer technology products constantly struggle to strike an ideal balance between convenience and strong security. Most of the vulnerabilities in SIM swapping are rooted in the fact that it requires users to put in effort to educate themselves about proper security practice. This includes, but is certainly not limited to, the following:

- Using a PIN number for any account changes with a telecom carrier
- Using a VoIP phone number like Google Voice for 2FA
- Using Google Authenticator or a hardware device like a YubiKey for secondary 2FA
- Using a secure password manager like 1 Password
- Changing passwords regularly with a password generator

Summary

The early days of cryptocurrency saw plenty of less-than-ideal activity occurring on blockchains. However, as regulators and law enforcement catch up with the technology, the promise of legitimate uses for blockchain has exploded. The next chapter takes a look at how businesses and other organizations are deploying blockchain applications to solve real-world problems—often with no cryptocurrency required.

CHAPTER 9

Other Blockchains

The success of Bitcoin and Ethereum has provided the genesis for many developers to begin working on blockchain technology. As previous chapters have shown, the decentralized nature of both networks leads to some interesting use cases.

Businesses must secure and protect corporate and user data, and blockchains are a novel technical idea for how to do so. Blockchain technology could be put to many uses within organizations. However, in practice this often requires rethinking the way that Bitcoin, Ethereum, and other open consensus networks operate in order to conform with data security, regulatory, and other requirements businesses must comply with.

What Are Blockchains Good For?

For open blockchains like Bitcoin and Ethereum, the main use cases thus far have been mostly speculative—the coverage of markets, dapps, and DeFi in this book have made that clear, we hope. But for businesses and other organizations, blockchain has some other interesting uses, and there are many trials occurring in this area.

Let's look once again at the basics of what blockchain is useful for besides cryptocurrencies and speculation. Here are the core technologies that are put together to create what is known as blockchain today:

Consensus
Validates new records to prevent corruption

Hashing
Solidifies records to retain an audit trail

Encryption
Secures the transfer of digital data

Distribution
Enables sharing of public ledger records

What are the specific properties derived from blockchain technology? On a basic level, a blockchain does the following:

Self-organizes (consensus)
A blockchain, without prompting, is capable of processing data at a consistent increment of time—generally whatever the block generation interval happens to be.

Permanently records (hashing)
Blockchain technology makes it very hard for any party to alter records that have already been placed into a block.

Transfers assets (encryption)
The first use case for blockchain was to transfer an asset without the involvement of a third party. That began with units of cryptocurrency.

Shares data (distribution)
Multiple parties that don't necessarily trust one another can use blockchain to collaborate on various data structures.

Many who are interested in blockchain are looking for reasons to use it to solve problems that existing technology hasn't solved. Open blockchains provided a way to make a payment to someone without a third party's involvement, but the main use for them today has become speculation. Unfortunately, speculation is not a use case that's relevant or attractive to organizations with technology issues.

So what are some use cases for businesses? Consider databases. Securing and sharing databases is a challenge for many organizations, and it has been made even more complex by the advent of technologies like cloud and mobile, which open up new security vulnerabilities. Blockchain could finally provide a way for organizations to coordinate information that needs to be secured yet shared by multiple parties.

Companies can ask questions like the following:

- Is blockchain a transactional mechanism counterparties can agree on?
- Can parties agree on what kind of data is to be written using blockchain?
- Can problems be solved with this technology?

The answer is definitely yes in each case.

Databases and Ledgers

A database is a structured set of information stored inside a computer system. Databases are key to storing information, and can often be accessed in several different ways depending on the data's use. *Database management systems* (DBMSs) are interfaces end users can use to categorize and retrieve data. These users are often critical components of an organization, working in areas such as communications, payroll, and human resources, among others. The most popular databases today are *relational* databases, which use tables to arrange information. The data is organized in such a way that it does not repeat across columns.

Replication systems are used with databases to make them distributed. Replication involves storing data in multiple places in a way that allows it to be easily updated or synchronized. This increases the availability of the data. Database systems must balance high availability with efficiency, and replication also allows users to work with various datasets in parallel. Replication systems must continuously work to update data in order to make sure everyone is working on the same set of information. There are various replication models that keep data up-to-date.

Ledger is a term used to describe a record-keeping system. The term *permissionless ledger* is sometimes used to describe cryptocurrency-based blockchains. This includes Bitcoin, Ethereum, various forks, and most altcoins. These networks are called permissionless because anyone can join in and participate; there is no central authority that grants or denies permission.

Blockchain in the permissionless world is a distributed computing system with accounts and payments built in. However, some organizations don't particularly see the benefit of this. Permissionless systems need accounts, payments, and cryptocurrencies to properly incentivize users, but that may not necessarily be the case for *permissioned* ledgers. In the permissioned world, providing infrastructure for payments and accounts is optional.

Distributed ledger technology (DLT) is enterprise terminology that describes a more blockchain-type ledger database. Database structures generally follow specific schemas that allow developers to read, write, and query them. DLT brings a new schema to database infrastructure, enabling reading and querying to occur in real time (writing in a consensus-based system is not always done in real time, and akin to following a clock).

Databases are centralized portals. In organizations, an administrator usually controls access to the entire system. Using a ledger system can allow multiple parties to access information without requiring one single gatekeeper.

There's nothing wrong with centralized databases. However, blockchain technology enables the sharing of information through consensus incentives instead of centralized rent-seeking (e.g., targeted advertising on social networks or taking a fee like online marketplaces do).

Decentralization Versus Centralization

Early cryptocurrency proponents embraced decentralization as a core part of the technology. However, many other blockchain platforms—particularly those being developed for organizations—are much more centralized. Let's take a look at some of the differences.

Participants

In open blockchains like Bitcoin, anyone with mining equipment can join the network and begin hashing. With private blockchains, such as for business use, there is a need to control who participates. In fact, centralized control is a key component that makes the system work. "Composition is more important than consensus" is an axiom used to express this. While having a way to agree upon transactions or data that is published in a block is important, it's more important to ensure that only authorized participants are involved. This is a big difference between decentralized and centralized blockchains.

Key Properties of Distributed Verifiable Ledgers

Ben Laurie, founder of the Apache Foundation and a cryptographer working at Google Research, has laid out a Framework for Distributed Verifiable Ledgers (*https://oreil.ly/5Kta5*) that outlines characteristics that are desirable in blockchains that are not of the open permissionless variety.

We're calling these *other blockchains* in this chapter because there is a good amount of variety between the different implementations. However, in all these systems it is important to consider the following aspects:

Admission control
> There must be some definition of what is permitted in the ledger, and how it should be formatted. Admission control is common in IT systems; it is a key element in system security.

Consensus
> Consensus means agreeing on the validity of information published on a chain or ledger. This could be achieved via proof-of-work, majority rule, union, or some other method. Bitcoin and Ethereum use the longest chain rule to resolve forks.

Verification
> Verification ensures that behavior on the network is correct and as intended. Admission control, consensus, and ledger reviews—some method of examination—are all components of this.

Enforcement
> Some form of enforcement is required to keep order. Blockchains such as Bitcoin provide enforcement by adding checkpoints corresponding to certain blocks that everyone on the network agrees were on the longest chain. At each fork, the new "longest chain" must contain all these checkpoints.

Ethereum-Based Privacy Implementations

Public blockchains and cryptocurrency networks don't make good implementations for businesses. This is because many organizations need to keep control of their information for competitive reasons, compliance, or other factors. However, blockchain technology potentially has many uses if the privacy concerns can be worked out. One option some enterprises have pursued is to fork the Ethereum blockchain and create a custom implementation including the privacy features they require.

Nightfall

Nightfall (*https://oreil.ly/FSkNE*) is an implementation of Ethereum by the accounting firm EY. It adds privacy features to the network's smart contract technology, enabling ERC-20 and ERC-721 tokens to be transacted on the Blockchain privately. Nightfall accomplishes this by using zk-SNARKs, generating proof via ZoKrates. This provides Nightfall with readable proofs that come from computation. There is a Java wrapper for ZoKrates functions.

Quorum

Developed by investment bank JPMorgan, Quorum (*https://oreil.ly/GKAUV*) is an Ethereum-based blockchain that supports private transactions and private contracts. It's compatible with development tools that Ethereum engineers are familiar with. Quorum uses Zether, which is an encrypted value tracking system. It "attaches" to ERC-20 contracts, creating Zether accounts that are private. This is done by using ElGamal ciphertext to encrypt each account balance under a public key.

Enterprise Implementations

There are also groups working on more specific proprietary blockchains. Many of these groups started with Ethereum and then decided to build their own solution from the ground up for specific use cases.

Hyperledger

Hyperledger (*https://www.hyperledger.org*) is an open source platform for blockchain development hosted by the Linux Foundation. The most well-known Hyperledger project is Fabric (*https://oreil.ly/BPLlZ*), a ledger technology that uses the programming language Go. There are other implementations, including a C++ implementation called Iroha and Sawtooth, which is multilanguage. Hyperledger Fabric offers support for smart contracts, transactions, and consensus, similar to Ethereum. Many enterprise blockchain projects, including those by IBM and Oracle, are based on this framework.

Corda

Developed by the consortium R3, Corda (*https://github.com/corda/corda*) focuses on institutions seeking privacy. The platform is based on the Java Virtual Machine (JVM), familiar to the existing base of developers in the finance industry. There is no global blockchain or representation of state. Instead, Corda uses a ledger system that replicates to relational databases for easy querying. Its smart contracts are basic legal terms instead of code.

How Corda works

Corda is designed to make transactions between businesses more trustworthy and efficient, as illustrated in Figure 9-1. Without Corda, the databases of the two companies are siloed. With Corda, the companies can safely collaborate to manage transactions.

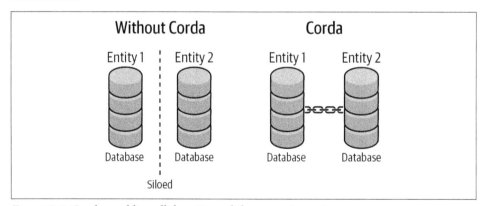

Figure 9-1. Corda enables collaboration while preserving privacy

Usually, when two separate entities perform transactions they each maintain a ledger, and at intervals they reconcile them. For example, a toy manufacturer receives constant shipments of parts from its supplier. Each company keeps track of those shipments using its own software and processes. Every month the two companies reconcile their ledgers when the supplier sends an invoice, and the manufacturer checks the invoice to confirm that the numbers are the same in its system.

Every business has multiple relationships like this. The more partnerships a company has, the more effort and resources are required to keep track of them.

There are two main attributes of public blockchains that businesses can benefit from:

Transaction immutability
Once a transaction has been added to the ledger, it cannot be modified or removed.

Peer validation
Before a transaction can be added to the ledger, other network participants check whether the transaction is valid or not.

However, there are also several attributes that are not attractive to businesses:

Transaction transparency
When businesses complete a transaction, they may not want everyone else in the network to know about it. Only the participants involved in the transaction should know the details.

Limited scalability
Centralized databases can process millions of transactions per second, whereas public blockchains at most can process a few hundred per second.

New programming languages and concepts
Dapps that run on top of public blockchains are mostly written in new languages, like Solidity and Vyper, and require developers to learn new skills.

Permissionless
Public blockchains allow anyone to participate in the network, but businesses want to control who can transact with them.

Hidden identities
Participants on public blockchains are identified by their blockchain address, which can make many participants essentially pseudo-anonymous. Businesses want to know who they are transacting with.

The Corda protocol was built to satisfy all those business requirements.

The Corda network

A Corda network is a peer-to-peer network of nodes. Each node represents a legal entity, and each runs an instance of Corda with one or more Corda applications. Figure 9-2 illustrates.

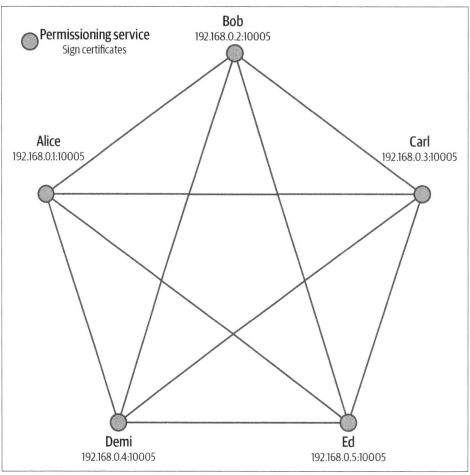

Figure 9-2. Example of a Corda network

Anyone can start their own Corda network, but every node in the network must receive permission by the network operator to join, and must also be identified to all participants in the network. Every node in the network communicates directly and in private with every other node in the network through Transport Layer Security (TLS).

Corda ledger

Each node in the network hosts its own centralized database, and all transactions are performed peer-to-peer. Two or more nodes can perform a transaction. After multiple nodes complete a transaction, the nodes each store the transaction in their own database. Only the nodes involved in the transaction or nodes that are given access have visibility into the transaction, as illustrated in Figure 9-3. Transactions are tamper-resistant and include digital signatures by some of the parties involved.

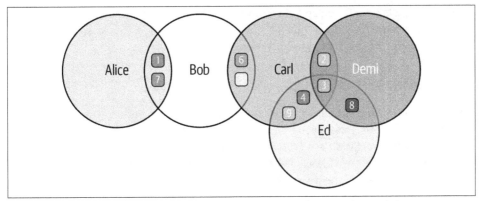

Figure 9-3. Example of a Corda network showing which nodes have visibility into transactions

In Figure 9-3, Bob has performed transactions #1 and #7 with Alice, and performed transactions #5 and #6 with Carl. Bob can see all four transactions, but Alice can only see transactions #1 and #7.

Corda consensus

In order for a transaction to be included on the ledger, it must pass the following two checks:

1. *Validity consensus.* All nodes involved check to make sure the following are true:
   a. All signatures that are required in the transaction are valid.
   b. The transaction satisfies all of the constraints that are defined in the associated smart contracts.
2. *Uniqueness consensus.* Corda follows a UTXO accounting model, similar to Bitcoin. Uniqueness checks prevent a double spend, confirming that inputs included in the transaction have not already been spent.

Corda language

The skills required by engineers to build a Corda solution for enterprise are well known and widely used in the tech industry, making it easy to find and train qualified engineers. Corda dapps are written in Java and can work with enterprise databases Azure SQL, SQL Server, Oracle, and PostgreSQL.

DAML

Developed by a company called Digital Asset, DAML (*https://github.com/digital-asset/daml*) is a blockchain-agnostic smart contract language for distributed applications. It supports all of the previously mentioned blockchain platforms. Developers work on

DAML contracts on a layer separate from its blockchain. The focus on smart contract development depends on the business use cases. It is thus easier to shift ledgers or storage models after a contract has been created.

Blockchain as a Service

The concept of *Blockchain as a Service* (BaaS), where vendors provide easy-to-implement solutions that can be customized, is likely to grow as use cases for the technology increase. Similar to Software as a Service (SaaS) and cloud offerings, these blockchain products provide elements such as centralized management of users and distribution of nodes. Here are a few examples:

Amazon Quantum Ledger
Part of Amazon Web Services, the Quantum Ledger Database (QLDB) is a ledger that is secured by cryptography and uses the Ethereum and Hyperledger Fabric frameworks. However, the system is centralized, because node-based distributed blockchains are harder to set up. Its strong point is that it offers users the ability to set up an immutable and cryptographically secure ledger.

Azure
Microsoft's Azure cloud platform offers a distributed model, allowing developers the ability to deploy different blockchains like Quorum and Corda. Because of the blockchains used, Azure supports smart contract development. Developers can also set up validators inside their blockchain implementations. The Azure framework makes it easy to export blockchain information to databases that allow for more complex querying.

VmWare
With support for the EVM, DAML, and Hyperledger, VmWare Blockchain is a multiblockchain platform. Developers are also able to use VmWare's cloud technology to set up various types of infrastructure implementations, including the option of hybrid cloud capabilities to increase security and privacy. It also uses a Byzantine fault-tolerant consensus engine to provide features of decentralization.

Oracle
Oracle's Blockchain Platform is built on Hyperledger Fabric and supports multi-cloud implementations—hybrid, on-premise, or a mix of the two for greater flexibility. The purpose is to be able to configure specific environments depending on regulatory requirements. Oracle also supports tamper-resistant blockchain tables within its existing enterprise database offerings to provide fraud protection; examples include chain of custody, escrow, and audit log capabilities within databases.

IBM

IBM provides a toolset that offers support for Hyperledger Fabric as the core technology. The toolset provides Visual Studio Code extensions for enterprise development, with smart contract programming capabilities available in Node.js, Go, Java, and Solidity, among others. Hosting options are flexible using IBM Cloud on-premise, remote, or hybrid offerings, with deployment via Red Hat's OpenShift container platform, which is managed with Kubernetes.

SAP

The company supports Hyperledger Fabric and Ethereum mainnet with deployment and services provided via its Cloud Platform. SAP Blockchain Business Services protects documents and data from tampering. SAP also allows external blockchains and nodes to plug into its various systems, including SAP "landscapes," which are its various server architectures, and SAP HANA, its custom data platform.

Banking

Large financial institutions and central banks have been looking at blockchain implementations in a search for ways to circumvent what may be outdated, inefficient, or otherwise expensive processes. Not all of these fully work yet, but experimentation in this sector is a sign of blockchain progress.

The Royal Mint

The Royal Mint, which produces coins in the United Kingdom, partnered with the Chicago Mercantile Exchange (CME) to create a blockchain-based asset tied to gold. The cryptocurrency company BitGo was brought in to provide wallet and KYC technology for the project. However, the effort was shelved in late 2018 after CME dropped out, leaving questions about where the asset would be traded.

Banque de France

The central bank of France was early in exploring ways to utilize blockchain. In 2016, it ran a trial based on digital identity for euro payments. The bank has been calling for global regulations within the blockchain industry. Most recently, it has published job postings looking for blockchain experts familiar with both crypto-economics and the Hyperledger, Corda, and Quorum platforms.

China

In 2019, president Xi Jinping announced an acceleration of development in blockchain for the country. China is moving toward central bank cryptocurrency, and a digital yuan is expected to use blockchain tech. The plan is for the system to be two-tiered, offering some degree of features similar to cash as well as an offline feature for mobile transactions.

US Federal Reserve

The United States' central bank has been observing cryptocurrencies over the years. In 2019, the Boston Federal Reserve published a paper (*https://oreil.ly/QW7ut*) describing Ethereum- and Hyperledger-based blockchain tests that it had run (Figure 9-4). It used wallets representing various banks and smart contracts to reconcile payments made to the Federal Reserve, which the Boston branch is in charge of.

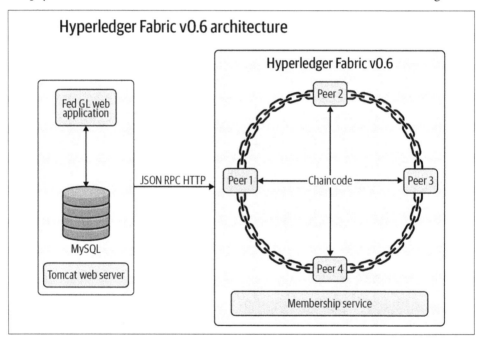

Figure 9-4. Design for the Boston Fed test—in Hyperledger, "chaincode" is a smart contract

JPMorgan

Investment bank JPMorgan has developed Quorum as its own blockchain based on Ethereum. It has also created its own stablecoin, JPC Coin. The cryptocurrency will be used as a method of making cross-border payments, which can be expensive and inefficient, via the Quorum blockchain. Users will be able to deposit fiat with the bank, be issued JPM Coin, and redeem it for fiat payment elsewhere.

Permissioned Ledger Uses

The use cases for permissioned systems are often very different from those of open blockchains. As we've pointed out, open blockchains can be good for speculation, tokenization, and storing digital value, but enterprises have other requirements. These include speed, privacy, and development capabilities. These requirements have led to the development of an array of new use cases for blockchain, after extensive testing of permissioned platforms.

IT

Security is an ever-present component of enterprise IT systems. Digital Asset's DAML SDK supports editing in Visual Studio, which is popular in many companies. Smart contracts tied to ledgers can help verify the validity of data critical for systems. This arrangement can include network management, database monitoring, and service desks. An example could be to use a contract to validate a software package or a Docker image.

Banking

As mentioned earlier, from securitization to settlement to rethinking fiat money, banks and central banks alike have increasingly been looking at blockchain technology. Banks must operate with a number of other organizations, and blockchain could serve as a trustless intermediary that disparate groups can all agree upon. One example that has gained traction and exemplifies this is *digital bonds*, which the bank Santander has issued. Custodians, issuers, and investors use tokens in this process, illustrated in Figure 9-5.

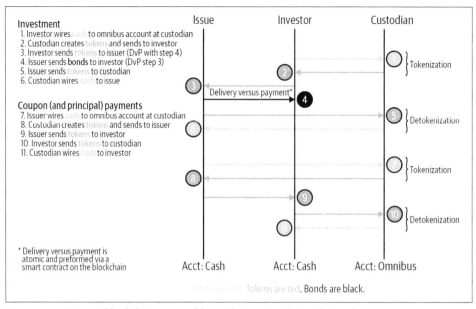

Investment
1. Investor wires cash to omnibus account at custodian
2. Custodian creates tokens and sends to investor
3. Investor sends tokens to issuer (DvP with step 4)
4. Issuer sends **bonds** to investor (DvP step 3)
5. Issuer sends tokens to custodian
6. Custodian wires cash to issue

Coupon (and principal) payments
7. Issuer wires cash to omnibus account at custodian
8. Custodian creates tokens and sends to issuer
9. Issuer sends tokens to investor
10. Investor sends tokens to custodian
11. Custodian wires cash to investor

Issue   Investor   Custodian

Tokenization

Delivery versus payment*

Detokenization

Tokenization

Detokenization

* Delivery versus payment is atomic and preformed via a smart contract on the blockchain

Acct: Cash   Acct: Cash   Acct: Omnibus

Tokens are red. Bonds are black.

Figure 9-5. How a blockchain-issued bond by Santander is devised

Central Bank Digital Currencies

Central bank digital currencies (CBDCs) are digital forms of a country's fiat currency. Instead of requiring intermediaries or third parties like banks, CBDCs could enable real-time payments directly between parties. While CBDCs may use existing databases for implementation, there is consideration of deploying blockchain or distributed ledger technologies. China, the US, Sweden, and the United Kingdom are among the countries considering or testing CDBC concepts.

Legal

The legal industry is by its nature adversarial. It involves opposing parties making claims while a neutral judiciary makes decisions. Blockchain, as an immutable technical innovation, can help to verify information during legal proceedings. In addition, technology to automate a number of legal processes is advancing; using concepts from smart contract development could be helpful. The law firm BakerHostetler, for example, is using smart contracts for freight agreements (*https://oreil.ly/_aeAI*).

Gaming

Anyone who has played video games understands the value of items like virtual weapons, power-ups, or clothing. In-game these items often have tremendous value, but they are normally locked into one particular game or ecosystem. The concept of items connected to a digital asset to signify uniqueness is gaining popularity, thanks in part to the Ethereum-based CryptoKitties.

Blockchain technology can also be used to combat cheating. On-chain chess, illustrated in Figure 9-6, is a project conducted by the Technical University of Berlin using Ethereum smart contracts. Players knew the game could not be cheated because of the public contract code.

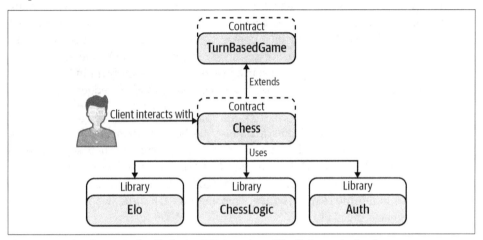

Figure 9-6. A schematic for Technical University of Berlin's on-chain chess

Health Care

The health-care industry generates a lot of data, and much of that data is scattered around. Patients go to general practitioners, specialists, hospitals, outpatient care clinics, and other locations for health needs. All of these visits generate data. Regulations are coming into place that will require that health-care providers enable patients to access all of their digital data. Google is working on something called a *verifiable data audit*, a ledger-based system that will cryptographically verify data records.

Internet of Things

Billions of smart devices, from power strips to light bulbs, can run more efficiently when cooperating with a larger network. To date, businesses are still struggling with ways to pay for all of these devices to connect into the Internet of Things (IoT) and provide verifiable information. Blockchain, with accounts and even payments in a controlled infrastructure, may be part of the solution. IBM's artificial intelligence platform Watson interacts with IoT devices and securely stores data with the IBM Blockchain Platform, which is based on Hyperledger Fabric.

Payments

There is a role for blockchain-based payments, but open blockchains have struggled to compete with the likes of existing networks such as Visa. Still, many still see an opportunity to use blockchain for specific payments use cases, such as the following:

Corporate payments
> The administrative costs involved when large organizations make payments are immense. An example would be ensuring that a check for an invoice matches a purchase order as stipulated in a contract. Also, making payments to various countries is complex. Some processes involved could be automated and verified with blockchain technology. Visa started working on this problem in 2016, and it launched a service in 2019 called B2B Connect that uses Hyperledger.

Interbank payments
> Large banks also have problems making cross-border payments. Some of these problems involve a lack of information about a payment when sending it to banks around the world. JPMorgan, with its JPM Coin, has developed something called the Interbank Information Network (IIN). This is a Quorum-based system that sends along interbank payment information. IIN now has more than 320 members using the platform.

Person-to-person payments
> There's a lot of interest in the idea of using blockchain ledgers to make payments cheaper and faster, which has been problematic on public blockchains. In 2019, PayPal invested in a company called Cambridge Blockchain for its identity technology, which has also been a challenge. Facebook, which possesses lots of information about its users, may have already solved that problem, as outlined in the next section.

Libra

Most enterprise blockchain experiments are focused on behind-the-scenes business processes. However, there is an opportunity for companies to use cryptocurrency and blockchain fundamentals to offer new features to users and customers. It's early in this game, but consumer-focused companies like Facebook want to bring blockchain to everyone, particularly in terms of making payments on the internet. *Libra* is the name of the effort being spearheaded by the company.

The Libra Association

With its billions of users, Facebook has been exploring blockchain implementations for some time. The company's Libra Association is a consortium of organizations that have come together to implement an entirely new blockchain system called Libra. The following are some of the companies involved, and their roles:

- *Payments*: PayU
- *Technology*: Facebook, FarFetch, Lyft, Spotify, Uber
- *Telecom*: Iliad
- *Blockchain*: Anchorage, BisonTrails, Coinbase, Xapo
- *Venture capital*: Andreessen Horowitz, Breakthrough Initiatives, Union Square Ventures, Ribbit Capital, Thrive Capital
- *Nonprofits*: Creative Destruction Lab, Kiva, Mercy Corps, Women's World Banking

Borrowing from Existing Blockchains

The Libra Association intends to create an entirely new payments system on the internet by using a proof-of-stake consensus Byzantine fault-tolerant algorithm developed by VMware, known as HotStuff. The association's members will be the validators of the system.

HotStuff uses a lead validator. It accepts transactions from the clients and uses a voting mechanism for validation. It is fault tolerant because the other validators can take the lead's place in case of error or downtime. Byzantine fault tolerance is used in other blockchain systems, most notably on some smaller open networks utilizing proof-of-stake. Figure 9-7 illustrates Libra's consensus mechanism.

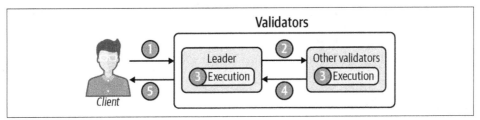

Figure 9-7. Consensus mechanism for Libra

The Libra cryptocurrency is expected to hold a stable value, backed by a basket of assets that will include fiat currencies and treasuries. Unlike most stablecoins, it does not plan to peg to the US dollar and will instead exist as a digital currency with its own valuation against fiat.

Libra is expected to support the use of smart contracts by third-party developers to create applications. This will be accomplished through a new programming language called Move. This language will allow programmers to create contracts and even update the state of the Libra blockchain. Move is being labeled as a language "with programmable resources." With vetted validators and specific resource types, Libra's smart contracts will likely be more limited in scope than those of open blockchains such as Ethereum.

Novi

Facebook itself will develop its own wallet, known as Novi, to facilitate transactions. The impact of the Novi wallet could be large given Facebook's billions of users across its many platforms, including Messenger, Instagram, WhatsApp, and Oculus VR.

Libra will also support a number of third-party wallet implementations. The network itself is expected to be open, with wallets being the gateways for financial services. KYC/AML will need to be a component of Novi, and this is something Facebook can easily implement into its products since it already has a trove of user data at hand.

Libra's Centralization Challenge

Libra faces many challenges. One of them is the plan for the network to be centralized while slowly building out a larger proof-of-stake consensus network. Achieving this could prove challenging from a technical standpoint.

Regulatory issues will likely shape the formation of this network, which is expected to launch slowly over time. For example, unlike most cryptocurrencies, Libra payments will need to be reversible in order to conform with regulations regarding consumer protections.

However, Libra does show that the underlying technologies discussed in this book are being experimented with and possibly deployed at a scale blockchain has not been capable of before. While the Libra Association has advocated for decentralization of the network, there may have to be a balance between centralization and decentralization in order for it to be efficient, stable, and scalable.

How the Libra Protocol Works

Libra's network contains two types of nodes: *validator nodes* and *full nodes*. Validator nodes are permissioned and are made up of organizations in the Libra Association. These nodes manage governance of the network and process Libra transactions using the LBFT consensus protocol.

Full nodes can be run by anyone and serve two purposes:

1. They act as real-time broadcasters of the current state of the Libra blockchain. Full nodes maintain a full copy of the blockchain and answer client requests to read from the blockchain.

2. They revalidate transactions that have been processed by validators.

Full nodes make Libra more scalable by removing the burden of validator nodes servicing read requests. This also protects validator nodes from potential DDoS attacks.

When a client application—for example, a Libra mobile wallet—wants to interact with the network, it reads data from full nodes and sends transaction requests to validator nodes.

The LBFT protocol is a set of rules that define how transactions and governance are performed on the Libra blockchain. Even though all validator nodes on the network are identified and trust each other, there is still a risk that at some point one or many of them could become a bad actor and try to include invalid transactions on the network. One example is if hackers compromise a couple of validator nodes. The hackers could then try to process transactions that send funds from other accounts to their own.

Blocks

Each block of transactions added to the blockchain in LBFT is proposed by the leader of a round. Validators rotate as the leader, each taking a turn. Unlike in proof-of-work consensus, no energy or time is spent deciding which node gets the right to generate a block. This makes LBFT fast and scalable. Libra is anticipating a speed of one thousand transactions per second—compare that to Bitcoin's seven transactions per second.

After a leader proposes a new block of transactions, all network validators vote on whether the block is valid or not. If more than $2f + 1$ validators agree that the block is valid, a Quorum Certificate is generated. This Quorum Certificate is attached to the next block, cryptographically connecting every block to its parent block.

A block can only be committed to the Libra blockchain when it has three consecutive child blocks that all have Quorum Certificates as well. Until this point, the block could possibly become an orphaned block. Figure 9-8 illustrates.

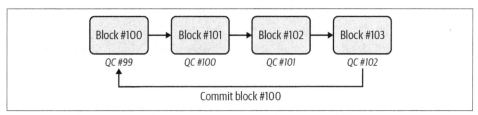

Figure 9-8. Block #100 is not committed to the blockchain until block #103 is proposed to the network, provided that block includes the Quorum Certificate for block #102

Transactions

Transactions in Libra are structured in a similar fashion to Ethereum. Libra follows an account model, as opposed to a UTXO model like Bitcoin, so there are no inputs or outputs. The structure of a Libra transaction is illustrated in Table 9-1.

Table 9-1. Structure of a Libra transaction

Field	Description
Sender address	The account address of the sender of the transaction.
Sender public key	The public key that corresponds to the private key used to sign the transaction.
Program	The program is comprised of the following: • The bytecode from the Move transaction script. • An optional list of inputs to the script. For a peer-to-peer transaction, the inputs contain information about the recipient and the amount transferred to the recipient. • An optional list of Move bytecode modules to publish.
Gas price (in microlibra/gas units)	The amount the sender is willing to pay per unit of gas (*https://oreil.ly/1RktS*) to execute the transaction. Gas is a way to pay for computation and storage. A gas unit is an abstract measurement of computation with no inherent real-world value. 1 microlibra = 0.000001 LBR (10^{-6}).
Maximum gas amount	The maximum units of gas the transaction is allowed to consume.
Sequence number	An unsigned integer that must be equal to the sequence number stored under the sender's account.
Expiration time	The time after which the transaction ceases to be valid.
Signature	The digital signature of the sender.

Summary

Some businesses want totally private blockchains, and for them an R3 Corda implementation might be useful. Some want a usable network for the general public. That's the kind of role the Libra project is trying to fill.

No one knows yet which service will become the Amazon of the blockchain business. AWS is so easy to deploy and develop on that, while it does have its competitors, it reigns supreme in cloud computing. No one reigns supreme in these other blockchain systems—at least, not yet.

Open networks like Bitcoin and Ethereum created the world of blockchain. Now businesses have taken blockchain concepts and are using them to improve many aspects of their operations.

This is just the beginning. There will be continued experimentation in the future— the subject of the next chapter.

CHAPTER 10

The Future of Blockchain

The comparison of blockchain and cryptocurrencies today to the early days of the internet isn't entirely incorrect. As those of a certain age may remember, the consumer internet in its early days was slow and lacked most of the features we are accustomed to now.

Blockchain is at a similar stage. Consumer adoption is still pretty low, and doing things is often confusing and difficult. This means developers have a tremendous opportunity to shape the future of the blockchain industry.

In general, new technologies are being adopted ridiculously fast—faster than ever before (see Figure 10-1). Blockchain could be the next great consumer technology that takes off, *if* the right applications are found for it.

Of course, not everything ends up succeeding. The internet offers the lesson that being flexible and adaptable is the path to advancement. The world of blockchain can move at a dizzying pace, and therefore having views that adjust to the changing market and developer ecosystem is key.

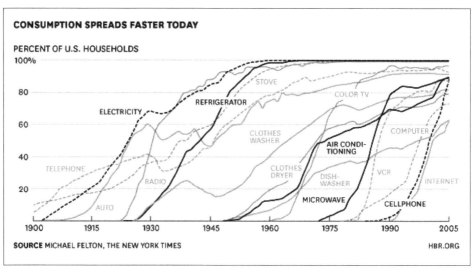

Figure 10-1. Rate of adoption of different technologies over time

The More Things Change

In the 1970s, at the dawn of the internet, a group of computer industry representatives from the United States, the United Kingdom, and France got together and devised the Open Systems Interconnection (OSI) (*https://oreil.ly/Ur4hJ*) model. Their aim was to create an open and multilayered set of standardized protocols for data exchange on the internet. By the 1980s, the effort had been backed by many stakeholders, including engineers, regulators, and computer and telecommunications companies. However, by the early 1990s two more efficient and nimble standards had come to dominate instead: Transmission Control Protocol and Internet Protocol, or TCP/IP. Here's a brief look at how this relative upstart took over:

1960s

Data transmission technology evolves from old-school circuit switching in telephone networks. Packet switching breaks information into blocks, transmits them, and then reassembles the data at the receiving end. ARPANET, an early version of the internet, is the first network to use packet switching.

1970s

Telephone carriers explore the idea of packet switching via "virtual" circuits, proposed in order to protect analog circuit revenue. However, the original proponents of packet switching propose a more innovative distributed datagram model. Following this divide, the OSI model is devised.

1980s

The reference model for OSI is published, including options for both packet switching implementations. The US government, the main sponsor for internet research, mandates purchasing OSI-standard computers by 1990.

1990s

TCP/IP, first used and developed throughout the '80s and used in the ARPANET as the successor to its Network Control Program (NCP), gains traction. A revolt among engineers attempting to scale TCP/IP leads to the rejection of the OSI standard; while OSI is mired in standards and procedure, TCP/IP is free and open for use.

2000s

TCP/IP is the de facto standard for internet communications on all devices, beating out standards-based OSI because of its more permissive framework for engineers to build upon.

What does this snapshot history of internet communication protocols have to do with the future of blockchain? Decades ago, early internet pioneers probably thought OSI would rule the world. Instead, TCP/IP accomplished that feat. The blockchain world, over time, will likewise see promising projects fade for various reasons because the ecosystem today is still evolving.

The internet is not something anyone ever sees. They just see the applications built on top of it, like the web and email. Blockchain is much the same. Just like the internet, blockchain is a backbone for consumer-facing applications.

Cryptocurrency networks and the blockchains that underpin them are similar in essence to software. Software is dynamic, never finished, and part of a larger ecosystem. Cryptocurrency is also dynamic, and blockchain, as the recording device for cryptocurrencies, moves in a dynamic way too. Lots of things are set to change in a few short years. The future is bright, but it's definitely not set in stone.

Blockchains to Watch

Besides Bitcoin, Ethereum, and various enterprise-type blockchains, there are lots of other projects available for developers to build on. Whether because of privacy, efficiency, or improved smart contract capabilities, these will be three of the platforms to watch out for in the near future:

EOS (https://github.com/EOSIO/eos)

An operating system and smart contract platform, EOS increases the number of transactions included in each block and requires no fees, using a resource-leasing model to provide transaction bandwidth for users on its blockchain by only utilizing a small set of concentrated nodes. The trade-off is that the nodes are part of a membership that is centralized. These *block propagators* use special hardware configurations to handle blockchain storage and smart contract execution on the network. The propagators receive rewards for block generation and for governance.

Cardano (https://cardano.org)

A smart contract platform that uses proof-of-stake, Cardano's consensus mechanism chooses random stakers to validate each block. Users are also able to "delegate" their stake in-wallet to stakers that are consistently online, a requirement for rewards. While delegating, users can still spend the native ADA cryptocurrency thanks to a structure of multisignature addresses. The project has been notable for its academic nature and its use of Haskell libraries, existing and established in programming, for the protocol.

Monero (https://www.getmonero.org)

A blockchain that has implemented privacy and is gaining traction for its ability to execute cash-like transactions, Monero makes transaction details private by implementing three cryptographic strategies: ring signatures, ring confidential transactions, and stealth addresses. Monero's currency symbol is XMR.

Privacy in blockchains is an important component of the future. In the next section, we'll briefly explore Monero in a little more detail.

How Monero Works

To demonstrate how Monero works, we'll look at an example transaction of 0.5 XMR between two addresses.

Transaction details that are visible to the public are as follows:

- *Transaction ID*: 7de8...53f1
- *Block #*: 2015291
- *Miner fee*: 0.00017681
- *Inputs*: Only 1 real input and 10 decoy inputs
- *Key image*: b142...da7e

These are the inputs that are publicly viewable:

	Ring members	Block	Timestamp
1	3154...a729	1936368	2019-10-03 6:07
2	60c9...de58	1970318	2019-11-19 13:11
3	F6a2...b1e3	1997733	2019-12-27 2:14
4	9a62...a1a8	2006400	2020-01-08 2:01

	Ring members	Block	Timestamp
5	d0aa...c50b	2014276	2020-01-18 22:55
6	31b6...0bbf	2014635	2020-01-19 11:20
7	d3a6...6ef1	2014688	2020-01-19 12:41
8	754e...3a4d	2015113	2020-01-20 3:11
9	ce8b...6f7a	2015154	2020-01-20 4:34
10	0bab...594d	2015200	2020-01-20 5:58
11	228d...1bd0	2015278	2020-01-20 8:38

And these are the outputs:

	Stealth address	Amount
1	0152...19e4	?
2	c44f...e531	?

The inputs that are hidden from the public are as follows:

	Monero address	Amount	Viewable by
1	43Ao...GHU9	0.01	Owner of this address, who also generated the transaction

And these are the outputs that are not visible to the public:

	Monero address	Amount	Viewable by
1	41qp...NxdK	0.005	Owner of this address
2	43Ao...GHU9	0.00482319	Owner of this address

Ring signatures hide the public address of a sender in a Monero transaction. Monero follows a UTXO accounting method, similar to Bitcoin. With Bitcoin, when the sender builds a transaction, they only include inputs from addresses for which they control the private keys. This is so the sender can sign the transaction that provides authorization to send those funds.

However, in Monero, when a sender builds a transaction they include decoy inputs chosen randomly from addresses that are owned by others. So, even though many inputs are included in the transaction, only one is actually sending funds. Publicly it is impossible to know which input is sending funds.

In the preceding example, funds are being sourced from only one input. There are 11 addresses in the ring signature, meaning that there are 10 decoy inputs. The generator of the transaction knows that the address sending the funds is #11 (228d...1bd0), but they are the only one who knows which one is the real input.

To prevent double spending, every Monero transaction includes a *key image*, which is generated by the true transaction sender. If the sender tries to send funds from an input that has already been sent, the key image they generate will be identical to the key image that was generated in the first transaction that sent those funds. The Monero miners won't validate the double-spend attempt because the same key image has already been included in a previous transaction on the blockchain.

 The key image is Monero's equivalent to Bitcoin's transaction signature. It's generated by the sender, and miners use the key image to prevent a sender from double spending. In the preceding example, the key image is b142…da7e.

The purpose of a *ring confidential transaction* (ring CT) is to hide the amount sent in a Monero transaction. It's a privacy feature that masks the amounts sent to an output through cryptography—only the sender and receiver of the transaction know the actual amount of funds being sent.

To recap:

- The sender is the one who generated the transaction details, and who therefore knows the transaction amount.
- Every Monero address has a private/secret view key. In a Monero transaction, the owner of the address that received XMR can decrypt the amount sent using their private/secret view key.

The miners don't care about the exact amount sent; their goal is simply to determine whether the transaction is valid or invalid. To validate a transaction, a miner must do a *range proof*. That is, they have to check if the following are true:

1. The sum of the inputs is equal to the sum of the outputs.
2. The amount sent to each output is greater than 0.

The miners can accomplish both these checks through cryptography without knowing the amount sent.

In the preceding example transaction, the funds were sent to two outputs. The first output goes to address 41qp…NxdK, and the owner of that address can use their secret view key to decrypt the amount value of 0.005 XMR. They cannot view the amount value for the second output.

Stealth addresses hide the receiver of a Monero transaction. The sender of a transaction creates a new stealth address for the receiver, using the receiver's public view key, the receiver's public spend key, and a random value.

Mimblewimble, Beam, and Grin

Mimblewimble (*https://oreil.ly/k3W6J*) is a blockchain protocol that emphasizes privacy paired with scalability. A zero-knowledge proof technology called Bulletproofs verifies that transactions are valid, and the state transition is recorded on the blockchain, obscuring the details.

Two other projects have emerged from this: Beam (*https://beam.mw*) and Grin (*https://grin.mw*). These two projects are governed quite differently: Grin is a loosely organized open source group, whereas Beam's team is backed by investors.

Both Beam and Grin share some key attributes, such as ASIC resistance, scalability, and privacy, but there are some differentiating features other than governance.

Beam characteristics include the following:

- Implemented in C++
- Uses Equihash proof-of-work
- Supply capped at 263 million to encourage store of value
- Sender and receiver wallets can create transactions without being online
- Uses "scriptless script" for extension beyond transactions like escrow and atomic swaps

Grin characteristics include the following:

- Implemented in Rust
- Uses Cuckoo Cycle proof-of-work
- Infinite supply to encourage spending
- Transactions require sender and receiver to be online
- Limited scripting, designed to be as simple as possible

The Scaling Problem

A lot of research in the coming years will center on increasing transaction capacity while remaining efficient, where fees are low and the crypto is still easy to use. Bitcoin and Ethereum definitely need to increase their scalability given their current limitations—Bitcoin can only process 3 to 7 transactions per second, and Ethereum can only get up to around 20 transactions per second. That's not nearly enough for cryptocurrency networks to truly take off on a massive scale. This is why new ideas, some of which are discussed in this section, are needed to solve the scalability problem.

Sidechains

As a method to offload some on-chain data, *sidechains* carry additional information about network transactions off of a main blockchain. A *federated* sidechain, such as Bitcoin's Liquid Network (*https://blockstream.com/liquid*), uses a trusted set of parties to sign blocks and hold funds in a multisignature address. *Trustless* sidechains, still under development, use the concept of a "two-way peg," which enables users to move funds from one chain to another in a more decentralized manner.

Sharding

A process to break up bigger chunks of data, *sharding* is used in database systems and is a proposed solution for scaling cryptocurrency networks. In peer-to-peer networks underpinned by blockchains, sharding would split datasets between nodes. The information would then be shared with other nodes on the network. Sharding on blockchain networks adds another layer of complexity since there has to be a secure communication protocol to share data.

STARKs

Scalable Transparent Arguments of Knowledge, or STARKs, takes advantage of the privacy-focused zk-SNARKs technology mentioned in previous chapters. The zero-knowledge proofs can be used as verifiers to make sure transactions are honest. This is done by using "prover" nodes. The transactions are then batched, creating smaller blocks. Individual balances are stored off-chain. Contracts that show balance commitments and a verification of the proofs are stored on-chain.

DAGs

Directed acyclic graphs (DAGs) rethink the way blockchains are constructed. Instead of blocks in a chain, DAGs are interconnected data structures, as Figure 10-2 illustrates. Transactions validate one another in a system where users act as both miners and validators. This design eliminates efficiency problems like orphaned blocks and long block times. Transactions are able to complete across this network in a more decentralized and faster method.

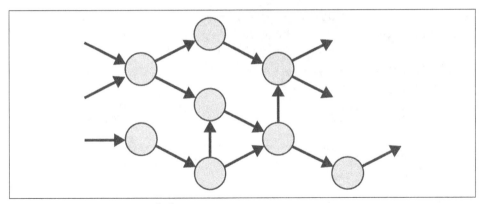

Figure 10-2. A DAG network design

Avalanche

A new type of consensus mechanism for cryptocurrencies, Avalanche (*https://www.avalabs.org*) relies on a dynamic population sampling voting mechanism to create a fluid blockchain with highly adaptable rules, with a "leaderless" model where all nodes are considered equal. This eliminates the hardware-based mining found in other cryptocurrency networks. Setting up nodes that have separate rules while still being part of the network is possible. In this way, the platform can use multiple scripting languages and virtual machines.

Liquid

Liquid is technology from Blockstream (*https://blockstream.com*), a company that provides technical products and services around Bitcoin. It's a multisignature wallet where users deposit bitcoin to be locked for interoperability purposes. Sidechains allow these locked bitcoin to be used on another chain, which may utilize a different set of rules than Bitcoin. This means potentially changing performance and security requirements.

The basis for Liquid comes from the Elements (*https://oreil.ly/fw3q5*) open source project. Elements allows developers to build sidechains and also standalone blockchains based on Bitcoin technology. As a result, it offers the ability to issue new assets. The platform also supports what it calls *confidential assets*, which means identifiers and amounts are obscured on the blockchain.

Lightning

A solution to the limitations of Bitcoin's throughput in transactions per second, Lightning (*https://lightning.network*) uses *channels*, as illustrated in Figure 10-3, that parties open with one another outside of the main Bitcoin blockchain. It uses a main chain-backed commitment scheme called Hash Time Locked Contracts to keep track of balances, providing settlement when a channel is closed or goes offline. There are several implementations for Lightning, including Blockstream's c-lightning (*https:// oreil.ly/w8onX*) and Lightning Labs's lnd (*https://oreil.ly/KXMrs*). Square Crypto is also planning to release a Lightning Developers Kit (LDK) in the near future.

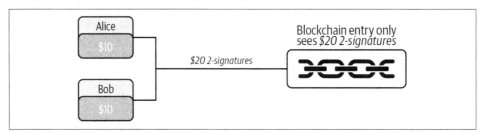

Figure 10-3. Lightning channels are created by two or more participants, who then assign value to the Bitcoin blockchain

The scaling problems that exist in cryptocurrency today aren't all that different from what computer networks once faced. Necessity, as they say, is the mother of invention. As the internet's popularity increased, the growing need for capacity led to numerous technical solutions. These included *dark fiber*, or fiber optic cable laid long before it was needed. Investment in numerous scaling solutions for cryptocurrency networks could be similar, as the research will likely be utilized as adoption picks up, including in Bitcoin and Ethereum.

Lightning aims to make Bitcoin more usable by solving the following scalability issues:

Transaction speed
> As mentioned, Bitcoin can only process up to about seven transactions per second. If masses of consumers wanted to use Bitcoin, the network currently couldn't support that level of demand.

Block times
> On average a new block of transactions is generated every 10 minutes, and once a block is full, no more transactions can be processed by the network until the next block is discovered. If someone buys something with bitcoin, they are likely not willing to wait more than 10–20 minutes to receive confirmation that their transaction was processed.

Bitcoin blockchain size
> Every miner and full Bitcoin node must maintain a copy of the entire Bitcoin blockchain, which was around 285 GB in size as of June 2020.

The Lightning Network solves these problems by enabling Bitcoin addresses to trans-act bitcoin through a payment channel. This channel acts as a ledger that two Bitcoin addresses manage peer-to-peer. Transactions through a payment channel are not recorded on the Bitcoin blockchain, but rather off-chain.

 This is a simplified explanation of payment channels that is meant only to give an idea of how they work. True payment channels involve a hashed secret and potentially several peer hops before they reach the intended recipient and sender.

Let's say Alice visits Bob's coffee shop every day and wants to buy a cup of coffee from Bob each day. One way she can pay conveniently is by buying a $100 gift card and using that each day. In this situation, Alice commits $100, and the gift card company controls a ledger of all her transactions.

The Lightning Network's version of this situation would be Alice opening a payment channel with Bob and funding that channel with 0.01 BTC. In this situation, Alice commits 0.01 BTC, and instead of a third party controlling the ledger, Alice and Bob both control the ledger together. Cryptography and the cost associated with funding the channel force both Bob and Alice to act appropriately.

Funding transactions

Alice can open a payment channel by sending Bob a *funding transaction* to a newly generated multisignature address that holds the payment channel funds. This funding address is mutually controlled by both Bob and Alice, like a joint bank account. In our example, illustrated in Figure 10-4, Alice sends 0.01 BTC to the payment channel address.

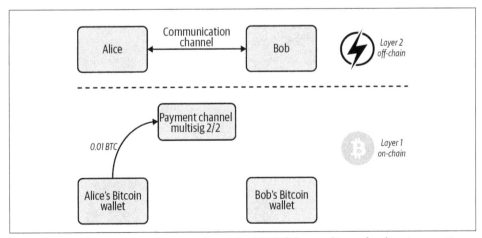

Figure 10-4. Alice opens a payment channel with Bob by sending a funding transaction

Once the funds are held in the payment channel, there are only two ways that they can leave that channel's address:

2/2 multisig transaction
This means that 2 out of 2 possible signatures must be provided to generate a valid transaction. Both Alice and Bob must sign a transaction with their private keys in order to perform a valid multisig transaction.

Refund contract
Since Alice is the one committing her funds to the payment channel, there is a risk that Bob might back out of the relationship and not provide a signature to help Alice recover her funds. To protect Alice, embedded in the funding transaction is a refund contract that says "after x number of blocks, refund all the funds in the payment channel address to Alice's address." This refund contract uses nLockTime, an attribute of a bitcoin transaction.

Off-chain transactions

At some time in the future, Alice and Bob will perform a withdrawal transaction (Figure 10-5) that requires both of their signatures. The question is, how much will Alice and Bob each receive from that future transaction? If they perform the multisig transaction before Alice buys anything at Bob's coffee shop, the multisig transaction should send all the funds back to Alice's address.

Here is possible future withdrawal transaction #1:

Inputs		Outputs	
bc1q...3ktl (Payment channel)	0.01 BTC	3DZ5...2NZU (Alice)	0.01 BTC
Signature 1: 001443692e0c9ce1c70840847495c3216318b04a7793 (Alice's signature)			
Signature 2: cb8b99f482852b6c0d40a2f5bc249743ea6d5a80 (Bob's signature)			

However, if Alice spends 0.007 BTC at Bob's shop, the multisig transaction should send Bob 0.007 BTC and Alice 0.003 BTC. So here is possible future withdrawal transaction #2 (illustrated in Figure 10-5):

Inputs		Outputs	
bc1q...3ktl (Payment channel)	0.01 BTC	3DZ5...2NZU (Alice)	0.003 BTC
		38iS...E8SE (Bob)	0.007 BTC
Signature 1: 9a791cf4d808afec90ed7051314f80f4a9310372 (Alice's signature)			
Signature 2: 104f28ca0bf87c07ef5b97d33dae38f547d0435b (Bob's signature)			

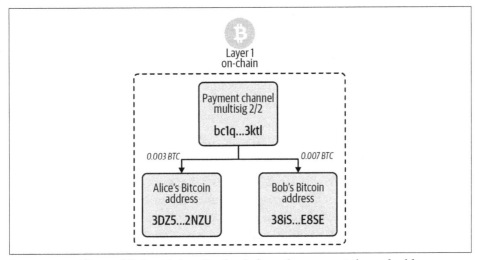

Figure 10-5. Alice and Bob withdrawing funds from the payment channel address

Each day, as Alice buys a coffee from Bob's shop, the values of how much each receives in the future withdrawal transaction change. And each time the values change, Alice and Bob need to generate and sign a new unique transaction, to authorize the future withdrawal transaction and prove to the miners that the new withdrawal transaction is valid. This process of generating and signing new withdrawal transactions is essentially the same as Alice and Bob performing off-chain transactions.

Lightning nodes and wallets

A *Lightning wallet* is a Bitcoin wallet with additional features that allow one to open/ close a payment channel and perform Lightning transactions. A common mistake first-time Lightning users make is trying to open a payment channel with no BTC sitting in their wallet. A Lightning wallet must have some BTC in it to pay for mining fees, and some funds to commit to the payment channel.

Lightning requires a blockchain to have no *transaction malleability*, which is a vulnerability that can allow an exploiter to modify some transactional data. Segregated Witness, or SegWit, is an update to the Bitcoin protocol that separates base transaction data and signature data. Since transactions are serialized using the original transaction data, signature-based malleability attacks are prevented. The signature data goes into the transaction witness area, used by SegWit-capable full nodes to confirm that the transactions are authorized.

 SegWit moves the witness data needed to check transaction validity to a different part of each bitcoin transaction generated. Before SegWit was implemented on the Bitcoin blockchain, for example, it was possible for a node to change prehash information, which was not originally included in a signed transaction. This resulted in malleability attacks on the network. In order for Lightning nodes to be feasible, the risk of these malleability attacks needed to be eliminated.

Once a user is running a Lightning node, they can open a payment channel. Multiple parties with open payment channels can then collaborate on a transaction. This is done using a commitment transaction.

Since Lightning uses channels instead of a blockchain, transactions are private. However, if a node drops or otherwise loses its connection in one of these bidirectional channels, it will close the channel and settle transactions on the blockchain. In addition, payment routing occurs in this system. This routing means that if a channel is not open for some reason, the payment can go through nodes to have channels open with other parties.

Optimistic Rollups

Designed with Ethereum in mind, *Optimistic Rollups* is a technique that uses an on-chain smart contract to hold funds for a sidechain. The sidechain is a Merkle tree that contains user information, including balances. On-chain information is then "rolled up" into a single block for efficiency. Aggregators collect transactions to publish to the smart contract. These aggregators post a bond to the smart contract to participate and are rewarded with fees as a result. Unipig Exchange (*https://unipig.exchange/welcome*) is an example of a project using Optimistic Rollups.

Ethereum Scaling

Ethereum is planning to make major changes to its network in order to increase its capacity. In its next iteration, known as Ethereum 2.0, the network will move to a form of proof-of-stake called Casper that will enable greater efficiency without adding complexity. It will also be split into shards, as described earlier in this chapter. It's an ambitious plan that brings together a number of novel research ideas in order to help the network move into the future.

The first phase of Ethereum 2.0 involves the following specifications:

Beacon chain
A new blockchain that will ensure the network stays in sync by providing consensus to all the shard chains. Each shard chain will have validators responsible for adding transactions to shard blocks and proposing new blocks to add to the beacon chain and all the shard chains. Validators are activated by the beacon chain and can be deactivated either voluntarily or due to misconduct.

Casper
A proof-of-stake algorithm designed specifically for Ethereum 2.0. It is expected to operate as a hybrid with Ethereum's existing proof-of-work system in the beginning. Casper is Byzantine fault tolerant, which means consensus can be reached even if some nodes are unreliable and there is accountability, so misbehaving validators are penalized by their staked balance. As long as two-thirds of the staked validators reach consensus, the chain can be validated.

Fork choice rule
A rule that will help validators decide which chain to follow in the event of a fork (the one whose blocks have received the most votes from validators). While the network will use something called a *random number heartbeat* in order to choose validators at block generation, fork choice is another protection mechanism. An attacker would need to be able to modify the fork choice rule somehow to be effective.

Deposit contract
The contract that will hold balances for the beacon chain. It will exist on the Ethereum 1.0 network. The ETH in this contract will not be able to be used on the 1.0 network once it is deposited. The minimum deposit required to become a validator is 32 ETH. As with most proof-of-stake systems, there will be some kind of financial reward for acting as a validator, the calculation of which is not yet set.

Honest validator framework
A set of standards validators are expected to abide by in order to help secure the Ethereum 2.0 network. These include having an available private key for signing

proposed blocks and for miscellaneous voting (the signing key, stored in a hot wallet) and a separate private key for withdrawing funds generated by being an active validator, which should be securely stored offline (the withdrawal key). The corresponding public keys are registered as part of the transaction with the validator deposit contract.

 It may take years for the transition from Ethereum 1.0 to 2.0 to be completed. For example, the execution environment for dapps is not part of the initial phase of Ethereum 2.0, so mainnet Ethereum 1.0 will remain an active developer platform for years to come.

Sharding in the network will result in an increase in gas costs and will remove the ability for atomic transactions, or the ability to make transactions all at one. This will increase the likelihood of Ethereum 2.0 becoming more of a software platform than a financial one used by traders.

Privacy

Privacy is expected to be one of the biggest growth areas for blockchain technology in the coming years. Developers and other stakeholders are realizing the need to *not* publicly transmit all data about transactions. Here are a few privacy-related projects that are in the works:

Secret Network
> Originally an MIT-based project called Enigma, Secret Network is a type of peer-to-peer network enabling computation of data in private. A blockchain manages access control and identities, with the ERC-20 SCRT token used to compensate "secret nodes" for providing computing power to the network. This allows users to share data while keeping it private using cryptography, removing the need for a third party to store information for users (which can be susceptible to breaches).

Schnorr
> A form of digital signature, the Schnorr algorithm enables simple, efficient, and short signatures. This will allow for several signatures in a transaction to be combined into one, which can obscure some data. For example, multisignature transactions can look the same as regular transactions. It also enables a cryptographic technique called "tweaking," which makes it possible to use Taproot (discussed next). Bitcoin is expected to soft fork in order to enable Schnorr signatures.

Taproot
> One of the interesting things that can be done with Schnorr key pairs is to use the Taproot scheme for signing transaction scripts. Taproot utilizes Merkelized

Abstract Syntax Trees (MAST), a data structure that allows some script information to remain obscured. This is done with a Merkle tree that encodes several different paths of script logic flow.

Interoperability

Interoperability is considered an important precursor to blockchain's mass adoption. There are numerous projects working on this, including Polkadot and Cosmos. The goal is to enable smooth information sharing, easier execution of smart contracts, and a more user-friendly experience between different blockchains.

Tokenize Everything

The original intention of this book was to clear up some of the misinformation and many misconceptions that surround the blockchain industry. But as we began writing, we realized just how fast the industry is changing, making it very difficult for *anyone* to keep up with all the innovations—including us.

This book was as much a process of learning for us as for you. Its scope would have been much narrower if we had only written about what we knew when we started. That's why we reached out to innovators in the blockchain industry—we needed to rely on the community's expertise.

Using our newfound knowledge, we wanted to end with an example that solves a problem we have. Our first thought was to tokenize every book, so that you knew it was an authentic O'Reilly book—but we realized that storing the serial number of each copy of *Mastering Blockchain* on the Ethereum blockchain would be extremely expensive. (The cost of storing data on Ethereum is high due to the blockchain's scaling bottleneck, which this chapter already covered.)

So instead, we decided to tokenize 50 limited edition copies. The only way someone can own one of these tokenized copies is by signing an Ethereum transaction with one of 50 private keys that are associated with each copy.

Summary

Blockchain lets developers build systems that distribute and decentralize trust by shifting agreements from paper to code. Someday, there likely will be millions of blockchains in operation, representing many different types of data structures.

Now it's *your* turn to solve a real-world problem using blockchain.

Index

A

ABI (application binary interface), 96
addresses
   Bitcoin, 24
      associating with an identity, 190
      generating with public/private keys, 24
      in UTXO transaction model, 25
   Ethereum
      for smart contracts, 96
   stealth addresses on Monero, 236
   whitelisting, 137
adjustable blocksize cap (Bitcoin), 66
adoption of blockchain, 231
airdrops, disbursement of cryptocurrencies via, 107
airgapped computers, 136
altchains, 61
altcoins, 61, 67-70
   earlier, sample of, 67
   Litecoin, 68
   other, 69
Amazon Quantum Ledger, 220
analysis, 139-143
   analytics services for cryptocurrency block-chains, 56
   fundamental cryptocurrency analysis, 140-142
      tools for, 141
      Tullip Mania or the internet, 140
   technical cryptocurrency analysis, 142-143
      looking for Bart pattern, 143
Anti-Money Laundering (AML) rules, 147, 197
   implementation in Novi wallet, 228
APIs

exchange APIs and trading bots, 148-153
   characteristics of high-quality API, 149
   Coinbase Pro and Kraken APIs, 149
   important API calls, 151
   market aggregators, 153
   open source trading tech, 151
   rate limiting, 152
   REST versus WebSocket, 152
   testing in a sandbox, 152
application binary interface (ABI), 96
application-based blockchain transactions, 86
application-specific integrated circuits (ASICs), 42
   ASIC-resistant Scrypt algorithm, 68
   deterring use for mining, 67
   X11 ASIC-resistant proof-of-work, 71
arbitrage, 131, 135, 144-146
   basic, 144
   basic mistakes in, 148
   exchange risk, 148
   involving fiat currency, banking risk, 147
   regulatory, 196-199
   timing and managing float, 144
      float configuration 1, 145
      float configuration 2, 145
      float configuration 3, 146
   triangular, 144
arbitrageurs, 135
assets, real-wold
   B-Money digital currency price based on, 9
   backing digital blockchain cryptocurrencies, 82
   enabling representation on Bitcoin, 80

problems when represented on blockchain, 81

asymmetric cryptography, 24
  (see also public/private key cryptography)

auditors, third-party, for smart contracts, 106

authentication issues in cryptocurrency losses, 39-41

autoliquidation, 134

Avalanche consensus mechanism, 239

Azure, Blockchain as a Service, 220

B

B-Money, 9

BaaS (Blockchain as a Service), 220

Back, Adam, 8

Bahamas, regulatory arbitrage, 198

banking risk, 147

banking, blockchain implementations, 221-223
  Banque de France, 221
  China, 222
  JPMorgan, 223
  permissioned ledger uses of blockchain, 223
  Royal Mint, 221
  US Federal Reserve, 222

Banque de France, 221

Bart pattern, 143

basic arbitrage, 144

Basic Attention Token (BAT), 186

Basis, 200

beacon chain, 245

Beam, 237

bidirectional payment channels, 75

BIP39 for generating wallet seeds, 41

bit gold, 9

Bitcoin, 10-17
  Bitcoin Cash fork, 62-66
  block times, 146
  bringing the network to life, 17-21
    achieving consensus, 18-20
    adoption, 21
    compelling components, 17
    early security vulnerability, 20
  evolution of, 79
  Liquid Network federated sidechain, 238
  mining difficulty, history of, 43
  Omni Layer protocol on top of, 82
  predecessors, 7-10
  proof-of-work consensus, problems with, 72
  Satoshi Nakamoto's whitepaper, 11

scalability issues, solving with Lightning, 240

SHA-256 hash algorithm, 33

storing data in chain of blocks, 13

timestamp system to verify transactions, 13

transaction life cycle, 50

2008 financial crisis, 10

why you can't cheat at, 16

bitcoin, 14
  evolution of its price, 123
  futures, 134
  halving, 132
    impact on market, 132

Bitcoin Cash (BCH), 62-65

Bitcoin Improvement Proposals (BIPs), 59, 108

Bitcoin Satoshi's Vision (SV), 66

"Bitcoin: A Peer-to-Peer Electronic Cash System", 11

Bitfinex, 205

BitGo, 56

BitLicense, 194

BitPay, 55

Bitstamp, 55

blind signature technology, 7

block explorers, 138

block hashes, 14, 34-36
  valid, criteria for on Bitcoin, 45

block height, 14

block propagators (EOS), 234

block reward, 31

Block.One, 196

blockchain explorers, 56

Blockchain.com, 56, 139, 190

blockchains
  creating new platforms for the web, 186
  future of, 231-247
    blockchains to watch, 233-237
    interoperability, 247
    privacy, 246
    similarities to internet, 233
    tokenizing everything, 247
  illegal uses of, 189
  information on the industry, 57
  oracles interacting with, 159
  origins of, 1-22
    Bitcoin experiment, 10-17
    Bitcoin predecessors, 7-10
    bringing Bitcoin network to life, 17-21

distributed versus centralized versus decentralized, 2-7
electronic systems and trust, 1
other
 banking implementations, 221-223
 Blockchain as a Service (BaaS), 220
 databases and ledgers, 213
 decentralization versus centralization, 214
 enterprise implementations, 215-220
 Ethereum-based privacy implementations, 215
 key properties of distributed verifiable ledgers, 214
 Libra, 226-230
 permissioned ledger uses, 223-226
 use cases, 211
scaling, 73-76
tokens, questioning necessity for, 106
2.0 chains, 70
blocks
 adjustable blocksize cap on Bitcoin SV, 66
 attributes of each Bitcoin block, 14
 Bitcoin, anatomy of, 34
 blocksize on Bitcoin SV fork, 66
 discovery of, 45
 generation in proof-of-stake networks, 52
 generation of, through mining, 43
 Libra blockchain, 229
 storing data in chain of blocks, 13
 valid, contents of on Bitcoin, 48
Blockstack, 187
Blockstream
 c-lightning, 240
 Liquid technology, 239
Bloomberg TV BTC stolen, 206
Brave browser, 186
broadcasting transactions (on Bitcoin), 50
brokerages, 55
brute force and dictionary attacks on passwords, 184
brute force attacks on private keys, 32
BTCPay Server, 55
burning, 159
business, blockchain uses for, 211
 (see also enterprise blockchains)
 questions to ask, 212
Byzantine agreement, 53
Byzantine fault-tolerant agreement, 72

HotStuff algorithm, 227

C
Cardano, 234
Casper algorithm (proof-of-stake), 245
CCXT (CryptoCurrency eXchange Trading Library), 151
cell phone porting attacks, 39
central bank digital currencies (CBDCs), 224
centralization
 caused by proof-of-work consensus on Bitcoin, 72
 decentralization versus, 214
 distributed versus centralized versus decentralized systems, 2-7
 Libra's centralization challenge, 228
centralized exchanges, 119, 125, 129
 decentralized exchanges versus, 164-173
 custody and counterparty risk, 168
 exchange rate, 172
 infrastructure, 164
 Know Your Customer (KYC) rules, 172
 scalability, 173
 token listing, 167
 infrastructure differences from decentralized exchanges, 119
CFTC (Commodity Futures Trading Commission), 193
Chainalysis, 57
channels (Lightning), 239
Chaum, David, 7
Chia, 53
Chicago Mercantile Exchange (CME), partnership with Royal Mint, 221
China, central bank cryptocurrency, 222
Coburn, Zachary, 195
Coin ATM Radar website, 125
Coinbase, 36, 56
Coinbase Pro, 55
 API example, BTC/USD ticker call, 149
 arbitrage trading on, 144-146
 custody solutions, robust, 136
 example order book, 128
coinbase transaction, 14, 31
 Bitcoin Genesis block, 18
Coincheck, 206
CoinDesk, 57
coins, 7
Coinye, 69

cold storage wallets, 136
cold wallets, 37
collisions, cryptographic hashes and, 33
colored coins, 70, 80
Commodity Exchange Act (CEA), 131
Commodity Futures Trading Commission
    (CFTC), 193
conferences on blockchain industry, 57
confidential assets, 239
confirmations, 50
confirmed transactions, 26
    confirmed by miner, 50
    confirmed by network on Bitcoin, 50
consensus, 44-54
    Avalanche mechanism, 239
    in Bitcoin network, 18-20
    Corda, 219
    in decentralized systems, 4
    Libra mechanism for, 227, 228
    other concepts for, 53
    proof-of-stake, 51-53
    proof-of-work, 44-51
        block discovery, 45
        confirmations by miners of block to
            include in blockchain, 50
        mining process on Bitcoin, 47
        transaction life cycle, 49
    SCP protocol, 73
    XRP Consensus Protocol, 72
ConsenSys, 89
    Truffle Suite tools for smart contracts, 92
contentious hard forks, 61-65
    replay attacks vulnerability, 64
Corda, 216-219
    consensus, 219
    how it works, 216
    ledger, 218
    network, 217
    programming language, 219
Counterparty blockchain, 70
counterparty risk, 135
    on centralized versus decentralized
        exchanges, 168
    reduced, on decentralized exchanges, 120
cross-shard communication complexity, 76
crypto laundering, 190-192
    how funds are laundered, 191
cryptocurrencies, 23-57

additional, Mastercoin introducing notion
    of, 80
backing DAI multi-collateral token, 160
and blockchain, leading to new platforms
    for the web, 186
blockchain systems and unit of account, 14
consensus, 44-54
    other concepts for, 53
    proof-of-stake, 51-53
    proof-of-work, 44-51
cryptographic hashes, 33-36
custody, 36-39
ICOs or fundraising for projects, 87
illegal uses of, 189
methods of buying and selling, 124
mining, 41-44
privacy-focused, 71
public and private keys in systems, 24-25
regulatory bodies in the US, 193
security, 39-41
stablecoins based on, 199-200
stakeholders in ecosystem, 54-57
    analytics services, 56
    brokerages, 55
    custody solutions, 56
    exchanges, 55
    information services, 57
theft from owners
    exchange hacks, 203-206
    other hacks, 206-209
transactions in, 26-32
UTXO model for Bitcoin transactions,
    25-26
cryptocurrency ATMs, 124
CryptoCurrency eXchange Trading Library
    (CCXT), 151
cryptography
    Bitcoin's use on transactions, 13
    cryptographic hashes, 33-36
    ECDSA encryption, signing and verifying
        transactions, 30
    enabling proof-of-work on Hashcash, 8
    public/private key, Bitcoin's use of, 19-20
    use by DigiCash, 7
CryptoKitties, 112-114
    causing scaling problems on Ethereum, 91
    digital cats as nonfungible tokens, 105
CryptoLocker and ransomware, 207
CryptoNote protocol, 71

currencies, exchanges for, 55
  (see also exchanges)
custodial wallets, 36
  (see also wallets)
custody, 36-39
  counterparty risk with exchanges, 135, 168
  crypto custody solutions, 56
custody providers, 136
cyberbucks, 7

D

DAGs (directed acyclic graphs), 238
DAI stablecoin, 160
  savings rates for, 163
Dai, Wei, 9
DAML, 219
DAOs (decentralized autonomous organizations), 87-88, 159
  The DAO project on Ethereum, 201
dapps (see decentralized applications)
Dash, 71
database management systems (DBMSs), 213
databases
  backend/database differences between centralized exchanges and Uniswap, 166
  and ledgers, 213
decentralization
  versus centralization, 214
  decentralizing the web, 186
  distributed versus centralized versus decentralized systems, 2-7
decentralized applications (dapps), 86, 90-91
  building decentralized web frameworks, 187
  challenges in developing, 91
  Corda, 219
  running on top of a blockchain, 91
  use cases, 90
decentralized autonomous organizations (DAOs), 87-88, 159
  The DAO project on Ethereum, 201
decentralized exchange contracts, 119-121
decentralized exchanges, 125, 164-173
  versus centralized exchanges, 164-173
    custody and counterparty risk, 168
    exchange rate, 172
    infrastructure, 164
    Know Your Customer (KYC) rules, 172
    scalability, 173
    token listing, 167

decentralized finance (DeFi), 155-164
  flash loans, 173-182
    creating the flash loan smart contract, 174-176
    deploying the contract, 176
    executing a loan, 177-180
    Fulcrum attack, 180
  important definitions, 158
  privacy and information security, 182-186
    ring signatures, 186
    Zcash, 186
    zero-knowledge proof, 183
    zk-SNARKs, 185
  redistribution of trust, 155-157
    identity and dangers of hacking, 155
    naming services, 157
  services, 163-164
    derivatives, 163
    lending, 163
    savings, 163
  stablecoins, 160-162
  traditional versus decentralized financial system, 158
DeFI Pulse website, 163
delegated proof-of-stake, 54
deposit contracts, 245
depth charts, 129
  sell wall on, 132
derivatives, 133
  in decentralized finance, 163
  derivatives exchanges, 125
desktop wallets, 38
DEXes (see decentralized exchanges; exchanges)
dictionary attacks on passwords, 184
difficulty of discovering valid block hash, 45
DigiCash, 7
digital bonds, 223
digital money, 7
  (see also cryptocurrencies)
  creation of, in B-Money, 9
  use of hashing to limit double spend, 8
digital signatures
  multisignature system, Hash Time Locked Contracts, 75
  Schnorr algorithm, 246
  signing transactions, 30
Digix, 199
directed acyclic graphs (DAGs), 238

disintermediation, 156
distributed ledger technology (DLT), 213
distributed systems, 90
    Bitcoin, 17
    distributed versus centralized versus decentralized systems, 2-7
Dogecoin, 69
Domain Name System (DNS), decentralized version of, 67
dot-com crash, 140
double spend problem, 8
    in Satoshi Nakamoto's whitepaper, 12
dumping of a cryptocurrency, 131

E

E-gold, 8
EEA (Enterprise Ethereum Alliance), 89
Elements open source project, 239
Elliptic Curve Digital Signature Algorithm (ECDSA) encrytion
    secp256k1 function, 25
    signing and validating transactions with, 30
Elliptic Curve Digital Signature Algorithm (ECDSA) secp256k1 function, 19
Enigma, 196, 246
enterprise blockchains, 215-220
    Corda, 216-219
    DAML, 219
    Hyperledger platform, 216
    zero-knowledge proofs used in, 185
Enterprise Ethereum Alliance (EEA), 89
EOS, 233
    origins of, 104
ERC-20 token standard, 105, 108-112
    creating your own custom token, 112
    DeFi's reliance on Ethereum and ERC-20 assets, 158
    events supported by ERC-20 compliant smart contracts, 109
    example of ERC-20 smart contract, 109-112
    listing of tokens on Uniswap, 168
    methods, 108
    push and pull transactions to move tokens, 114
    wrapped tokens outside of Ethereum ecosystem, 159
ERC-721 token standard, 105, 112-114
ether, 85
    denominations of, 100

EtherDelta redirection, 206
Ethereum, 79-101
    block times, 146
    cost of storing data on, 247
    decentralized applications (dapps), 90-91
    decentralized exchange, IDEX, 119
    DeFi's reliance on Ethereum and ERC-20 assets, 158
    deploying and executing smart contracts, 91-101
        Ethereum Virtual Machine (EVM), 92-99
    Ethereum Classic fork, 77
    Etherscan analytics service, 56
    improving Bitcoin's limited functionality, 79-84
    improving Bitcoin's lmited functionality
        colored coins and tokens, 80
        Mastercoin and smart contracts, 80
        Omni Layer, 80-84
    Keccak-256 hash algorithm, 33
    maximum transaction rate, 173
    origins of, 103
    privacy implementations based on, 215
    scaling in Ethereum 2.0, 245-246
    scaling solutions, 76
    taking Mastercoin to the next level, 84-89
        decentralized autonomous organizations, 87-88
        ether and gas, 85
        key organizations in ecosystem, 88
        use cases, ICOs, 86
    tokenize everything via ICOs, 103
    tokens on, 105-108
        airdrops and, 107
        deciding whether a token is necessary, 106
        different token types, 107, 107
        many different token types, 106
Ethereum Classic (ETC), 87
Ethereum Foundation, 88
Ethereum Improvement Proposals (EIPs), 108
Ethereum Naming Service, 157
Ethereum Requests for Comment (ERCs), 108-116
    ERC-1155, 116
    ERC-20, 108
    ERC-721, 112-114
    ERC-777, 114

viewing all ERC standards online, 121
Ethereum Virtual Machine (EVM), 92-99
   authoring a smart contract, 92
   deploying a smart contract, 93-96
   executing a smart contract, 98
   interacting with a smart contract, 96
   reading a smart contract, 97
   writing a smart contract, 98
Etherscan.io, 139
exchange traded funds (ETFs), 134
exchange traded notes (ETNs), 134
exchanges, 55, 124, 125-126
   APIs and trading bots, 148-153
   as custodial wallets, 36
   basic types of, 125
   Bitcoin addresses, 191
   custody over customer funds, 135
   custody setup, how it might work, 136
   decentralized, 164
   decentralized exchange contracts, 119-121
   decentralized exchange on Omni Layer, 82
   decentralized versus centralized, 164-173
   hacking attacks on, 203-206
      Mt. Gox, 203-205
   jurisdiction over cryptocurrency exchanges,
      130
   order types in cryptocurrency exchanges,
      126
   risks of, in cryptocurrency trading, 148
   types of cryptocurrency exchanges, 129
externally owned account (EOA) wallets, 116

F

Fabric (Hyperledger), 216
Facebook
   Libra Association, 226
   Novi wallet, 228
false stake attacks, 53
faucets (Ethereum testnets), 93
Federal Reserve (see US Federal Reserve)
federated sidechains, 238
fiat currencies, 2
   blockchain-based assets pegged to, 160
   mint-based model, 12
file storage in web applications, 187
Financial Action Task Force (FATF), Travel
   Rule, 194
Financial Crimes Enforcement Network (Fin-
   CEN), 192

financial crisis of 2008, 2, 10
financial transactions, reliance on trust, 2
flash loans, 173-182
   creating a smart contract for, 174-176
   deploying the smart contract, 176
   executing, 177-180
float
   configuration 1, 145
   configuration 2, 145
   configuration 3, 146
   timing and managing, 144
Force, Carl, 195
forks, 61-65, 67
   (see also altcoins)
   contentious hard forks, 62-65
      fork of Bitcoin Cash into Bitcoin SV, 66
      replay attacks vulnerability, 64
   different types of, 61
   Ethereum Classic, 77, 87
   fork choice rule in Ethereum 2.0, 245
   other Ethereum forks, 88
   in proof-of-stake networks, 53
fraud risk as seen by banking audits, 147
Fulcrum attack, 180
full nodes (Libra), 228
funding amount, 75
funding transactions, 241
fungible tokens, 105
   ERC-20 standard for, 108
   ERC-777 proposed standard for, 114
futures, 134

G

gambling, on Web 3.0, 187
gaming
   permissioned ledger uses of blockchain, 224
   tracking virtual goods in games, 116
Garza, Homero Joshua, 196
gas, 86
   ETH Gas Station, 100
   list of gas prices by opcode, 99
GAW Miners, 196
GeistGeld, 67
Gemini, arbitrage trading on, 144-151
   API example, BTC/USD ticker call, 150
Genesis block (Bitcoin), 18
Gitcoin, 187
Gnosis, 104

government-backed currencies (see fiat currencies)
graphics processing units (GPUs), 42
Grin, 237

H
halting problem, 86
hard forks, 61
hardware wallets, 37, 156
hash algorithms, 44
hash power, 45, 82
hash rates, 44
Hashcash, 8
hashes, 8, 33-36
    Bitcoin hash function, double SHA-256, 28
    block, 14, 34-36
    of information generated by transactions in
        Bitcoin, 13
    MD5 password hashes, 183
    Merkle root, 28-30
    in proof-of-work cryptocurrency mining, 44
    public key hash on Bitcoin, 25
    in Satoshi Nakamoto's whitepaper, 12
health care, permissioned ledger implementations of blockchain, 225
height number (block), 14
hex value arguments to smart contract calls,
170
Honest validator framework, 245
Hong Kong, regulatory arbitrage, 197
hot or cold storage wallets, 136
hot wallets, 37
HotStuff algorithm, 227
Hyperledger, 216

I
IBM
    IoT interaction by Watson and data storage
        in Blockchain Platform, 225
    toolset offering support for Hyperledger
        Fabric, 221
identify
    verification of, 39
identity
    and dangers of hacking, 155
    associating with Bitcoin addresses, 190
    identification services, 157
IDEX decentralized exchange, 119
illiquidity, signs of, 138

infinite recursion, 87
information on blockchain industry, 57
Infura, 101
initial coin offerings (ICOs), 80, 103, 200-203
    as example of regulatory arbitrage, 201
    DAOs and, 87
    Ethereum, 103
    founder intentions, 201
    funds collected into multisignature wallets,
        117
    illegal activities in, 195
    legal, regulatory, and other problems with,
        104
    Mastercoin, 103
    motivations for founders versus venture-
        funding startups, 203
    other terms for, 201
    spectrum of ICO viability, 201
    token economics, 202
    use of Ethereum platform, 86
    whitepaper, 202
intermediary trust, 1
internet
    data exchange protocols, evolution of, 232
    dot-com crash, 140
    evolution of, 1
Internet of Things (IoT), permissioned ledger
    implementations of blockchain, 225
interoperability between different blockchains,
247
Interplanetary File System (IPFS), 187
issuance trust, 1
IT systems, permissioned ledger uses, 223
Ixcoin, 67

J
Java, 219
JPMorgan, 223
    interbank payments using permissioned
        ledger, 226
jurisdiction over cryptocurrency exchanges,
130

K
Keccak-256 hash algorithm, 33
Know Your Customer (KYC) rules, 147, 161
    on centralized and decentralized exchanges,
        172
    crypto laundering and, 192

implementation in Novi wallet, 228
in Singapore, 197
stablecoins requiring/not requiring, 162

L

LBFT consensus protocol, 228
Ledger wallet, 156
ledgers, 14, 213
    Corda, 218
    distributed verifiable, key properties of, 214
    Hyperledger Fabric technology, 216
    permissioned ledger uses of blockchain, 223-226
    Ripple, 72
legal industry, permissioned ledger uses, 224
legal requirements, cryptocurrency and blockchain technology skirting the laws, 194
lending services (DeFi), 163
less than 5% rule, 137
Libra, 226-230
    borrowing from existing blockchains, 227
    centralization challenges, 228
    how the Libra protocol works, 228-230
        blocks, 229
        transactions, 230
    Libra Association, 226
    Novi wallet and other third-party wallets, 228
Lightning, 75, 239
    funding transactions, 241
    nodes and wallets, 243
    off-chain transactions, 242
    solving scalability issues on Blockchain, 240
Liquid multisignature wallet, 239
liquidity, 135
    or depth in a market, 143
Litecoin, 68
longest chain rule, 49
lottery-based consensus, 54

M

MaidSafe, 81
    ICO for, 87
Maker project's DAI, 160
    savings rates for DAI, 163
Malta, regulatory arbitrage, 196
man in the middle attacks, 184
margin/leveraged products, 134

market capitalization, low, cryptocurrencies with, 131
market depth
    considerations in cryptocurrency trading, 148
    lacking in cryptocurrency market, 134
market infrastructure, 123-153
    analysis, 139-143
        fundamental cryptocurrency analysis, 140-142
        technical cryptocurrency analysis, 142-143
    arbitrage trading, 144-146
    cryptocurrency market structure, 134-139
        aribtrage, 135
        counterparty risk, 135
        market data, 138-139
    depth charts, 129
    derivatives, 133
    exchange APIs and trading bots, 148-153
        market aggregators, 153
        open source trading tech, 151
        rate limiting, 152
        REST versus WebSocket APIs, 152
        testing trading bot in sandbox, 152
    exchanges, 125-126
    order books, 126
    regulatory challenges, 146-148
    slippage in cryptocurrency trading, 128
    wash trading, 131
    ways to buy and sell cryptocurrency, 124
    whales, 131
market size, 126
Mastercoin, 80, 103
    Ethereum and, 84
    raising cryptocurrency funds to launch a project, 87
Meetup.com, 57
mempool, unconfirmed transactions on Bitcoin, 50
Merkelized Abstract Syntax Trees (MAST), 246
Merkle roots, 14, 28-30
    in block hashes, 34
Merkle trees, 29
MetaMask wallet, 89, 156
    using in writing smart contracts, 98
Middleton, Reggie, 195
Mimblewimble, 237
mining, 41-44, 124

Bitcoin, problems with, 72
block generation, 43
GAW Miners, 196
impacts on market data, 129
incentives for, 42
miners discovering new block at same time, 48
process on Bitcoin for block discovery, 47
Scrypt, 67
transactions confirmed by miner on Bitcoin, 50
mint-based currency model, 12
minting, 159
MKR token, 161
mobile wallets, 38
Moesif's binary encoder/decoder, 170
Monero, 71, 186, 191, 234
how it works, 234-236
money laundering, 147
(see also Anti-Money Laundering (AML) rules)
evolution of crypto laundering, 190-192
Money Services Business (MSB) standards, 194
MoneyGram, 73
Mt. Gox exchange, 138
hacking attacks on, 203-205
multisignature wallet contracts, 116-119

N

Namecoin, 67
naming services, 157
network hash rate, 45
networks
centralized versus decentralized versus distributed design, 3
Corda, 217
nodes having visibility into transactions, 218
DAG design, 238
Libra's centralization challenge, 228
transactions confirmed by network on Bitcoin, 50
New York Department of Financial Services (NYDFS), 194
NiceHash, 206
Nightfall blockchain, 215
nodes, 3
in Avalance consensus mechanism, 239
Libra, validator and full nodes, 228

Lightning, 244
in proof-of-stake networks, 52
nonces, 48
in block discovery on Bitcoin, 48
running out of nonce space or overflow, 48
in Satoshi Nakamoto's whitepaper, 12
noncustodial wallets, 37
(see also wallets)
nonfungible tokens, 105
ERC-721 standard for, 112
Nothing-at-Stake problem, 53
Novi wallet, 228
NuBits, 199
NXT blockchain, 70

O

oligarchical model dominating the web, 186
Omni Core, 81
limitations of, 91
Omni Layer, 80-84
adding custom logical operations to Bitcoin, 82-84
how it works, 82
limitations of, 91
technical stack, overview of, 81
Tether project built on, 81
opcodes, 99
Open Systems Interconnection (OSI) model, 232
operating system platform (EOS), 233
operators, 115, 116
Optimistic Rollups, 76, 244
options, 133
OP_RETURN field, 83
translation of metadata in, 84
Oracle, Blockchain Platform, 220
oracles, 159
manipulation in Fulcrum attack, 180
order books, 126
thin, slippages and, 128
over-the-counter (OTC) market, 128

P

paper wallets, 37
Parity, 89
Parity hack (2017), 89
participants, 214
passwords
security vulnerabilities, 183

Thinbus Secure Remote Password protocol, 184
pay-to-play, 141
payment channels, 241
    node dropping or losing connection to, 244
    opening by sending funding transaction, 242
    withdrawing funds from, 243
payment systems
    Libra, 227
    permissioned ledger uses of blockchain, 226
    physical cash versus digital, 2
Permacoin, 53
permissioned ledger uses of blockchain, 223-226
    banking, 223
    central bank digital currencies, 224
    gaming, 224
    health care, 225
    Internet of Things, 225
    IT systems, 223
    payments systems, 226
permissioned ledgers, 213
permissionless ledgers, 213
person-to-person trading of cryptocurrency, 124
phishing attacks, 39
Plasma implementation of sidechains, 76
Ponzi schemes in cryptocurrency, 195
PotCoin, 70
precompilation of zk-SNARKs, 185
premining
    issues with, 68
    premined altcoin, Ixcoin, 67
prices (gas), 100
Primecoin, 68
privacy
    and censorship resistance with dapps, 90
    Ethereum-based privacy implementations, 215
    future developments in blockchains, 246
    information security in decentralizing finance and the web, 182-186
        ring signatures, 186
        Zcash, 186
        zero-knowledge proof, 183
        zk-SNARKs, 185
    insufficient anonymity on Bitcoin, 191

paired with scalability, Mimblewimble blockchain protocol, 237
privacy-focused blockchains, 183
    Monero, 234-236
    Zcash, 186
privacy-focused cryptocurrencies, 71
    Dash, 71
    Monero, 71
    Zcash, 71
private blockchain networks, 183
private blockchains, 89
private keys, 19
    (see also public/private key cryptography)
products/services, buying or selling, 124
proof-of-history, 54
proof-of-stake, 51-53
    Byzantine fault-tolerant algorithm, Hot-Stuff, 227
    Casper algorithm in Ethereum 2.0, 245
proof-of-stake velocity, 70
proof-of-storage, 53
proof-of-work, 43, 44-51
    bit gold's client puzzle function type, 9
    block discovery, 45
    confirmations by miners of blocks to include in blockchain, 50
    criticisms of, 52, 72
    CryptoNote protocol, 71
    Ethereum's Ethash protocol, 85
    longest chain rule, 49
    mining process for block discovery on Bitcoin, 47
    mining process on Bitcoin, 47
    in Satoshi Nakamoto's whitepaper, 12
    transaction life cycle, 49
    use by B-Money, 9
    use by Hashcash, 8
    X11 ASIC-resistant, 71
protocols, 1
pseudonimity, KYC rules and, 162
public keys, 19
    (see also public/private key cryptography)
public/private key cryptography
    Bitcoin's use of, 19
    examples of public and private keys, 157
    generating keys, 19
    private key storage for digital wallets, 92
    private keys for wallets, 157

public and private keys in cryptocurrency systems, 24-25
unauthorized access to private key, 32
use in controlling access to personal information, 156
pull transactions, 31, 114
push transactions, 31, 114

Q

Quantum Ledger Database (QLDB), 220
Quorum blockchain, 215, 223

R

ransomware, CryptoLocker and, 207
rate limiting, 148, 152
real estate transactions, using tokens on a blockchain, 105
recovery seed, 40
recursive call vulnerability, 87
regulation
    of cryptocurrency exchanges, 130
    FATF and the Travel Rule, 194
    FinCEN guidance and beginnings of, 192-194
    regulatory challenges in cryptocurrency market, 146-148
    regulatory issues with ICOs, 104
regulatory arbitrage, 196-199
    ICOs as example of, 201
relational databases, 213
replay attacks, 64
    protecting against, on Ethereum and Ethereum Classic, 77
replication systems, 213
REST APIs
    Ethereum network, 101
    WebSocket versus, 152
ring confidential transactions, 234, 236
ring signatures, 71, 186, 234
    hiding public address of sender on Monero, 235
Ripple, 53, 72
    block times, 146
Robinhood mobile app, 55
Rollups, Zero Knowledge (ZK) and Optimistic, 76, 244
Royal Mint, 221

S

Santander, blockchain-issued bonds, 223
SAP, Blockchain as a Service, 221
satoshi, 100
Satoshi Nakamoto
    bitcoin address related to, 191
    efforts to establish identity of, 16
    identity, guesses at, 198
    Satoshi's Vision group (Bitcoin SV), 66
    whitepaper, 11
savings services (DeFi), 163
scalability
    centralized versus decentralized exchanges, 173
    discontent over Bitcoin network's scaling, 65
    EOS solution to blockchain issues, 104
    privacy paired with, Mimblewimble blockchain potocol, 237
Scalable Transparent ARguments of Knowledge (STARKs), 238
scaling blockchains, 73-76, 237-246
    Avalanche consensus mechanism, 239
    DAG network design, 238
    Ethereum, 245-246
    Lightning solution, 75, 239-244
    Liquid multisignature wallet, 239
    other altchain solutions, 76
    SegWit, 74
    sharding, 238
    sidechains, 238
    STARKs, 238
Schnorr algorithm, 246
Scott, Mark, 196
SCP consensus protocol, 73
scripted money, 79
Scrypt mining, 67, 68
Secret Network, 246
securities
    tokens proposed in ICOs, 107
    unregistered securities offerings, 195
Securities and Exchange Commission (SEC), 193
security
    Bitcoin transaction security, 31
    custody infrastructure for exchanges, 135
    detection of blockchain tampering with Merkle roots, 30
    early vulnerability on Bitcoin, 20

exchanges taking care of private keys, 137

flash loans exploiting vulnerabilities in DeFi platforms, 180

fundamentals for cryptocurrencies, 39-41

identity and dangers of hacking, 155

information security in decentralizing finance and the web, 183

Lightning Network vulnerabilities, 76

proof-of-stake consensus algorithm, criticisms of, 53

recursive call vulnerability, 87

replay attacks vulnerability, 64, 77

sharding, vulnerabilities with, 76

theft of cryptocurrencies in exchange hacks, 203-206

theft of cryptocurrencies in other hacks, 206-209

transaction malleability vulnerability, 244

security token offerings (STOs), 108

security tokens, 202

seeds (recovery), 40
  storage of, 92

SegWit (Segregated Witness), 74, 244

self-sovereign identity, 156

SHA-256 hash algorithm, 13, 33

SHA256 and RIPEMD160 functions, 19

shadow market for disinformation, 141

sharding, 76, 238
  in Ethereum 2.0, 245

Shavers, Trendon, 195

Shrem, Charlie, 195

sidechains, 76, 238
  Liquid technology and, 239
  Optimistic Rollups and, 244

Silk Road, 189
  criminal investigation tracking bitcoin address to operator, 191
  provision of bitcoin to users without KYC/AML, 195

SIM swapping, 207-209

Singapore, regulatory arbitrage, 197

single-shard takeover attacks, 76

slashing algorithms, 53

slippage, 128

smart contracts, 80
  DAML language for distributed applications, 219
  for decentralized exchanges, 119, 168

deploying and executing in Ethereum, 91-101
  authoring a smart contract, 92
  deployment, 93-96
  Ethereum Virtual Machine (EVM), 92
  executing a smart contract, 98
  gas and pricing, 99
  interacting with a smart contract, 96
  programmatically interacting with Ethereum, 101
  reading a smart contract, 97
  writing a smart contract, 98

deployment for dapps, 91

EOS platform, 233

ERC-20 compliant
  events supported by, 109
  example of, 109-112
  methods implemented, 108

ERC-compliant, library of, 121

flash loans
  creating the contract, 174-176
  deploying the contract, 176
  manipulation of oracles in Fulcrum attack, 180
  steps in process, 173

Libra support for, 227

Omni Layer providing, 81

publicly viewable record of method call to Uniswap smart contract, 169-172

sending tokens to via push and pull transactions, 114

third-party auditors of, 106

Uniswap contract viewable on Ethereum, 167

social media, campaigns to influence cryptocurrencies, 142

soft forks, 61

software development, changes from use of cryptcurrency and blockchain, 187

software forks, 61

software wallets, 156

Solidcoin, 67

Solidity language, 92

South Korean exchanges, 147

speculation in cryptocurrency, 123, 141

spoofing, 131

spot exchanges, 125

Square's Cash App, 55

stablecoins, 160-162

DAI, 160
JPC Coin, 223
JPM Coin, 226
Know Your Customer rules and pseudo-
    nymity, 162
    problems with, 199-200
        Basis, 200
        Digix, 199
        NuBits, 199
        Tether (USDT), 200
    TrueUSD, 162
    USDC, 161
    use by unregulated exchanges, 131
stakeholders in cryptocurrency ecosystem,
    54-57
    analytics services, 56
    brokerages, 55
    custody solutions, 56
    exchanges, 55
    information services, 57
STARKs, 238
state channels, 76
stealth addresses (Monero), 234, 236
Stellar, 53, 73
STOs (security token offerings), 108
Synthetix DeFi platform for derivative assets,
    164
Szabo, Nick, 9

T
Taproot, 246
target value in block discovery, 45
TCP/IP, 232
Tenebrix, 67
testing
    Ethereum testnets, 91, 92
    sandbox environment for exchange APIs,
        152
Tether, 81, 200
    transaction in Omniexplorer, 83
Thinbus Secure Remote Password (SRP) proto-
    col, 184
thinly traded market, 143
timestamps
    creation through proof-of-history, 54
    use to verify transactions in Bitcoin, 13
tokens, 7, 80
    EOS, sale on Ethereum, 104
    ERC-1155 standard for, 116

ERC-777 proposed standard for, 114
on Ethereum, 105-108
    airdrops and, 107
    deciding whether a token is necessary,
        106
    fungible and nonfungible tokens, 105
    many different types of, 106
Ethereum Requests for Comment (ERCs),
    108-116
    ERC-20, 108
    ERC-721, 112-114
listing on decentralized versus centralized
    exchanges, 167
multi-collateral, DAI, 160
sending/receiving on decentralized
    exchanges, 119
Tether use case for tokenization, 81
token economics in ICOs, 202
tokenizing everything, 247
use to create new cryptocurrencies on
    blockchain protocols, 81
Torcoin, 53
trading bots and exchange APIs, 148-153
trading technology, open source, 151
TradingView, 57
transaction fees, 26
    in coinbase transaction, 31
transaction flows, 139
transaction malleability problem, 74, 244
transactions, 26-32
    coinbase, 31
    Corda, 218
    difficulty of changing past transactions, 16
    Ethereum versus Bitcoin, 85
    events in execution of bitcoin transaction,
        27
    funding, 241
    generating on Bitcoin, 20
    Libra, structure of, 230
    life cycle, 49
    Merkle root, 28-30
    Monero, privacy of details, 234
    off-chain, 242
    Omni transaction on Bitcoin, 83
    push and pull, for ERC-20 tokens, 114
    in Satoshi Nakamoto's whitepaper, 12
    security on Bitcoin, 31
    signature generation, replay attacks on hard
        forks, 64

signing and validating, 30
signing, ring signatures, 186
Tether transaction in Omniexplorer, 83
UTXO model, 25-26
view in blockchain explorer, 56
transparency
greater, on decentralized exchanges, 120
ICOs and multisignature wallet code, 117
lack of, in 2008 financial crisis, 10
transaction transparency, 217
Travel Rule (FATF), 194
triangular arbitrage, 144
TrueUSD (TUSD) stablecoin, 162
Truffle Suite tools for smart contracts, 92
trust
blockchain's effort to reestablish, 2
challenge of, Bitcoin's effort to overcome, 13
intermediary, 1
issuance, 1
trustless sidechains, 238
Tulip Mania, 140
2.0 chains, 70
two-factor authentication, 39

U

Ulbricht, Ross, 189
unconfirmed/mempool (transactions on Bit-coin), 50
uniqueness consensus, 219
Uniswap exchange, 164
backend/database differences between cen-tralized exchanges and, 166
frontend differences between centralized exchanges and, 165
publicly viewable record of method call to Uniswap smart contract, 169-172
smart contract viewable on Ethereum, 167
token listing on, 167
Unobtainium, 69
unspent transaction output (see UTXO model)
US agencies and regulatory bodies regulating cryptocurrencies, 193
US Dollar Coin (USDC), 161
US Federal Reserve
blockchain implementation, 222
raising interest rates to control housing bubbles, 10
USDT, 200
users, ownership of their data, 155

utility tokens, 107, 202
UTXO model, 20, 25-26
on Corda, 219
Ethereum's version of, 85

V

validator nodes (Libra), 228
validators, 52
in Ethereum 2.0, 245
Honest validator framework, 245
validity consensus, 219
value
bitcoin as store of, 79
in Bitcoin, 17
transfer of, with dapps, 90
venture capital-backed startups, founder moti-vations versus those of ICOs, 203
verifiable data audit, 225
verifying transaction signatures, 30
virtual asset service providers (VASPs), require-ment to provide user data on transactions, 194
VmWare blockchain, 220
volatility of cryptocurrencies, 106
Maker creating stable asset from volatile markets, 160
Voorhees, Erik, 195
voting-based consensus, 54

W

wallets, 36-38
custodial versus noncustodial, 36
Ethereum, interacting with smart contracts, 92
for funds deposited into exchanges, 136
Lightning, 243
Liquid multisignature wallet, 239
MetaMask, browser-based Ethereum wallet, 89
multisignature, 116-119
necessity for using DeFi services, 156
Novi wallet, development by Facebook, 228
private keys, 157
security vulnerability in Parity multi-signature wallets, 89
variations on primary wallet types, 37
warm wallets, 136
wash trading, 131
Web 3.0, 186

web browsers, giving away user data, 186
web wallets, 38
Web3.js library, 101
WebSocket versus REST APIs, 152
whales, 131
whitelisting addresses, 137
whitepapers
    "Bitcoin: A Peer-to-Peer Electronic Cash
       System" , 11
    for ICOs, 202
WikiLeaks, Bitcoin and, 17
withdrawals wallet, 137
wrapped tokens, 159, 181

X
XCP cryptocurrency, 70

XRP consensus protocol, 72
XRP cryptocurrency, 72

Z
Zcash, 71, 186
Zero Knowledge (ZK) Rollups, 76
zero-knowledge proof, 183
    Bulletproofs, 237
Zero-Knowledge Succinct Non-Interactive
    Arguments of Knowledge (see zk-SNARKs)
Zether, 215
zk-SNARKs, 185, 215, 238
ZoKrates functions, 215

About the Authors

Lorne Lantz is the founder of Breadcrumbs (*https://breadcrumbs.app*), the blockchain investigation tool. He was a technical editor for the book *Mastering Bitcoin* and has produced educational videos on blockchain. With almost a decade worth of blockchain experience spanning from Silicon Valley to Asia, Lorne has founded several startups from a Bitcoin remittance service, a cryptocurrency wallet, a Bitcoin point of sale system, to a crypto trading platform. Lorne has a computer engineering degree from the University of Manitoba and an MBA from McMaster University.

Daniel Cawrey first became involved with blockchain technology at CoinDesk, the largest information resource in the cryptocurrency industry, where he has contributed since 2013. For almost a decade, Daniel has worked on and advised many blockchain-based projects, including running a cryptocurrency hedge fund for several years. He has an information science degree from Central Michigan University.

Colophon

The animal on the cover of *Mastering Blockchain* is a southern rockhopper penguin (*Eudyptes chrysocome*), a penguin found on islands and in the surrounding waters of the subantarctic off the coasts of South America, Australia, and New Zealand. The majority of the population breeds on the Falkland Islands off of Patagonia.

These birds are among the smallest penguins, averaging 20 inches tall and weighing 6 pounds. Their most distinctive features are the yellow stripes above each small red eye that extend into eccentric yellow crests. Their blue-black waterproof coat is comprised of small feathers. Opportunistic eaters, southern rockhoppers feed on crustaceans, squid, and small fish—sometimes participating in group dives to depths of over 300 feet.

The rockhopper gets its name from the penguin's tendency to jump over boulders and across cracks, unlike other penguins that typically navigate obstacles by sliding on their bellies or climbing using flippers. These penguins breed annually in large colonies, many returning to the same colony and even the same nest and partner, when possible.

The ICUN lists the conservation status of the southern rockhopper penguin as threatened, likely due to commercial fishing reducing available prey. Many of the animals on O'Reilly covers are endangered; all of them are important to the world.

Color illustration by Karen Montgomery, based on a black and white engraving from *Meyers Kleines Lexicon*. The cover fonts are Gilroy Semibold and Guardian Sans. The text font is Adobe Minion Pro; the heading font is Adobe Myriad Condensed; and the code font is Dalton Maag's Ubuntu Mono.

O'REILLY®

There's much more where this came from.

Experience books, videos, live online training courses, and more from O'Reilly and our 200+ partners—all in one place.

Learn more at oreilly.com/online-learning

Printed in the USA
CPSIA information can be obtained
at www.ICGtesting.com
JSHW061405091124
73248JS00008B/197